The Aesthetics of Necropolitics

EXPERIMENTS/ON THE POLITICAL

Series Editors

Iain Mackenzie, University of Kent
Amanda Giorgio, UMass Amherst

This series reflects on how interdisciplinary and/or practice-led thought can create the conditions for experimental thinking about politics and the political. What if the domain of the political is not what we usually think it is? Are there ways of thinking about the nature of politics and the political that can take us beyond frameworks of conflict and cooperation? These questions derive from a commitment to the idea that political thought has not yet exhausted its creative potential with regard to what constitutes the political domain. It is also motivated by the desire for political theory to become a genuinely creative discipline, open to collaborative interdisciplinary efforts in innovation. Moreover, if our understanding of the political world is to keep pace with political events then it is important that political theorists do not simply presume that they express one or other of these dominant models of the political; rather they should remain open to the possibility that experiments in politics may be happening 'on the street' in ways that require theorists to think differently about what is meant by 'the political'.

Titles in the Series

The Political Space of Art: The Dardenne Brothers, Ai Weiwei, Burial and Arundhati Roy
Benoît Dillet and Tara Puri

Comedy and Critical Thought: Laughter as Resistance
Edited by Iain MacKenzie, Fred Francis and Krista Bonello Rutter Giappone

Meanderings Through the Politics of Everyday Life
Robert Porter

The Aesthetics of Necropolitics
Edited by Natasha Lushetich

The Aesthetics of Necropolitics

Edited by Natasha Lushetich

ROWMAN &
LITTLEFIELD
INTERNATIONAL
London • New York

Published by Rowman & Littlefield International Ltd.
6 Tinworth Street, London SE11 5AL
www.rowmaninternational.com

Rowman & Littlefield International Ltd. is an affiliate of Rowman & Littlefield
4501 Forbes Boulevard, Suite 200, Lanham, Maryland 20706, USA
With additional offices in Boulder, New York, Toronto (Canada), and Plymouth (UK)
www.rowman.com

British Library Cataloguing in Publication Data

A catalogue record for this book is available from the British Library

ISBN: HB 978-1-78660-685-3

Library of Congress Cataloging-in-Publication Data Available

ISBN: 978-1-78660-685-3 (cloth : alk. paper)
ISBN: 978-1-5381-5868-5 (pbk : alk. paper)
ISBN: 978-1-78660-686-0 (electronic)

∞™ The paper used in this publication meets the minimum requirements of American National Standard for Information Sciences—Permanence of Paper for Printed Library Materials, ANSI/NISO Z39.48-1992.

Printed in the United States of America

Contents

Acknowledgements ix

Prologue 1
Natasha Lushetich

The Sensorial and Temporal, Less-than-Conscious Political 3
The Impasse of the 'Break or Mend' Aesthetic Narratives 5
The Structure and Organisation of this Volume 7

PART I: SEDIMENTATIONS: RACE AND GENDER

1 What Is the Aesthetics of Necropolitics? 17
Marina Gržinić

Biopolitics 18
Racialisation 20
Necropolitics 26
Necroaesthetics 27
Coda: Resisting the Necropolitical 32

2 *Get Out*: From Atlantic Slavery to Black Lives Matter 37
Sarah Juliet Lauro

Social Death 37
Sedimented Space and Time 40
The Master-Slave Struggle 43
Internalised Oppression 45

3 Aesthetic Autonomy at the Border: Notes on Necro-Art 55
Verónica Tello
Theories of Social Practice 58
Instituent or Postautonomous Practice 59
The Silent University: 'Autonomous Knowledge Platform' 61
Authorship and the Division of Labour 63
Necro-Art 66
Reframing Autonomy via Reproductive Labour 68

PART II: ABSTRACTIONS: TECHNOLOGICAL, FINANCIAL, CULTURAL, SCIENTIFIC

4 Inside the Corpse of Abstraction (An Apotropaic Text) 79
Franco Berardi
The Automaton 79
Immortality 82
Money 84
Extermination 86
Suburbicon 91
The End 93

5 Greenness: Sketching the Limits of a Normative Fetish 97
Jens Hauser
Undisciplined Metaphors 100
The Paradox of Symbolic Fetishes 102
Prismatic Mediations 104
Measuring Greenness 106
Epistemological Debunking in Artistic Practice 107
Toxicity Remediated 108

6 Desire, DNA, and Transgenetic Technology: Life after Necropolitics 119
Mi You
Overcodification and DNA as Signifier 120
Abstract Sex and Meta-Stable Bodies 121
Content and Expression or How DNA Became Overcodified 123
Inorganic Becoming against Death: Spiess/Strecker's *Hare's Blood +* 126

Desire, Death and Capitalism 127
Hypernature 130
Hypernatural Future 133

PART III: TACTICS: DETOURNING THE LIMIT, OVERBIDDING, MOURNING

7 Necropolitics and the Dark Comedy of the Posthuman 141
Critical Art Ensemble
Humans 141
Cyborgs 142
Transhumanists and Extropians 145
Green Posthumans 147

8 Dirty Your Media: Artists' Experiments in Bio-Sovereignty 157
Tiffany Funk
Big Data in Psychopolitics and Biometrics 158
Alternative Economies 161
Glitch and Dirty New Media 162
Obfuscation and Camouflage 166
Activist Destruction 171
Dirty Your Media: *Détourne*, Decentralise and DIY 173

9 Intimacy, Ignorance and Mourning in Iowa Hog Confinement 181
Malin Palani
Touching This Decomposing Body 183
Modes of Partitioning the Perceptible 185
Unknown Knowns 191
With (Death) Care 194

Epilogue: Archipelagoes of the Unseen 203
May Joseph
Islands of the Forgotten 204
Walking the Archipelagic Necropolis 206

Index 209

About the Contributors 215

Acknowledgements

Most of all, I would like to thank the contributors to this volume for the many interesting discussions that have animated this venture, in verbal and written form. I am also grateful to Jesse Holmes, Lucas van der Put and Kiven Strohm for their astute comments, big and small, and to Adeline Kueh for a particularly illuminating conversation about transcultural conceptions of death and necropolitics that took place in Singapore in June 2017.

Thanks are also due to the organisers and panelists of the 'Necro-Capital, Necro-Excess: Comparative Death-Worlds in Theory and Culture' panel at the ACLA conference in Utrecht in July 2017. Both the panel and the conference provided an excellent plateau for the discussions relevant to this volume. I am indebted to Iain McKenzie, the Experiments/On the Political series editor at Rowman & Littlefield International, for his continuing support, encouragement and very useful feedback. My heartfelt thanks also go to Amanda Giorgio and, last but certainly not least, to my publishers, Dhara Snowden and Rebecca Anastasi, for all their help and care.

Prologue

Natasha Lushetich

> Politics can only be traced as a spiral transgression, as that difference that disorients the very idea of the limit.[1]

Today's global semiocapitalism—a recombinant machine that deracinates knowledge and habit and floods the nervous system with information deluge[2]—is coated in smooth aesthetics. The aesthetics of uninterrupted connectivity, of shiny Macs and iPhones, of Brasilian depilation that erases the difference between actual and virtual bodies, of transglobal food, fashion and telecommunication chains that make landing in Paris, New York or Taipei into a relatively undifferentiated experience[3]; finally, the aesthetics of big data working imperceptibly in the background integrating financial, medical and consumer records into a new (digital) class that segregates (human) 'trash' from 'stars'[4].

In such a universe, death has a bad name. It is avoided, devalued or it returns to the scene in an overbidding gesture[5] of cataclysmic destruction. In the Western world, unspectacular death does, of course, have a long history of exclusion from the public domain. Not only do the majority of natural deaths occur in hospitals where the fiction of a likely recovery is maintained until the very end, but the deceased are often shown to family only after they have been shaven, coiffured, dressed and made up to appear as if asleep. In a society preoccupied with accelerated accumulation and rampageous consumption, death has no value as it can be neither accumulated nor consumed. Worse still, death is that final consumption that puts an end to all possibilities of 'having fun'. Consequently, the dead and the dying are seen as a class of the 'less fortunate' and any association with them is regarded as best kept to a minimum. In recent years, the obstinate denial of death has been punctured by the so-called senseless violence—mass murder and suicide—conveniently attributed to individual psychopathy rather than seen for what it is: infested, putrid social tissue, a horrifying yet utterly ineffectual attempt to 'trump'[6] systemic biosocial violence in a gesture imitative of the avant-garde shock tactics that propelled experimental composer Karlheinz Stockhausen to dub the terrorist attacks of 9/11 'a work of art'[7]. (It's important to mention that Stockhausen doesn't exonerate killing, only draws attention to the long history of destructive gestures in art that operate in the manner of the speech act[8].)

At the heart of these outrageous yet, it would appear, unstoppable tendencies, is endemic necropolitics in Achille Mbembe's dual sense of the word: necropolitics as the expression of sovereignty that resides in the power to 'dictate who may live and who must die'[9], and necropolitics as the 'generalized instrumentalization of human existence' and 'material destruction of bodies and populations'[10]. Rooted in Michel Foucault's biopower[11] and in Giorgio Agamben's (Schmittian) state of exception—which initially referred to the concentration camp's suspension of law[12] but has, since then, come to stand for engineered crisis—necropolitics shapes the conditions 'for the acceptability of putting to death'[13]. By extension, it also shapes the conditions for the acceptability of ubiquitous exploitation and denigration. This phenomenon or, rather, process can be observed in many domains: in the grand-scale destruction of the earth's ecosystems, in the overt and covert forms of genocide (the co-called refugee crisis), in the feeding of dead poultry to genetically modified legless pigs, or in the more recent 'ecological' inventions such as biocremation, in which human remains are used to produce heat for leisure centres[14]. Given that *necri-fice* (sacrifice without sanctity) is built into the first principle of capitalism—the subjection of one thing to another with the speculative aim of producing some future 'value'—it comes as no surprise that in the age of 'absolute capitalism'[15], necropolitical tendencies have ramified and intensified. The problem, however, is that the increasingly automated, logic-locked conduits of exploitation and denigration—in short, conduits that lead to irreparable destruction, systemic violence and devalued death—also function as a discursive and sensorial loop that produces hopelessness and devalues death and, by implication, also life.

This volume is an attempt to think necropolitics otherwise, as an *emergent practice* that operates in and through interpersonal synchronisation[16], existential refrains[17], asignifying semiotics[18], in infospheric, atomised time[19]. In order to move beyond the notion of necropolitics as a logic- and sequence-locked destiny, contributors to this volume chart the sensorial-affective cartography of temporal, spatial, embodied, embedded, affectively, culturally and scientifically transmitted memes and ideologies. Using divergent methodologies, such as exegesis, ethnographic fieldwork, interviews, auto-ethnography and peripatetic decolonial knowledge production, they identify resistive potential in the manner of the judo throw. The judo throw is a martial arts move that does not oppose or block the opponent's attack, nor does it launch a counterattack. Instead, it uses the impetus of the opponent's attack to redirect its force. Like the spiral transgression Mbembe speaks of, it is an oblique and iterative rather than a frontal tactic aimed at destabilising existing positions and well-rehearsed moves.

THE SENSORIAL AND TEMPORAL, LESS-THAN-CONSCIOUS POLITICAL

Invariably, the political is both a residue of past practices and relations and an emergent phenomenon. To borrow from Claude Lefort, it is 'the *mise en forme* of human coexistence'[20] that includes conscious, unconscious and purposefully ignored regions of being, seeing and doing. It is therefore necessary to situate the political at the threshold of perceptibility and knowability, in spatial, temporal and sensorial terms. Arguing against the conception of politics as the (more or less consensual) governance of the commons, Jacques Rancière foregrounds that which *precedes* consensus: precognitive attunement to rhythm and patterns, shared space and time, divergent perceptual habits, affect and the correspondingly divergent ideas about *what constitutes* the commons. The difference here is one between sound heard and understood as speech and sound registered as mere 'noise'[21]. Lurking in the background of Rancière's aesthetic conceptualisation of politics is Maurice Merleau-Ponty's notion of perception *as* action[22], further developed by many phenomenologists[23] as well as artists such as George Brecht, for whom every perception is an *active arrangement*, in spatial and temporal terms[24]. Perception partitions; it includes and excludes, organises and delimits. It lends duration to a thing or an occurrence; it engages in its development, or it does not. Although partially culturally formatted by a culture's 'phenomenological vector', which organises ambiguous perceptual possibilities into what is experienced as uncontestable physical phenomena—surfaces, images and sounds[25]—perception is also increasingly shaped in and by the infosphere. Consisting of perpetual communication, cultural production, symbolic and affective regimes, the infosphere configures the grids of sociopolitical possibility by recoding spatial, temporal and corporeal parameters and by modifying (our understanding of) attention, memory, care, support, empathy and value.

As Byung-Chul Han suggests, in the informational age, time is fragmented not because it is accelerated; rather, time *appears* accelerated because things and objects have become disposable[26]. Designed to last a year or two at best, they are no longer repositories of memory; instead, they recede from the world and from human experience with speed and indifference. While mythical (preindustrial) time was, for Han, anchored in the figure of god and, for this reason, immobile—it resembled an image—historical (industrial) time was anchored in the figure of the human being; it resembled a running line. Digital (postindustrial) time, which resembles vacillating points, is anchored in the algorithm but has no gravity[27]. It is unhinged. Uprooted now-moments vacillate without a direction, or they are strung into interminable yet empty durations that create a sense of provisionality, unfinished-ness and thus also diminished importance. This problem, which is a problem of value, places an enormous emphasis on the temporal, actual-virtual domain of the imperceptible, on the less-than-conscious working of the senses as well as on memory, which, arguably, is a meta-sense—the sense of all senses. In the informational age, learning and memory are entwined with technical objects (the computer, the mobile phone, the camera), which function as a perceptual-mnesic motorway of sorts. As Bernard Stiegler notes, new generations are socialised into a world in which ways of seeing, being, experiencing and memorising are already grammatised. Grammatisation here doesn't refer to the articulation of the sensible only but also to the isolation and automatic reproduction of the producers' gestures[28], that is, to the *mise en forme* of possibility. It *overwrites* perception by means of a technocultural practice, which, in turn, overwrites the 'affective activity of the nervous system'[29].

The inseparability of atomised time, technical objects, mnesic networks and the nervous system are the reasons why the political cannot be thought as separate from the interplay of perceptibility and imperceptibility, spatio-temporal and medial dynamics. 'Process-based' accounts of 'co-action', of coexistence in time, such as those discussed by John Protevi, that do not focus solely on communication as speech or on information as a message but foreground body postures, conversational rhythms, signals and patterns that trigger interpersonal and group 'impulses' and that can, for this reason, be seen as forms of entrainment[30] cannot be overestimated. The role of temporality is crucial in this context not only because, as humans, we are profoundly temporal but also because in the deterritorialised and deterritorialising universe of global capital, technical objects incessantly proliferate new forms of entrainment by incessantly proliferating new existential refrains. In his prescient, McLuhanesque[31] theorisation of human-machine assemblages, Félix Guattari suggests that an existential refrain couples 'heterogeneous leitmotifs to the existential territory of the self' and installs itself within the 'sensible and significational chaos' like a 'strange attractor'[32]. Suffice it to think of everyday refrains such as checking one's mobile devices for messages every five minutes or of the phantom phone vibration[33] to understand the extent to which these new biosocial patterns choreograph relations. Significantly, they bypass consciousness. They do not communicate representations to the conscious mind but, instead, operate through asignifying semiotics—languages that act directly on the nervous system[34]. Aided by digital 'diagrams'[35], existential refrains channel flows in a way similar to Bentham's panopticon, in which the incarcerated's behaviour is spatially and temporally orchestrated through the interplay of visibility and invisibility embedded in the architecture and independent of human agency (a particular prison guard's intentions, views of or attitudes to surveillance). When combined with aggressive financialisation and precarity, grammatisation and existential refraining (which, according to Stiegler, lead to 'affective and cognitive proletarisation'[36]) make precognitive perception of phenomena—or aesthesis—into an urgent political concern.

THE IMPASSE OF THE 'BREAK OR MEND' AESTHETIC NARRATIVES

Unsurprisingly, 'agentless' biosocial violence and systemic denigration have created a sense of enclosure, even hopelessness, which has, in turn, given rise to two dominant aesthetic accounts. The first rationalises the breakdown of perceptual orders and symbolic universes. In this category we find Paul Virilio's aesthetics of disappearance that focuses on the epileptic state of consciousness produced by speed—gaps, glitches and speed bumps[37]—Eldritch Priest's aesthetics of failure, which foregrounds boredom and formlessness produced by the overload of sensory information[38], and Kieran Cashell's transgressive aesthetics that reformulates (neo)avant-gardist practices reliant on affective deterritorialisation and cognitive disorientation[39]. Since the 1960s, and concomitantly with the progressive invisibilisation of control mechanisms increasingly immanent to the social field (and therefore increasingly difficult to identify and discuss[40]), there has been a veritable boom of staged pain, suffering and abjection. Between 1960 and 1990 the work of many 'abject' artists made a significant contribution to identity politics[41]. But we have to ask ourselves whether staging transgression of a visceral kind in a universe in which visceral transgression is the norm—and here I'm thinking of the run-of-the-mill online profiles that combine images of well-groomed individuals with the images of discharging vast amounts of urine, or similar, in a drunken state[42]—has any *politically* transgressive potential. Even artists who once articulated invisible violence with astounding poignancy, for example, Paul McCarthy in his 1970s orgies with urine, blood, ketchup, mayonnaise and excrement, are now resorting to more tongue-in-cheek references to their formerly radical work such as dropping giant inflatable plastic poop on cities with serious pollution problems, like Hong Kong[43].

The second aesthetic account, rooted mostly in H. G. Gadamer's dialogic hermeneutic tradition, acknowledges the erosion of sociality, the increasing economic injustice and pervasive biodigital violence and proposes a remedy. In this category we find Nicolas Bourriaud's relational aesthetics[44], which seeks to remedy social fragmentation produced by neoliberal precarisation and market fundamentalism, found in such works as Carsten Höller's giant slides that cue ludic sociality in an attempt to (re)create a temporary community[45]. Grant Kester is even more adamant about the need to engage participants in social utopias. Arguing vehemently against the shock tactics exemplified by the work of the abject artists who continue to stage (what is seen as) blasphemy, incest, deformity and disgust, Kester claims that such symbolic order–annihilating works do nothing but cut even deeper into the already damaged *clinamen* and destroy all hope of a hermeneutic community, coordinated action or, in fact, all hope *tout court*. For Kester, such works make viewers 'viscerally aware of their own complicity in an oppressive specular economy' which only adds 'both to social and symbolic oppression'[46]. Consequently, Kester advocates projects that defy the erosion of the social by engaging the haptic and the visceral and by facilitating the process of collaborative interaction and ameliorative co-creation. But doesn't this take us back to consensual politics and the unwavering faith in human rationality, only more attuned to the demands of emotional capitalism?

Bypassing the hegemony of the 'break or mend' aesthetic narratives, this volume's chapters focus on specific aesthetic and pre-aesthetic dimensions that are *spirally*, not frontally, political: the emptied image, the folding of the past in the present, the incompatibility of global contemporaneity and the outdated notions of autonomy, sensorial saturation, scientific and semantic overdetermination, the aesthetics of annihilation narratives, indeterminacy, other-species proximity and embodied encounters with the environmentally embedded abuse and humiliation. Instead of formulating a political aesthetic—or defending the aesthetic space as autonomous, a gesture appropriate in, say, Herbert Marcuse's time[47], but one decidedly out of place in the accelerated semiocapitalist infosphere in which art, technology, science and politics all form part of a variegated topography—the authors gathered in this volume articulate a necropolitical aesthetic *as* a political space.

THE STRUCTURE AND ORGANISATION OF THIS VOLUME

This volume is divided into three sections, each of which serves a different purpose. The first—'Sedimentations: Race and Gender'—examines the inherited 'conditions' that create the 'acceptability for putting to death' and denigration[48]. The three chapters in this section make transparent the formation, continuation and, in some cases, perverse sophistication of past necropolitical practices, while engaging critically with their normalisation. In chapter 1, 'What Is the Aesthetics of Necropolitics?' Marina Gržinić traces the historical progression from biopolitics to necropolitics. Through a cross-temporal reading of Hortense J. Spillers, Michel Foucault, Étienne Balibar and Achille Mbembe, she identifies strategies of racial, gender and, more generally, identitarian entrapment that are as violent as colonial subjugation. In a single blow, these strategies imprison European citizens (third- or fourth-generation descendants of immigrants from former European colonies) in a foreign identity, much like they blame the supposedly 'historically dysfunctional' black family on the female line. Key to Gržinić's conceptualisation of necroaesthetics is the simultaneous invisibility and overvisibility of the image—or the emptied image—which articulates a spectrum of imperceptibility reliant on amnesia and aphasia.

In chapter 2, '*Get Out*: From Atlantic Slavery to Black Lives Matter', Sarah Juliet Lauro offers a reading of Jordan Peele's 2016 fantastical film about body snatching (Peele refers to the film as 'a documentary') to accentuate the similarity between Atlantic slavery and the lives of African Americans in the United States today. Engaging with the metaphor of social death and drawing comparisons with the Domingue slave revolt and the figure of the zombie, Lauro reassesses the Hegelian master-slave dialectic in light of Alexandre Kojève's, Paul Gilroy's and Achille Mbembe's arguments. Relying on Ian Baucom's concept of temporal accumulation, she proposes a broadened spectrum of resistance that death, killing and suicide provide.

In chapter 3, 'Aesthetic Autonomy at the Border: Notes on Necro-Art', Verónica Tello analyses the legacy of artistic autonomy as an outdated phenomenon that continues to plague institutent practice, such as the Silent University (SU). Pointing to the fact that the utopistic nature of the project (which foregrounds the knowledge of refugees) depends on a practice that, although operative in the social realm in the manner of Joseph Beuys's social sculpture[49], remains indebted to the modernist idea of the artist as genius creator, Tello analyses the division of labour. Separating the transformatory work of SU's initiator and the 'banal' work of the (mostly female) administrators and coordinators, the SU, argues Tello, produces necro-art. Through a reading of postautonomy, based on feminist conceptual art and on theories of contemporaneity, she proposes that the concept-practice of maintenance replace outdated inaugurative gestures, as maintenance relies on low-key constancy and a distributed concept of autonomy that is far more attuned to the (uneven) global contemporaneity.

The second part of the volume—'Abstractions: Technological, Financial, Cultural, Scientific'—takes stock of the multiple processes of repartitioning the sensible via the various mechanisms of abstraction. This section accentuates emergent directions sprouting from the various abstracting mechanisms and focuses on the reorganisation of epistemic practices as well as on the resistive potential always already present in scientific procedures. Part II opens with Franco Berardi's 'Inside the Corpse of Abstraction', in which he discusses the entwined problematics of financialisation, technology and capitalist immortality (immortality achieved through the virtual transubstantiation of capital), which, in reality, is no more than dead labour, however dead labour that has usurped life and is now turning all its segments into automated (necrotic) abstraction. Focusing on issues as diverse as Narendra Modi's proposed demonetarisation, Trumpism, the return of American colonialism, and the increasingly present semiocapitalistically induced lack of empathy, Berardi diagnoses the current condition as one of global civil war in which aggressive identity politics is back as a form of forceful reterritorialisation, a revenge for the violent, unceasing deterritorialision of work, culture and, more broadly, life.

The following chapter, Jens Hauser's 'Greenness: Sketching the Limits of a Normative Fetish', develops a comprehensive analysis of the threefold trope 'green-greenness-greening' as a cultural and scientific fetish against whose symbolic value noxious environmental practices are ratified. The abstracted necropolitical line Hauser takes is less visible than the phenomena discussed by Berardi; however it is no less important. Employing a media-theoretical approach, Hauser deconstructs the pervasiveness of the 'green' metaphor and traces its technoscientific and art-historical roots while simultaneously articulating the absurd human need for reassurance through the conceptual construction of 'natural' otherness, regardless of the widespread (human and environmental) death and destruction resulting from programmed obsoleteness (of tools and apparata). For Hauser, what is needed is a reorganisation of epistemic practices to foreground the relationship between modelling technologies, measuring systems, media-specific technicity and the (human) thresholds of perception. In chapter 6, 'Desire, DNA, and Transgenetic Technology: Life after Necropolitics', Mi You presents an insightful analysis of scientific overdetermination and the necropolitical entanglement of capitalism and life, not as a force to be extracted from living human beings through labour but as a biotechnological product. Using two artistic practices, Paul Vanouse's and Lucie Spiess and Klaus Strecker's, You shows how Gilles Deleuze's notion of capitalist *desire for desire* permeates biotechnological necropolitics—the power to redesign, discontinue or annihilate—that concerns both the patenting of genetic data and the subjection of the so-called healthy bodies to medical monitoring. Pointing to the seemingly inescapable loop in which genetic-specific medication remains tied to large-scale diagnostic testing, which turns products, such as pills, and testing technologies back into information—databases, test results, marketing and media campaigns—You formulates a subversive strategy of inorganic becoming based on Luciana Parisi's concept of abstract sex.

Although all three sections ponder strategies of resistance, the third section—'Tactics: Detourning the Limit, Overbidding, Mourning'—is concerned with the formulation of tactics at the limit of the necropolitical horizon, the digital unconscious, indeterminacy and loss. The first chapter in this section, Critical Art Ensemble's (CAE) 'Necropolitics and the Dark Comedy of the Posthuman', examines posthuman scenarios associated with technoromanticism and technofatalism. Scrutinising cyborgs, transhumanists, green posthumans and their various scenarios for overcoming the unfortunate human condition, the CAE analyse existing proposals for mass extermination, such as those put forth by E. O. Wilson and Lierre Keith. Reappropriating the gesture of deliberative politics, they suggest that since the death of several billion people is what seems to be needed for the continuation of life on the planet, an open and democratic debate about who may live and who must die should be staged as a matter of urgency.

In 'Dirty Your Media: Artists' Experiments in Bio-Sovereignty', Tiffany Funk examines the integrated problematics of big data, medical and police surveillance and tracking. Analysing artistic-activist practices that focus on social and ethical problems inherent in the fact that medical and criminal records are shared across governmental agencies, she foregrounds the work of glitch and dirty new media artists who employ indeterminacy to detourn necropolitical operations that stigmatise individuals as criminal, ill or uninsurable. Discussing such practices as obfuscation and Trackmenot plugins created by Helen Nissenbaum et al., plugins that, in a gesture of overbidding, bombard tracking programmes with an overload of information, Funk argues against the foreclosure of the future. Despite the fact that big data predicts human behaviour and thus, arguably, confiscates the future, Funk's focus on the zone of imperceptibility, usually referred to as the 'digital unconscious', makes clear that resistance is not impossible, only that it has relocated to a different realm: the infosphere. In chapter 10, 'Intimacy, Ignorance and Mourning in Iowa Hog

Confinement', Malin Palani offers an auto-ethnographic account of caring for an injured pig. Analysing the confluence of entrepreneurism, the corporate tactics of evasion and cultivated agnotology in light of Foucault's biosecurity and Rancièrian blind spots, she arrives at an affirmative tactics of death care. Anchored in mourning—not as a state to be rid of but as a process grounded in the materiality of existence—Palani argues for the need to restore dignity and faith to, within and around death. This is not a weak strategy of acceptance but a form of articulating the full cycle of composition, decomposition and re-composition that is life-death. In the epilogue, 'Archipelagoes of the Unseen', May Joseph brings the multiple violent pasts of New York, a city often associated with what Berardi has termed the 'global civil war', triggered by 9/11, into the present moment. Using a decolonial methodology of reenvisioning what lies below the surface of ecological meaning, she roams the forty islands that shape the New York archipelago listening to 'quiet soundings', a form of ontological excavation of the erased (yet resurrectable) spaces of possibility, and a form of attunement to the longue durée of death. Death as a dimension of 'being otherwise' that needs to be valued and honoured as such.

NOTES

1. Achille Mbembe, 'Necropolitics', trans. Libby Meintjes, *Public Culture* 15, no. 1 (Winter 2003): 16.
2. Franco Berardi, *Heroes: Mass Murder and Suicide* (London: Verso Books, 2015), 68.
3. Byung-Chul Han, *Sauvons le Beau: L'esthétique à l'ère numérique* (Paris: Actes Sud, 2016), 9–10.
4. Byung-Chul Han, *Psychopolitics: Neoliberalism and New Technologies of Power*, trans. Erik Butler (London and New York: Verso, 2017), 65.
5. Overbidding, which refers to raising the stakes higher than the system can endure, is a concept first introduced by Jean Baudrillard in *The Illusion of the End*, trans. Chris Turner (Stanford: Stanford University Press, 1994).
6. It is, of course, ironic that in the age of perpetual stake-raising, in the vortex of abstraction that is the financial world, and overbidding in the form of terrorism or mass murder, the name of the president of the United States is (Donald) Trump.
7. See Anthony Tommasini, 'Music; The Devil Made him Do It', *New York Times*, 30 September 2001, http://www.nytimes.com/2001/09/30/arts/music-the-devil-made-him-do-it.html (accessed 22 December 2017).
8. Many radical performance art practices—the Viennese Actionists, Gina Paine, Carolee Schneemann, Paul McCarthy, ORLAN or, more recently, Michael Landy—used blood, semen, urine, excrement, self-inflicted pain and the destruction of material objects as a performative statement against the absence of the lived body from

social systems, the glossing of pain and misery, the suppression of nondominant knowledges, such as female knowledge, and against aggressive consumption.

9. Mbembe, 'Necropolitics', 11.

10. Ibid., 14.

11. Michel Foucault, 'Society Must Be Defended,' in *Lectures at the College de France 1975–76*, ed. Mauro Bertani and Alessandro Fontana, trans. David Macey (New York: Picador, 2003), 255.

12. See Giorgio Agamben, *Homo Sacer: Sovereign Power and Bare Life*, trans. Daniel Heller-Roazen (Stanford: Stanford University Press, 1998), 168–70.

13. Michel Foucault, quoted in Mbembe, 'Necropolitics', 17.

14. See Hannah Rumble et al., 'Disposal or Dispersal? Environmentalism and Final Treatment of the British Dead', *Mortality* 19, no. 3 (2014): 243–60.

15. Berardi, *Heroes*, 87.

16. See John Protevi, 'Political Emotion,' in *Collective Emotions*, ed. Christian von Scheve and Miko Selmela (Oxford: Oxford University Press, 2013), http://www.protevi.com/john/PoliticalEmotionOUP2014.pdf, 3.

17. Félix Guattari, *Chaosmosis*, trans. Paul Bains and Julian Pefanis (Bloomington: Indiana University Press, 1995), 17–19.

18. Maurizio Lazarrato, *Signs and Machines: Capitalism and the Production of Subjectivity*, trans. J. D. Jordan (Amsterdam: Semiotext(e), 2014), 80.

19. Byung-Chul Han, *Le Parfum de temps* (Paris: Edition Circé, 2016), 17–23.

20. Claude Lefort, quoted in Chantal Mouffe, 'Artistic Activism and Agonistic Spaces', *Art & Research* 1, no. 2 (2007): 4, http://www.artandresearch.org.uk/v1n2/mouffe.html.

21. Jacques Rancière, *Disagreement: Politics and Philosophy*, trans. Julie Rose (Minneapolis: University of Minnesota Press, 1999), 29.

22. Maurice Merleau-Ponty, *The Primacy of Perception*, trans. J. M. Edie (Evanston: Northwestern University Press, 1964), 162–63.

23. See, for example, Alphonso Lingis, *Sensation: Intelligibility in Sensibility* (New York: Humanity Books), 1996.

24. See Natasha Lushetich, *Fluxus: The Practice of Non-Duality* (Amsterdam and New York, 2014), 41–52.

25. Drew Leder, *The Absent Body* (Chicago and London: The University of Chicago Press, 1990), 150.

26. Han, *Le Parfum*, 17.

27. Ibid., 22–23.

28. Bernard Stiegler, *For a New Critique of Political Economy*, trans. Daniel Ross (Cambridge: Polity, 2010), 33.

29. Ibid.

30. Protevi, 'Political Emotion', 3.

31. For Marshall McLuhan, the medium is the message. It is not *what* we are watching on TV that matters—the news, a children show or a football match—but the fact we are receiving televised information passively. See Marshall McLuhan, *Understanding Media: The Extensions of Man* (London: Routledge and Kegan Paul, 1964).

32. Guattari, *Chaosmosis*, 17.

33. The phantom vibration syndrome refers to the mobile phone user's experience of vibration or, more precisely, his or her *hallucination* of vibration when the mobile phone is, in fact, not vibrating at all. As two separate groups of researchers have shown, one reason for the high percentage of such hallucinations (70 to 90 percent) is stress. The other is the close proximity of the phone—usually carried in the pocket or in a handbag—and the nervous system. See Michelle Drouin et al., 'Phantom Vibrations among Undergraduates: Prevalence and Associated Psychological Characteristics', *Computers in Human Behavior* 28 (2012): 1490–96.

34. Lazarrato, *Signs and Machines*, 80.

35. Lazzarato borrows this notion from Gilles Deleuze's reading of Michel Foucault's theoristation of nondiscursive power, found in such technologies as the panopticon. See Gilles Deleuze, *Foucault* (Paris: Editions de Minuit, 2004), 78–81.

36. Stiegler, *For a New Critique*, 30.

37. See Paul Virilio, *The Aesthetics of Disappearance*, trans. Philip Beitchman (Los Angeles: Semiotext(e), 2009).

38. See Eldritch Priest, *Boring Formless Nonsense: Experimental Music and the Aesthetics of Failure* (London: Bloomsbury Academic, 2013)

39. See Kieran Cashell, *Aftershock: The Ethics of Contemporary Transgressive Art* (London: I. B. Tauris and Co., Ltd., 2009).

40. Michael Hardt and Antonio Negri, *Empire* (Cambridge, MA: Harvard University Press, 2000), 23.

41. Abject art is a form of public outrage at the diffuse yet palpable effect of the increasingly invisible violence, perpetuated by all sorts of consumerist, class, and gender interpellations. Prominent examples are Paul McCarthy, Kiki Smith and Andreas Serrano, among others. For a discussion of abject art, see Hal Foster, *The Return of the Real* (Cambridge, MA: MIT Press).

42. For more information, see Natasha Lushetich, 'The Performative Constitution of Liberal Totalitarianism on Facebook', in *Žižek and Performance*, ed. Broderick Chow and Alex Mangold (Basingstoke: Palgrave, 2014), 101–5.

43. The reference here is to Paul McCarthy's 1974 performance *Hot Dog* and video work *Tubbing* and his 2013 mixed media work *Complex Pile*.

44. See Nicolas Bourriaud, *Relational Aesthetics* (Paris: Les Presses du Réel, 2002).

45. This is a reference to Carsten Höller's 2006 *Test Site*, made for Tate Modern, London.

46. Grant Kester, *The One and the Many: Collaborative Art in a Global Context* (Durham: Duke University Press, 2011), 62.

47. In 1979 Herbert Marcuse argued the following: 'The truth of art lies in this: that the world really is as it appears in the work of art . . . the political potential of art lies only in its own aesthetic dimension'. Herbert Marcuse, *The Aesthetic Dimension*, trans. Erica Sherover (London: Penguin Random House, 1979), xii.

48. Michel Foucault, quoted in Mbembe, 'Necropolitics', 17.

49. For Joseph Beuys, social sculpting was a socio-aesthetic practice aimed at transforming society through interdisciplinary multilogue, relationality and co-action.

BIBLIOGRAPHY

Agamben, Giorgio. *Homo Sacer: Sovereign Power and Bare Life.* Translated by Daniel Heller-Roazen. Stanford: Stanford University Press, 1998.

Baudrillard, Jean. *The Illusion of the End.* Translated by Chris Turner. Stanford: Stanford University Press, 1994.

Berardi, Franco. *Heroes: Mass Murder and Suicide.* London: Verso Books, 2015.

Berardi, Franco. *The Uprising: On Poetry and Finance.* Los Angeles: Semiotext(e), 2012.

Bourriaud, Nicolas. *Relational Aesthetics.* Paris: Les Presses du Réel, 2002.

Cashell, Kieran. *Aftershock: The Ethics of Contemporary Transgressive Art.* London: I. B. Tauris and Co., Ltd., 2009.

Deleuze, Gilles. *Foucault.* Paris: Editions de Minuit, 2004.

Drouin Michelle, et al. 'Phantom Vibrations among Undergraduates: Prevalence and Associated Psychological Characteristics'. *Computers in Human Behavior* 28 (2012): 1490–96.

Foster, Hal. *The Return of the Real.* Cambridge, MA: MIT Press.

Foucault, Michel. 'Society Must Be Defended'. In *Lectures at the College de France 1975–76*, edited by Mauro Bertani and Alessandro Fontana. Translated by David Macey. New York: Picador, 2003.

Guattari, Félix. *Chaosmosis.* Translated by Paul Bains and Julian Pefanis. Bloomington: Indiana University Press, 1995.

Han, Byung-Chul. *Le Parfum de temps.* Paris: Edition Circé, 2016.

Han, Byung-Chul. *Psychopolitics: Neoliberalism and New Technologies of Power.* Translated by Erik Butler. London and New York: Verso, 2017.

Han, Byung-Chul. *Sauvons le Beau: L'esthétique à l'ère numérique.* Paris: Actes Sud, 2016.

Hardt, Michael, and Antonio Negri. *Empire.* Cambridge, MA: Harvard University Press, 2000.

Kester, Grant. *The One and the Many: Collaborative Art in a Global Context.* Durham: Duke University Press, 2011.

Lazzarato, Maurizio. *Signs and Machines: Capitalism and the Production of Subjectivity.* Translated by Joshua David Jordan. Amsterdam: Semiotext(e), 2014.

Leder, Drew. *The Absent Body.* Chicago and London: The University of Chicago Press, 1990.

Lingis, Alphonso. *Sensation: Intelligibility in Sensibility.* New York: Humanity Books, 1996.

Lushetich, Natasha. *Fluxus: The Practice of Non-Duality.* Amsterdam and New York: Rodopi, 2014.

Marcuse, Herbert. *The Aesthetic Dimension.* Translated by Erica Sherover. London: Penguin Random House, 1979.

Mbembe, Achille. 'Necropolitics'. Translated by Libby Meintjes. *Public Culture* 15, no. 1 (Winter 2003): 11–40.

McLuhan, Marshall. *Understanding Media: The Extensions of Man.* London: Routledge and Kegan Paul, 1964.

Merleau-Ponty, Maurice. *The Primacy of Perception.* Edited and translated by J. M. Edie. Evanston: Northwestern University Press, 1964.

Mouffe, Chantal. 'Artistic Activism and Agonistic Spaces'. *Art & Research* 1, no. 2 (2007): 1–5. http://www.artandresearch.org.uk/v1n2/mouffe.html.

Priest, Eldritch. *Boring Formless Nonsense: Experimental Music and the Aesthetics of Failure.* London: Bloomsbury Academic, 2013.

Protevi, John. 'Political Emotion'. In *Collective Emotions*, edited by Christian von Scheve and Miko Selmela. Oxford: Oxford University Press, 2013. http://www.protevi.com/john/PoliticalEmotionOUP2014.pdf.

Rancière, Jacques. *Disagreement: Politics and Philosophy.* Translated by Julie Rose. Minneapolis: University of Minnesota Press, 1999.

Rumble, Hannah et al. 'Disposal or Dispersal? Environmentalism and Final Treatment of the British Dead'. *Mortality* 19, no. 3 (2014): 243–60.

Stiegler, Bernard. *For a New Critique of Political Economy.* Translated by Daniel Ross. Cambridge: Polity, 2010.

Tommasini, Anthony. 'Music; The Devil Made him Do It'. *New York Times*, 30 September 2001. http://www.nytimes.com/2001/09/30/arts/music-the-devil-made-him-do-it.html.

Virilio, Paul. *The Aesthetics of Disappearance.* Translated by Philip Beitchman. Los Angeles: Semiotext(e), 2009.

Part I

SEDIMENTATIONS

Race and Gender

Chapter One

What Is the Aesthetics of Necropolitics?

Marina Gržinić

Faced with two hegemonic operations—on the one hand, with aesthetics, and on the other, with necropolitics—I will attempt to articulate their present condition in order to discuss global neoliberal necrozones in which misery, exclusion and death are manufactured, administered, normalised and, ultimately, aesthetised. This task will necessitate a revisiting of biopolitics and the many bio-necro entanglements that form part of racialised differentiations, which continue to devalue bodies of colour—that are also bodies of knowledge—by relegating them to marginalised and ghettoised positions. As Ebony Rose suggests, race and racism are central to the bio-necro-political project that traps 'black bodies in a temporal ontological prison of anti-blackness grammar and the structure of suffering'[1]. Like the numerous catastrophes we have witnessed in the past decades—tsunamis, hurricanes and typhoons—necropolitical events have a cataclysmic dimension. They injure and scar humanity and animality by repeatedly showing the carefully differentiated, racialised ways in which help and government support are selectively administered to violently differentiated groups of beings. Decisions regarding whom to help and how much, and, conversely, whom not to help, follow a distinctly necropolitical logic. Simply put, this logic is political in that it refers to management and administration; it is 'necro' in that the objects of management are death zones and events produced by 'sovereign entities', entities that *have instituted themselves as* 'sovereign' after 2001—the sovereign war state, the sovereign bank, sovereign debt and the ubiquitous sovereign multinational corporation. Today, it is these 'sovereign entities' that decide 'who may live and who must die'[2].

We have long entered the zone of what, at first sight, appears to be an oxymoron: necropolitical *ethics*. In *A Theory of the Drone*[3], first published in French in 2013 and translated into English in 2015, Grégoire Chamayou discusses necroethics in light of the increasing use of drones. Chamayou's point is that killing from a distance allows for a 'clean shot', a consideration that has nothing to do with the choice of target or, for that matter, with killing itself. At the heart of necroethics lies the pervasive element of racism: technologically advanced weapons are used against what may be termed the 'disenfranchised collaterals', the expendable population that does not matter *in* or *to* the necro-military arrangement of forces prevalent in the United States. Chamayou insists that both necropolitics and necropower operate through the ethics of the 'clean shot'. The popular understanding of ethics and aesthetics, as supposedly related to individual 'moral' decisions and to a 'natural' affinity for the beautiful, is and always has been ideologically constructed. My purpose in analysing bio-necropolitical entanglements is therefore not to state the obvious but to articulate a *further disconnection* with the deeply ideologically constructed, necropolitically tainted ethics and aesthetics. In order to present a systematised reading of these entanglements, the following text is divided into four parts: biopolitics, racialisation, necropolitics and necroaesthetics. In the final section, I ruminate on the possibilities of resistance. But let me, first of all, make explicit and visible the authors who have allowed me to systematise my thoughts and come to certain conclusions about the conditions, practice, consequences and aftermaths of the aesthetics of necropolitics.

My analysis of racialisation as a key link between biopolitics and necropolitics is indebted to Hortense J. Spillers's 'Mama's Baby, Papa's Maybe: An American Grammar Book'[4], a text that, although published in 1987, is more relevant today than ever, as will be shown in a cross-reading with Étienne Balibar's 2011 text on race and culture[5]. My elaboration of the aesthetics of necropolitics is further anchored in Joshua Dunn's 2017 'Cross Roads of the Living and the Dead: Necropolitics and Market Logic in Chris Abani's *GraceLand*'[6], and in Ebony Rose's 2016 'Afro-Stasis: Understanding the Necro/Biopolitical Collaboration in the Creation of a Carceralization of Black Life/Death'[7]. In the last section that focuses on strategies of resistance, I turn to Katherine McKittrick's 2014 *Sylvia Wynter*: *On Being Human as Praxis*[8].

BIOPOLITICS

In *'Society Must Be Defended', Lectures at the College de France, 1975–76*[9], Michel Foucault lays out his theory of biopolitics and biopower. Foucault states that

> one of the greatest transformations political right underwent in the nineteenth century was precisely that sovereignty's old right—to take life or let live—was

> [not exactly] replaced, but came to be complemented by a new right which does not erase the old right but which does penetrate it, permeate it. This is the right, or rather precisely the opposite of right. It is the power to 'make' live and 'let die'.[10]

Foucault continues: 'After the anatomo-politics of the human body established in the course of the eighteenth century, we have, at the end of the century, the emergence of something that is no longer an anatomo-politics of the human body, but what I would call a "biopolitics" of the human race'[11]. The optimisation of life via politico-corporeal discipline takes on a particular significance when examined through the lens of Foucault's biopolitical framework, which posits a gradual historical shift in focus from 'man-as-body' to 'man-as-species'[12]. In other words, biopolitics asserts itself through the calculation and management of birth and death rates, as well as through the study and modification of epidemic disease and endemic illness. For Foucault, this juncture marks the birth of biopolitics because 'biopolitics deals with the population . . . as a political problem and as power's problem'[13]. There is a difference between disciplinary power and this new regulatory power developing in and alongside industrial capitalism in the nineteenth century. With this particular relation in mind, Foucault formulates the notion of state racism, which establishes

> the hierarchy of races, the fact that certain races are described as good and that others, in contrast, are described as inferior: all this is a way of separating out the groups that exist within a population. It is, in short, a way of establishing a biological-type caesura within a population that appears to be a biological domain.[14]

It's important to note here that Foucault's definition of state racism *exceeds* the common definition of racism. While including different subgroups, it also differentiates between these subgroups and the so-called normal population. This differentiation is the first function of racism; its purpose is 'to fragment, to create caesuras within the biological continuum addressed by biopower'[15]. The second function of racism is the following ultimatum: 'if you want to live, you must be able to kill'[16]. Seen from the point of view of state racism, the right to kill is not a deviation from the biopolitical; it is its very norm. This dynamic, or, rather, this *impasse*, in which the death of one human being is directly related to the life of another, is the epitome of Foucault's definition of state racism, which survived as a *positivist* notion with no connection to the post–World War II influx of people into the West (Europe) or the Occident, transformed into (sub)populations of migrants, postcolonial subjects, that is, the marginalised and the abandoned.

The task here, therefore, is to directly link the constructed category of race to such categories as nationals, citizens, second- and third-class citizens

and noncitizens. Moreover, it is to rethink the supposedly 'empty centre' of Western biopower as exempted from the processes of racialisation, much like it is to rethink the very rhetoric of the empty centre of power—a case in point is the refusal of many European countries to have their inner-city parks populated by 'migrants' as it is their 'citizens'' right to live in a harmonious, green city—which is a stumbling block that prevents us from seeing that racialisation is fundamental to all these processes of emptying in order to achieve 'harmony'. The endpoint of this process is the forced 'repatriation' of refugees, which is what is currently happening in the European Union (henceforth EU). It is plain to see that the supposedly empty centre of power (the empty public sphere) is not empty at all but is, on the contrary, directly linked to processes of intensified cleansing and control—an erased, cleansed and violently disposed centre. The main difference here is the passage from an empty to an erased, cleansed centre, rife with violent racialisation that transforms the so-called empty centre into a deathscape. As a result, the current border-control hypermilitarisation aided by hypersurveillance is not effective at the margins but operates from *within* the very centre of what is wrongly referred to as the empty centre of Western biopower.

RACIALISATION

Racialisation is a complex regime of hyperviolent discrimination, dispossession, exploitation and dehumanisation. In order to understand its central place in the necropolitical order, a structured analysis that frames its material-institutional and discursive logics is necessary. In 'Mama's Baby, Papa's Maybe: An American Grammar Book'[17], Hortense J. Spillers embroils histories of enslavement with family structure in order to expose the formation of the gender-and-race complex in the United States. In so doing she brings to the fore the implications of vocabularies, naming and, more generally, terminology. For Spillers, names used to describe black women are 'overdetermined nominative properties'; they are inextricably entwined with ethics, aesthetics and religious values. Spillers writes,

> Embedded in bizarre axiological ground, they [names] demonstrate a sort of telegraphic coding; they are markers so loaded with mythical prepossession that there is no easy way for the agents buried beneath them to come clean. In that regard, the names by which I am called in the public place render an example of signifying property plus.[18]

Everyday language has deep historical roots, as the 1965 Moynihan Report[19], the central point of Spillers's analysis, shows. Written by American soci-

ologist Daniel Patrick Moynihan, who, at the time, was serving as assistant secretary of Labour under U.S. president Lyndon B. Johnson, the Moynihan Report, *The Negro Family: The Case for National Action*, focused on the roots of black poverty in the United States. Controversially, the report suggested that one of the reasons for the black population's slow progress towards political and economic equality was the high percentage of single-mother families. Spillers points out that the report both *names* black women *responsible for* and *representative of* the historically 'dysfunctional' black family, seen as a deviation from the national norm, the 'American' way, the patriarchal family structure. Spillers states that,

> according to Daniel Patrick Moynihan's celebrated 'Report' . . . the 'Negro Family' has no Father to speak of; his Name, his Law, his Symbolic function mark the impressive missing agencies in the essential life of the black community, the 'Report' maintains, and it is, surprisingly, the fault of the Daughter, or the female line. This stunning reversal of the castration thematic, displacing the Name and the Law of the Father to the territory of the Mother and Daughter, becomes an aspect of the African-American female's misnaming.[20]

In the Moynihan Report, 'ethnicity', as in the example of the 'white' family, as opposed to the 'Negro family', is embroiled in a binary grid of meanings. Spillers reflects on the consequences of this reversal and concludes that 'ethnicity', perceived as mythical time, enables the writer (Moynihan) to perform a variety of conceptual moves all at once. Under its hegemony, 'the human body becomes a defenseless target for rape and veneration, and the body, in its material and abstract phase, a resource for metaphor'[21]. Spillers exposes ethnicity to be a myth, which, as 'a signifier has no movement in the field of signification . . . although one would be unwise not to concede its dangerous and fatal effects'[22].

In global neoliberal necrocapitalism, it is still this point on which decisions about who may live and who must die turn. Millions of blacks that were kidnapped, sold and enslaved represent the 'zero degree of social conceptualization'[23]. Referring to the triangular trade in which Africans were shipped to the New World as part of the Atlantic slave trade, as well as to the trading of manufactured goods for the kidnapped Africans, the former of which continued their journey to Europe, the latter of whom continued their journey across the Atlantic, Spillers speaks of the 'middle passage', related to the special status of the slave's flesh, insisting on the difference between body and flesh:

> I would make a distinction . . . between 'body' and 'flesh' and impose that distinction as the central one between captive and liberated subject-positions. In that sense, before the 'body' there is the 'flesh,' that zero degree of social

conceptualization that does not escape concealment under the brush of discourse, or the reflexes of iconography.[24]

Spillers continues,

> Under these conditions, we lose at least gender difference in the outcome, and the female body and the male body become a territory of cultural and political manoeuvre, not at all gender-related, gender-specific. But this body, at least from the point of view of the captive community, focuses a private and particular space, at which point of convergence biological, sexual, social, cultural, linguistic, ritualistic, and psychological fortunes join. This profound intimacy of interlocking detail is disrupted, however, by externally imposed meanings and uses: 1) the captive body becomes the source of an irresistible, destructive sensuality; 2) at the same time—in stunning contradiction—the captive body is reduced to a thing, becoming being for the captor; 3) in this absence from a subject position, the captured sexualities provide a physical and biological expression of 'otherness'; 4) as a category of 'otherness,' the captive body translates into a potential for pornotroping and embodies sheer physical powerlessness that slides into a more general 'powerlessness', resonating through various centers of human and social meaning.[25]

Alexander G. Weheliye's political demand to think humanity differently turns on the same point. For him, to think humanity means to think it as '*habeas viscus*' (as having flesh) not '*habeas corpus*' customarily reserved for the nation-state's biopolitical exercise of hegemonic power, and its brutal differentiations between the majoritarian national body and all other generations of 'ethnicities'[26]. Thinking 'humanity otherwise' means precisely this: thinking the *political flesh*. Based on William Goodell's descriptions of tortures in captivity, Spillers painfully yet accurately narrates the sufferings of the flesh:

> The anatomical specifications of rupture, of altered human tissue, take on the objective description of laboratory prose—eyes beaten out, arms, backs, skulls branded, a left jaw, a right ankle, punctured; teeth missing, as the calculated work of iron, whips, chains, knives, the canine patrol, the bullet. These undecipherable markings on the captive body render a kind of hieroglyphics of the flesh whose severe disjunctures come to be hidden to the cultural seeing by skin color.[27]

Spillers wonders whether this 'phenomenon of marking and branding actually "transfers" from one generation to another, finding its various symbolic substitutions in an efficacy of meanings that repeat the initiating moments'[28]. Étienne Balibar returns to this point in 2011, suggesting that, in the present-day EU, the transfer from generation to generation adapts and naturalises processes of racialisation, executed precisely along the lines of skin colour. For Spillers, the history of the slave trade should be understood not as a haphazard series of brutal, dehumanising historical moments but as representative of many and much deeper levels of meaning, indeed, as representing the logics and the regime within which Europeans and white Americans 'make sense' of the racial system they live in today. Elements of captivity that resonate with what might be termed necro space and necro time are revealed not to be intervals but spaces and times of absolute immobility that play a key role in the spatio-temporal conceptualisation of the aesthetics of necropolitics. Spillers suggests that

> those African persons in the 'Middle Passage' were literally suspended in the 'oceanic,' if we think of the latter in its Freudian orientation as an analogy for undifferentiated identity: removed from the indigenous land and culture, and not-yet 'American' either, these captive persons, without names that their captors would recognize, were in movement across the Atlantic, but they were also nowhere at all. Inasmuch as, on any given day, we might imagine, the captive personality did not know where s/he was, we could say that they were the culturally 'unmade,' thrown in the midst of a figurative darkness that 'exposed' their destinies to an unknown course.[29]

Today's situation is not one of liminality but of *immobility*; not an 'in-between', a 'neither-nor', a 'not quite' or 'not yet'—which could be seen as characteristic of modernity. The aesthetic dimension of necropolitics resides precisely in seizure, captivity and immobilisation. Once again, we have to search in the vocabularies and grammars, as Spillers suggests, in order to think outside of the dominant 'American grammar' so that we may account for the ruptures within the so-called legitimacy of the white, normative gender constructions, ruptures that may radically transform what it means to be a man or woman, instead of banishing the 'illegitimacy' of black family structures as 'lacking' something fundamental in the WASP United States and, by extension, in other countries too. Spillers writes,

> Relatedly, we might interpret the whole career of African-Americans, a decisive factor in national political life since the mid-seventeenth century. . . . According to this reading, gender, or sex-role assignation, or the clear differentiation of sexual stuff, sustained elsewhere in the culture, does not emerge for the African-American female in this historic instance, except indirectly, except as a way to reinforce through the process of birthing, 'the reproduction of the relations of production' that involves 'the reproduction of the values and behavior patterns necessary to maintain the system of hierarchy in its various aspects of gender, class, and race or ethnicity.[30]

In 'The Genealogical Scheme: Race or Culture?'[31] Étienne Balibar enumerates several reasons for researching the juncture of 'nationalism and racism'.

Apart from assembling his own (past) observations on the genealogical scheme, the purpose is, for Balibar, to rethink the relation between 'bourgeois universality and anthropological differences', to discuss 'fictitious ethnicity' and elaborate several 'discursive models' of the genealogical scheme[32]. Elsewhere, Balibar explains the genealogical scheme as consisting of

> studying the idea that generation after generation children inherit the 'qualities'—or, conversely, collective 'defects'—of their parents, be they physical, moral or intellectual. . . . A current example of great significance would be the way in which our liberal societies, which preach individualism and equal opportunities, trap the descendants of immigrants within a 'foreign identity' for two or three generations, even when they are societies formed by the mixing of populations and the contributions of immigrants, as is the case in North America and in certain European countries such as France.[33]

In the 2011 paper Balibar revisits the 'genealogical scheme' returning to the ghettoes of the French *banlieues* (where massive urban riots erupted in 2005 demanding the end of inequalities the French Republic imposed on French nationals and the second- and third-generation French citizens whose parents or grandparents originate from the former French colonies). He states that

> in the modern ghettoes like the French *Banlieues* . . . a quality like 'migrant' (which is in fact a stigma and a pejorative collective name) becomes absurdly attributed to youngsters who, precisely because they are discriminated, are seen as a threat, but who are only the children or the grand-children of the actual migrants, therefore enjoy the national citizenship . . . so that the quality 'migrant' becomes *socially and symbolically a 'hereditary' quality'*.[34]

Furthermore, the pseudo community effect of a certain natural collectivity is but a myth. It is

> a mythical construction allowing it [the collectivity] to imagine that reproduction, transmission, education, memory, tradition, etc., are taking place *within the limits of a community* which bears a certain recognizable 'identity'. Indeed this myth was anything but deprived of effectivity, which is the characteristic of all genuine mythical constructions: it was applied and 'forced' into reality, so to speak. With this idea, we can finally return to the idea that there is an intrinsic link between racism and sexism that the modern nation, not only does not suppress, but permanently reinforces, while it is bound in the end to produce permanent crises in its institutional life.[35]

In other words, Balibar affirms what Spillers suggested in 1987, that the community effect is but 'the representation of quasi- or pseudo- collective genealogy', a *myth*. Additionally, Balibar gives us the possibility—or at least that is my reading of Balibar—to develop three other theses that reflect the persistent, brutal necropolitical racialisation. The first is the fact that 'when the nation-form becomes challenged and undergoes a crisis (which occurs repeatedly throughout history)—the development of racist ideologies and practices appears as a natural "solution"'[36]. Indeed, what else are we seeing today in the EU, in Germany, Austria and France, and in the United States? Faced with a crisis (which is nothing else but a blatant power game of capital), these countries *racialise* refugees, marginalise migrants, fragment and destroy communities and reconstitute them as 'communities' cleansed of 'foreigners', marked by the skin colour line. Indeed, such ideas present themselves as 'natural solutions'. Secondly, Balibar reveals that the national ideal of a 'natural' community, which, needless to say, is a fictitious construct (based on race, language or both), is possible only as a result of a double rejection, of a prohibition and stigmatisation of the always anew constructed 'other'. Taking us back to the ghettoes of the French *Banlieues*, Balibar suggests that

> we cannot ignore the ultra-violent *double-bind* in which immigrants and children of migrants are burdened with, on one side, a *prohibited genealogy*, and, on the other side, with the *stigma of origin* or 'ethnic-cultural descent' that is imposed on them, so that the 'normalization' of family life (which in general also becomes increasingly problematic in today's society) is made into an impossible goal.[37]

Naturally, this is the central point of the protests of the so-called second and third generations of migrants (who are not migrants at all but French, British, Dutch and so forth citizens). Referring to two authors whose work is reflected in his previous writing on race, genealogy and community, Alys Eve Weinbaum, the author of the 2004 *Wayward Reproductions: Genealogies of Race and Nation in Transatlantic Modern Thought*, and Rada Iveković, the author of the 2003 *Le sexe de la nation* (*Nation's Gender*, or even *Nation's Sex*), Balibar unearths interesting dilemmas. He shows that 'ethnicity' is indeed of a quasi-genealogical order, a 'fictitious' relationship of domination based on race and gender while class exploitation is left out of the equation. He also emphasises his previous hypothesis that the 'racist community' and the 'sexist community' (the community of males excluding women) is not really different; they are, in fact, the same 'community', they rely on the same 'community effect'.[38] Thirdly, we cannot understate, much less dismiss, colonialism. Balibar's analysis of William Faulkner's 1936 novel *Absalom, Absalom*, which he defines as postcolonial *avant la lettre*, brings to light that the phenomenology of the

> 'foreign body's presence', the presence of the intruder in the middle of the bourgeois order, whose essential manifestation is the racialised body in terms

> of colour, derives not so much from a coherence of the sexual and racial dimensions, either formulated in biological or cultural languages, but from the invisible disruption or interruption within the genealogical scheme that slavery in particular has pushed to the extreme and installed in the very heart of the collective memory of our institutions.[39]

Balibar's claim is that colonisation (in this specific case the internal colonisation of the American South) 'anticipates a bourgeois order in which, ultimately, questions of degeneracy, inherited defects, eugenics, will entirely occupy problems of ancestry, lineage, thus making the progeny, offspring, children more decisively other than the ancestors'[40]. *Absalom, Absalom* articulates notions of '"alliance" and "inheritance", and the way they are "thrown" into crisis when the "foreign body" par excellence, that is, the racial other who had remained invisible, emerges in the middle of the generational connection'[41]. The outcome of this 'revelation' is terrifying for the regime of whiteness. Indeed, what emerges from Balibar's analysis is that the bourgeois nation-state order will more readily accept incest than it will accept *miscegenation*.

NECROPOLITICS

In his 2003 'Necropolitics'[42], Achille Mbembe builds on Foucault's idea of state racism but relocates the argument to spaces of colonial occupation and the apartheid state. Mbembe adds two key concepts to Foucault's analysis: 'the relation to enmity', which concerns the threat from a/n (fictional) enemy, and 'the state of exception', in which the rule of law is suspended in response precisely to this perceived threat. In a straightforward yet sharp manner Mbembe defines the necropolitical as the 'power and . . . capacity to dictate who may live and who must die'[43]. Such a politic of death management places Mbembe's notion of necropower not only within the state's prerogative to wage war but also, and equally importantly, within the neoliberal market technologies whose purpose and goal is '*the generalized instrumentalization of human existence and the material destruction of human bodies and populations*'[44]. Mbembe argues, 'in the economy of biopower, the function of racism is to regulate the distribution of death and to make possible the murderous functions of the state'[45]. But, as already mentioned in the section on biopolitics, the function of racism is also to *naturalise* abandonment via the tacit agreement to, for example, not talk about migrants—the labour force that played a crucial part in the revitalisation of the post-Nazi, post–World War II Western Europe. For Mbembe, the colony is the ultimate space of exception; it 'represents the site where sovereignty consists fundamentally in the exercise of a power outside the law (*ab legibus solutus*) and where "peace" is more likely to take on the face of a "war without end"'[46]. In such settings, necropolitics is a *structure*; the 'sovereign right to kill is not subject to any rule. . . . In the colonies, the sovereign might kill at any time or in any manner. Colonial warfare is not subject to legal and institutional rules. It is not a legally codified activity'[47]. Mbembe develops the necropolitical theme by drawing parallels between early modern colonial occupation and its late modern counterparts and, finally, contemporary warfare in which state actors are increasingly replaced by war machines. What is produced in all these cases, regardless of epoch or technology, is the necropolitical space. Mbembe writes,

> I have put forward the notion of necropolitics and necropower to account for the various ways in which, in our contemporary world, weapons are deployed in the interest of maximum destruction of persons and the creation of *death-worlds*, new and unique forms of social existence in which vast populations are subjected to conditions of life conferring upon them the status of *living dead*.[48]

In 2016 Ebony Rose revisited this relation and suggested that 'we rupture and deconstruct the theoretical preoccupations of both the material body and architectures to provide a close reading of the black body situated in a place and space as a negative one that's exclusively exposed to the highest form of vulnerability under the guise of Achille Mbembe's "Necropolitics," (insecurity/death) and life-optimization and population management under Michel Foucault's "Biopolitics" (security/life)'[49]. Therefore this includes the examination of political, material, economic and ideological conditions of the re/production of life but only and solely through processes of managed, administered death in contemporary global neoliberal societies. This relation is reproduced in the contemporary division of labour and in the new forms of exploitation and expropriation while, simultaneously, developing a racist basis for practices, structures and discourses in the field of culture and art.

NECROAESTHETICS

The effect of these destructive processes is disturbing and destabilising; it gives free reign to capital's most urgent task: the de/re/structuring of the working class by means of intensified precarisation—the fundamental contemporary form of labour devaluation in the shift from biopolitics to necropolitics. These de/re/structuring processes are ongoing in many different realms: in the imposed war on terrorism, in multiple forms of abandonment and immiseration, such as redundancy, rising unemployment, asset liquidation and forced evictions, while coexisting with the various art, cultural, health and economic institutions, such as banks and multinational corporations, that, too, are refused the choice to disobey the imperative of profit maximisation. As Chamayou points out, this is, indeed, the basis of necroethics. In neoliberal necrocapitalism, the entire society has been transformed into one *big investment sector* that provides new opportunities for the incessant capitalisation of capital in order to make surplus value. The situation created here, as Joshua Dunn poignantly notes, is the following:

> The [Western] biopolitical state must ultimately step in to install a secondary apparatus of security around the artificial milieu produced through the regulatory power of the market. This is the domain of labor laws, minimum wages, and environmental regulations. . . . It is the very dissolution of this state security apparatus, the unleashing of the market's necropolitical function, which marks the neoliberal turn, in which free market fundamentalism and an attack on the 'welfare state' come together to form a new biopolitical landscape.[50]

The racial logic which underlies this 'exclusion from biopolitical protection, unpalatable to the modern liberal imagination, is masked in discourses on the morality of debt repayment'[51]. Dunn goes on to propose another differentiation, which, in my opinion, is axiomatic of the relation between aesthetics and necrocapitalism: the relation between the biopolitical aesthetics and the necropolitical social, which is a key characteristic of the 'financialisation of the biopolitical technologies of power'. Dunn writes,

> The phenomenon of debt-collection and austerity can be understood as a financialization of the biopolitical technologies of power. When the aleatory elements of a population are regulated so that the objective is not the preservation and maintenance of life but rather the protection of a return on investment, and when the elements of risk to be secured against are not only those concerning human existence, but also the risks which are inherent to financial speculation, and when the latter supersedes the former, the technologies of biopower are converted into a financialized necropower in which a population is sapped of its vitality in order to prioritize debt repayment.[52]

Let me be even more precise. The financialised biopolitical aesthetics forms part of *Western* necropolitics. In the necropolitical South, in the so-called third world, in the Middle East (Afghanistan, Iraq, Syria) or at the Mexico–U.S. border, there is nothing but necroaesthetics. The global world is organised around the ordering of bodies—bodies that are expendable: black bodies, transgender bodies, Roma bodies, 'white trash' bodies, migrants; bodies that are collateral 'damage', as can be seen from the so-called human rights practiced in the EU which leave the refugees dispossessed, discriminated against, ghettoised and incarcerated (that is, captivated). Financialised bio- and necropolitical structures produce uncontrollable violence as the only aesthetic intensity that profoundly reorders space and time. Consequently, it is possible to state the following: if the body of the refugee is taken as the ultimate political figure of necrocapitalism, the emergent necroaesthetic parameters are: a) hyperviolence, b) the body as a corpse and c) hyperimmobilisation, all of which are predicated on the erasure of history. In addition, the necropolitical logic of the financialised biopolitical aesthetics implies a perverse ability of each now ultimately violently dehumanised 'necro-subject' to reflect on his/her position. What we are dealing with here is 'necrodistance' that allows the necrosubject to see her position clearly and understand that her experience, knowledges and practices are continually being erased or repossessed by the neoliberal necrocapitalist mode of (re)production.

But let's go through a detailed reading of these elements. First, hyperviolence is the central trope here; it 'behaves' as the 'spontaneous violence of the mob'[53], however, lurking under its surface is the well-organised repressive violence of the necrocapitalist government. In the 2011 London riot, in which the 'mob' looted shops, damaged and burnt property, was characterised in the media as an outburst of greed, vandalism and meaningless destruction, in other words, as spontaneous violence. But expunged from media reporting and the various opinion fragments was the central agenda of the riot's protest: against conspicuous consumerism reserved for the wealthy yet imposed as (what could be termed) a measure of 'dignity' on those working-class citizens who could not afford it. The riots took place one year into the Conservative and Liberal Democrat Coalition's government that had implemented many drastic cuts. This situation was exacerbated by the death of Mark Duggan, shot by the police several days before the Tottenham riot in an area historically steeped in racial turmoil, and the bloody battles between the police and the local black community that, to this day, resonate with the Broadwater Farm riot of 1985[54]. The same interweaving of necropolitics, biopolitics, economics and aesthetics is present in the violent demolition of the third-world slums or of unwanted parts of the Western mega-cities, as was the case with the French city of Calais and its 'Calais jungle', a refugee and migrant encampment, in use from January 2015 to October 2016, that was dismantled and demolished.

Western financialisation is, of course, inextricably entwined with the necropolitical regions of the global South via the extraction of goods and value, the ruination and dispossession of lands and lives and the exploitation of the ultra-cheap labour force. Although the Western imaginary may initially be shocked by the images of destruction and death, these images are soon enough 'normalised' through the routine sublimation of 'the biological racial caesura' as formulated by Foucault, further developed by Mbembe and mentioned earlier. Western biopolitical aesthetics is predicated on factual death and factual death-worlds. Amidst this state of affairs, the aesthetics deployed in films and television serials—in the Hollywood industry as such—serves as a link between the necroscapes of devastation and riot sites and commodified disasterscapes. Second, and in reference to the body—the body-corpse—every relation of violence invariably produces racialised immobilisation, although, in the West, there is a proliferation of bodies *as* stories (not histories) suffering from myriad sexual neuroses, while in the overtly necropolitical context of any given city, in the slums, or in the ghetto, bodies and entire communities are perceived as a disease, contagion, even when such ghettos are purposefully constructed, as is the case with many Western mega-cities[55]. This is why, when Alexander G. Weheliye in *Habeas Viscus: Racializing Assemblages, Biopolitics, and Black Feminist Theories of the Human* discusses the difference between the body and the flesh, he insists on '*habeas viscus*' (flesh), in contradistinction to '*habeas corpus*' (body). Via the category of '*habeas viscus*' Weheliye asks for recognition of the distinction between those who are seen as fully human bodies (the white, Western wo/men) and their (less-than-human) 'complements'.

The third and uncircumscribable problem is immobilisation. There are vast and—from the point of view of the EU—superfluous populations of refugees, noncitizens that are immobilised in enclaves and camps, either in the EU or in the bordering countries, such as Turkey, or in countries that have an agreement with the EU, such as Libya, which serves as a sanitary cordon to stop the refugees from entering the EU. Significant, in this respect, is Kirstine Nordentoft Mose and Vera Wriedt's analysis of the various seclusion and security measures/systems that resort to a vocabulary of violence encapsulated in abbreviations:

—FRONTEX (European Border Enforcement Agency)
—EUROSUR (European Border Surveillance System)
—NCC (National Coordination Center in EU countries)
—ENP (European Neighbourhood Policy, consisting mainly of bilateral policy agreements between the EU and partner non-EU countries).[56]

Apart from being spatially, physically and linguistically omnipresent, necroaesthetics is also (paradoxically) absent from sight because one of the goals of necropolitics—as management of death—is to destroy evidence. The necropolitical thus disappears into invisibility. The status of the image is key to this process as it protects the necropolitical project by emptying it of any content. Today, concomitant with the absence of real finance, if one is to go by the images that circulate in the media and in the nonghettoised part of any

Western city, one might conclude that there is also an absence of poverty, suffering or strife of any kind. Naturally, images of poverty, suffering and strife are present but they are present as a mirage, as an immense complexity that is incomprehensible and far removed from those living under the reign of necrocapitalism. The empty form of the image is coexistent with the empty balloon of economics and with financialisation that functions as appearance and abstraction. Such a situation of pseudo-invisibility is necessary to *naturalise* contemporary necroculture. The necropolitical regime is ultimately about death, visible or invisible. But it operates in such a way as to link aesthetics to the devastation of landscapes and bodies in order to produce the 'beauty' of death. Consequently, we have two processes that seem opposed but are, in fact, coextensive, even mutually structuring. The empty form of the image is directly related to the 'subliminal' empty form of death, which is a *mise-en-scène* of capturing death's 'beauty'. As Dunn suggests,

> the necropolitical regime does not make death any less unruly. . . . Instead, death exceeds logic, and transforms in ways which cannot be mastered, contained, or made uniform. . . . The constant exposure to death produces its own distinct logics and subjectivities which resist order and control.[57]

It's hardly a surprise that inventing new forms of death is one of the central tasks of Hollywood's blockbuster film productions. These death forms are empty, but meticulously, indeed, forensically elaborated. A good example is *Blade Runner 2049* (2017) that has no content whatsoever but is an abundant collection of empty forms of death. Here, death is not hidden; it acquires an almost sovereign status through its empty form. The question that remains is: What might be the consequences of the earlier discussed changes that are rapidly taking place? My proposed answer is: the contemporary necrocapitalist seizure of history.

The 1970s saw the imposition of what I term the biopolitical amnesia, not as a racialising process of forgetting but as a deficit of memory. After the fall of the Berlin Wall, in the 1990s, the suppression of counter-history continued as aphasia. In 'Colonial Aphasia: Race and Disabled Histories in France', Ann Laura Stoler presents the case of France that cannot put together the French Republic and the colonial empire. Stoler's notion of cultural aphasia points towards a lack of language with which to address the colonial past. This is, of course, yet another form of contemporary colonial violence, used, as Stoler argues, to displace 'amnesia' through three key features: 'an occlusion of knowledge, a difficulty generating a vocabulary that associates appropriate words and concepts with appropriate things, and a difficulty comprehending the enduring relevancy of what has already been spoken'[58].

In historical terms, processes and procedures for racialising aesthetic assemblages imposed on counter-histories turn from the biopolitical amnesia of the 1970s to the aphasic abandonment of the 1990s. From 2001 onwards, this process transforms into the sovereign necropolitical seizure, or confiscation, and a complete privatisation of communal counter-histories. The result of this process is both an aesthetic of erasure and an aesthetic of seizure, as Mbembe suggests in his definition of necropolitics as a 'concentration of bodies that allows to the sovereign to deploy weapons onto them and to construct death worlds'[59]. Seizure is therefore co-substantive with necropolitical racialising assemblages; it is, literally, a confiscation of history that paves the way for the erasure of counter-cultural histories.

CODA: RESISTING THE NECROPOLITICAL

Resisting the necropolitical aesthetisation of death and abandonment is a challenge. Suggestions for a possible praxis are drawn from a rereading of Katherine McKittrick's *Sylvia Wynter: On Being Human as Praxis*. In reference to Aimé Césaire, Wynter suggests that what needs doing is 'a rewriting of our present now globally institutionalized order of knowledge'[60]. The second suggestion comes from the title of the book itself, the first part of which consists of a long, meticulously knitted interview. In a question to Wynter, McKittrick emphasises the racial line of division that runs through neoliberal necrocapitalism, suggesting that

> the enactment of our present biocentric descriptive statement (and thus its eugenic and dysgenic sociogenic codes of symbolic life and death) is linked to the law-like normalization of the corporeal features of Western Europeans in their now ethno-class bourgeois aesthetic configuration. This normalization is most strikingly evident in the consumer marketing of skin bleaching creams and cosmetic surgery, as well as by the proposed mainline genetic engineering of designer babies.[61]

McKittrick also clarifies that the process of 'beautification' in bourgeois-consumer terms refers, 'most markedly, [to] blackness', which is furthest removed from the standard image of the '*homo oeconomicus* (the virtuous breadwinner, the stable job holder, the taxpayer, the savvy investor, the master of natural scarcity)'[62]. For Wynter, however, such a category reveals the *symbolic death* of the denizens of the 'planet of slums' and of the 'reality of climate change/instability, to which, inter alia, it gives rise'[63]. In reference to Frantz Fanon, Wynter suggests that what we need at this moment in time is

> to initiate the exploration of the new reconceptualized form of knowledge that would be called for by Fanon's redefinition of being human as that of skins (phylogeny/ontogeny) *and* masks (sociogeny). Therefore *bios* and *mythoi*. And notice! One major implication here: *humanness* is no longer a *noun*. *Being human is a praxis*.[64]

If we understand this suggestion without *naïveté*, we can begin to think a radical transformation of relations of necropower for a different future. For example, as T. L. Cowan suggests, by '*staging living*' in the 'apparently uninhabited/uninhabitable spaces', in borderline necrozones, in 'spaces marked for death'[65]. Such an aesthetic depends on a 'decolonial imaginary', characterised by lingering, dwelling and reflecting on the 'living that happens in the borderland necro-zones, living that happens in spite of being marked for an *unliveable life*'[66].

NOTES

1. Ebony Rose, 'Afro-Stasis: Understanding the Necro(bio)political Collaboration in the Creation of the Carceralization of Black Life/Death', *AAG Paper*, 2016, 4.
2. Achille Mbembe, 'Necropolitics', *Public Culture* 15, no. 1 (Winter 2003): 1.
3. Grégoire Chamayou, *A Theory of the Drone* (New York: The New Press, 2015).
4. Hortense J. Spillers, 'Mama's Baby, Papa's Maybe: An American Grammar Book', *Diacritics* 17, no. 2 (Culture and Countermemory: The 'American' Connection) (Summer 1987): 65–81, http://www.jstor.org/stable/464747.
5. Étienne Balibar and Immanuel Wallerstein, *Race, Nation, Class: Ambiguous Identities* (London: Verso, 1991); the original in French language was published in 1987.
6. Joshua Dunn, 'Cross Roads of the Living and the Dead: Necropolitics and Market Logic in Chris Abani's *GraceLand*', Master's Thesis, University of South Carolina, 2017.
7. Rose, 'Afro-Stasis', 4.
8. Katherine McKittrick, ed., *Sylvia Wynter: On Being Human as Praxis* (Durham: Duke University Press, 2014).
9. Michel Foucault, 'Society Must Be Defended', *Lectures at the College de France 1975–76*, ed. Mauro Bertani and Alessandro Fontana, trans. David Macey (New York: Picador, 2003).
10. Ibid., 241.
11. Ibid., 243.
12. Ibid.
13. Ibid., 245.
14. Ibid., 255.

15. Ibid.
16. Ibid.
17. Spillers, 'Mama's Baby, Papa's Maybe', 65–81.
18. Ibid., 65.
19. http://www.blackpast.org/primary/moynihan-report-1965.
20. Spillers, 'Mama's Baby, Papa's Maybe', 65–66.
21. Ibid., 66.
22. Ibid.
23. Ibid., 67.
24. Ibid.
25. Ibid.
26. Alexander G. Weheliye, *Habeas Viscus: Racializing Assemblages, Biopolitics, and Black Feminist Theories of the Human* (Durham and London: Duke University Press, 2014).
27. Spillers, 'Mama's Baby, Papa's Maybe', 67.
28. Ibid.
29. Ibid., 72.
30. Ibid., 79.
31. Étienne Balibar, 'The Genealogical Scheme', *Race* or *Culture*? (2011), 1–8, https://www.scribd.com/document/221186055/Balibar-the-Genealogical-Scheme-Race-or-Culture.
32. Balibar and Wallerstein, *Race, Nation, Class*.
33. 'A Racism without Races', an interview with Étienne Balibar by Clement Petitjean, 15 April 2014, http://davidmcnally.org/wp-content/uploads/2011/01/Balibar_A-racism-without-races1.pdf.
34. Balibar, 'The Genealogical Scheme,' 8.
35. Ibid.
36. Ibid., 2.
37. Ibid., 3.
38. Ibid., 2–3.
39. Ibid., 6.
40. Ibid., 5.
41. Ibid.
42. Mbembe, 'Necropolitics'.
43. Ibid., 11.
44. Ibid., 14 (italics originally in the text).
45. Ibid., 17.
46. Ibid., 23.
47. Ibid., 25.
48. Ibid., 40.
49. Rose, 'Afro-Stasis', 4.
50. Dunn, 'Cross Roads of the Living and the Dead', 5.
51. Ibid., 7.
52. Ibid.
53. Ibid., 10.

54. https://www.theguardian.com/commentisfree/2017/aug/04/a-moment-that-changed-me-london-riots-2011.

55. http://www.dw.com/en/brussels-district-molenbeek-fights-terrorist-label/a-19048396.

56. Kirstine Nordentoft Mose and Vera Wriedt, 'Mapping the Construction of EU Borderspaces as Necropolitical Zones of Exception', *Birkbeck Law Review* 3, no. 2 (December 2015).

57. Dunn, 'Cross Roads of the Living and the Dead', 26, 29.

58. Ann Laura Stoler, 'Colonial Aphasia: Race and Disabled Histories in France', *Public Culture* 23, no. 1 (2011): 121–56, http://publicculture.dukejournals.org/content/23/1/121.abstract.

59. Mbembe, 'Necropolitics', 40.

60. McKittrick, *Sylvia Wynter*, 18.

61. Ibid.

62. Ibid., 19.

63. Ibid.

64. Ibid., 23.

65. T. L. Cowan, 'The Land of the Living in the Necro-Zone: Linking Border Stories with Prison Stories in Yadira De La Riva's *One Journey* and Liza Jessie Peterson's *The Peculiar Patriot* on the Cabaret Stage', *Liminalities: A Journal of Performance Studies* 12, no. 4 (2016): 16. In this respect Cowan exposes the works of Yadira De La Riva and Liza Jessie Peterson, arguing that these two authors 'confound the exclusionary matrix of borderland necro-zones'.

66. Ibid.

BIBLIOGRAPHY

Balibar, Étienne. 'A Racism without Races', an interview with Étienne Balibar by Clement Petitjean. 15 April 2014. http://davidmcnally.org/wp-content/uploads/2011/01/Balibar_A-racism-without-races1.pdf.

Balibar, Étienne. 'The Genealogical Scheme', *Race* or *Culture*? (2011): 1–8, https://www.scribd.com/document/221186055/Balibar-the-Genealogical-Scheme-Race-or-Culture.

Balibar, Étienne, and Immanuel Wallerstein. *Race, Nation, Class: Ambiguous Identities.* Translated by Chris Turner. London: Verso, 1991.

Chamayou, Grégoire. *A Theory of the Drone*. Translated by Janet Lloyd. New York: The New Press, 2015.

Cowan, T. L. 'The Land of the Living in the Necro-Zone: Linking Border Stories with Prison Stories in Yadira De La Riva's *One Journey* and Liza Jessie Peterson's *The Peculiar Patriot* on the Cabaret Stage', *Liminalities: A Journal of Performance Studies* 12, no. 4 (2016).

Dunn, Joshua. 'Cross Roads of the Living and the Dead: Necropolitics and Market Logic in Chris Abani's *GraceLand*', Master's Thesis, University of South Carolina, 2017.

Foucault, Michel. 'Society Must Be Defended', *Lectures at the College de France 1975–76*. Edited by Mauro Bertani and Alessandro Fontana. Translated by David Macey. New York: Picador, 2003.

Mbembe, Achille. 'Necropolitics', *Public Culture* 15, no. 1 (2003): 11–40.

McKittrick, Katherine, ed. *Sylvia Wynter: On Being Human as Praxis*. Durham, NC: Duke University Press, 2014.

Nordentoft Mose, Kirstine, and Vera Wriedt. 'Mapping the Construction of EU Borderspaces as Necropolitical Zones of Exception', *Birkbeck Law Review* 3, no. 2 (December 2015).

Rose, Ebony. 'AfroStasis: Understanding the Necro(bio)political Collaboration in the Creation of the Carceralization of Black Life/Death', *AAG Paper*, 2016, 4.

Spillers, Hortense. 'Mama's Baby, Papa's Maybe: An American Grammar Book', *Diacritics* 17, no. 2 (Culture and Countermemory: The 'American' Connection) (Summer 1987): 65–81, http://www.jstor.org/stable/464747.

Stoler, Ann Laura. 'Colonial Aphasia: Race and Disabled Histories in France', *Public Culture* 23, no. 1 (2011): 12–156.

Weheliye, Alexander, G. *Habeas Viscus: Racializing Assemblages, Biopolitics, and Black Feminist Theories of the Human*. Durham, NC, and London: Duke University Press, 2014.

Chapter Two

Get Out

From Atlantic Slavery to Black Lives Matter

Sarah Juliet Lauro

SOCIAL DEATH

In Achille Mbembe's 2003 article 'Necropolitics', the author discusses the manner in which certain 'populations are subjected to conditions of life conferring on them the status of *living dead*'[1]. Mbembe's discussion of necropolitics applies equally to colonial and postcolonial operations of capital as it does to the devaluation of certain types of humans within the state. Chief among the examples provided is a sketch of plantation slavery of the U.S. antebellum era. Drawing on the well-established discussion of slavery as a form of 'social death', Mbembe suggests that the slave is 'kept alive but in a state of injury, in a phantom-like world of horrors and intense cruelty and profanity'[2]. As an exemplary form of necropolitics, 'slave life, in many ways, is a form of death-in-life'[3]. However, in his book *The Reaper's Garden*, Vincent Brown cautions that we ought not misconstrue the metaphor as 'an actual state of being'; to do so is an occlusion of the enslaved's overt acts of resistance and effaces the rebellion of mere survival[4]. This caveat is fleshed out more thoroughly in Brown's article 'Social Death and Political Life in the Study of Slavery', a critique of the uses of the trope of social death in slavery scholarship, such as in Ian Baucom's *Specters of the Atlantic* and *Lose Your Mother*, of which Brown writes, 'rather than pathologizing the slaves by allowing the condition of social death to stand in for the experience of life in slavery . . . it might be more helpful to focus on what the enslaved actually made of their situation'[5]. Attuned to Brown's criticisms of the danger of taking 'social death' literally, my interest, in this chapter, is in the complexity of the figural work of the metaphor in literary and cinematic instances in which the oppressed are depicted as less than living or already dead—be they a representation of historical slavery or of contemporary dispossession. To be more precise, I look to these figural models for an acknowledgement of real-world resistive potential.

I am haunted by the continued relevance of imagery of the living dead: by the 'spectres of the Atlantic' that I read in today's headlines about the murder of unarmed black citizens by police—the latest plot points in a century-long drama of an exercise of necropower—hashes on a timeline that stretches back through lynching in the Jim Crow era to the master's irreproachable execution of his human 'property', to the slave traders' murder of captured Africans unlikely to bring profit in the Zong Massacre of 1781, in which 133 slaves were heartlessly thrown overboard to drown when the ship ran low on drinking water so that the owners could collect an insurance payout[6]. In a 2015 opinion piece for the *New York Times* on the subject of police violence against people of colour, Roxane Gay concludes her article with a striking simile: 'Increasingly, as a black woman in America, I do not feel alive. I feel like I am not yet dead'—a powerful proclamation of the operations of necropower at work today, one that begs the question of whether the phantom-like status of enslaved peoples has been transmitted to the free citizens who are their descendants[7]. The 'precarious life'—to invoke Judith Butler's term[8]—of the black citizen is felt under the crush of recent instances of police brutality, a phenomenon short-handed in the United States with the expression 'Black Lives Matter'. This crisis is but one among many examples of contemporary necropower, in which some lives are deemed salvageable and others expendable. As Butler writes in *Precarious Life*,

> A certain level of dangerousness takes a human outside the bounds of law. . . . What counts as 'dangerous' is what is deemed dangerous by the state, so that, once again, the state posits what is dangerous, and in so positing it, establishes the conditions for its own preemption and usurpation of the law.[9]

That police officers are continually acquitted of any wrongdoing in cases in which unarmed black citizens are murdered is analogous to the usurpation of the law Butler describes in addressing the devaluation of Arab lives after 9/11. What makes these men and women so 'dangerous' in the eyes of the law as to justify the use of deadly force is only the colour of their skin, the same property that justified ownership of their bodies under the institution of slavery. Jordan Peele's 2017 film *Get Out* provides a perfect example of the *stakes* of the necropolitical metaphor that characterise the precarity of black life in the aftermath of slavery. Peele's cinematic text draws on imagery of living death as a figuration of necropolitics, simultaneously recalling the 'social death' of the slave and the devaluation of black lives in contemporary

U.S. society—in a way that acknowledges the temporal connection between the two. Many have classified the film as belonging to the horror or science fiction genres for, on the surface, it is a tale of hypnotic control and brain transplantation that renders black bodies under the control of white people and may call to mind films like Philip Kaufman's 1978 *Invasion of the Body Snatchers* or Brian Forbes's 1975 *The Stepford Wives*[10]. But the body-snatching theme is used in *Get Out* to recall that peculiar institution in which white people historically *commandeered* black lives; the most apt comparison may be to the early wave of zombie films. The Haitian zombie is a classic example of a figure of living death that acts as a political allegory. The folkloric zombies of Caribbean Voudou, controlled by a witch doctor profiting from his living dead labour force, were clearly coded descriptions of the colonial master's enslavement of the African[11]. However, Jordan Peele, who recently described *Get Out* as 'a documentary', situates the film's horrific context both in the (past) necroscape of the Atlantic slave trade and in the (present) state of necropower in the United States[12].

The film resounds with Baucom's treatment of history in *Specters of the Atlantic* wherein the author articulates the concept of 'temporal accumulation'[13]. Folding together the Benjaminian concept of 'now time' with Edouard Glissant's discussion of history as sediment, Baucom argues that we need to reconceptualise the present in a manner that recognises that the past is not separate from it: 'time does not pass, it accumulates, and as it accumulates it deposits an ever greater freight of material within the cargo holds of the present'[14]. Though it may not be a zombie movie per se, *Get Out* does similar work as does the Haitian zombie myth; the film allegorises both slavery *and* slave revolt, which I have elsewhere called the zombie's dialectic: the zombie has historically borne not only imagery of slavery in the entranced's servitude to the witch doctor but also a historical connection to the Haitian Revolution, the largest slave revolt on record[15]. In preserving the presence of resistance and rebellion in its plot, the film resonates with the ideas of those who, like Vincent Brown, question the limits of models like social death for conceptualising resistance. In depicting the struggle rather than just the plight, Peele's important film safeguards against fatalism and futility[16]. This is why, in this chapter, I use *Get Out* as a lens through which to reappraise Mbembe's address of slavery and social death. I focus on the film as offering a revision of the Hegelian master/slave dialectic, one more in keeping with that originary spark that kindled the allegory—the slave revolt of Saint Domingue, also known as the Haitian Revolution[17]. Along the way, I present the operations of necropolitics in the United States today and analyse what the film's depiction offers in terms of hope for resistance.

SEDIMENTED SPACE AND TIME

On the surface, the film's narrative concerns a young black man named Chris Washington, who must navigate numerous tensions as he meets his white girlfriend's family for the first time. As such, the film clearly foregrounds race relations from the beginning, well before Chris discovers that Rose's family has a nefarious agenda: the Armitages perform body snatching of African Americans through a hypnotic zombification and, ultimately, brain transplantation to give control of young black bodies over to ageing white people who pay handsomely for this privilege. The original inhabitant of the body remains trapped within the body but powerless, an allegorisation of the 'death-in-life' of the enslaved and the master's control over the bodies of his human chattel. Centrally, the film serves as a reminder that people were born—and normalised into—slavery on both sides. Rose, Chris's girlfriend, has been raised to accept the family business as the norm. Likewise, the disappearances of previous victims of the Armitages' plot have failed to trigger a serious enquiry by police. The film quite obviously signals to police discrimination, the exploitation of black domestics in white suburbia and to diverse types of racism, from micro-aggressions and the fetishisation of the black body to discomfort with interracial relationships. But as the narrative twists into the fantastical scenario of body snatching, the plot corkscrews, revealing a layer beneath, one that specifically connects society today to slavery and the plantation's complete mastery of the enslaved person's life.

My treatment of the film emphasises spaces—the suburbs, the city, the house and the garden—as the film's dual emphasis on space (in the presentation of the house as a stand-in for the plantation) and on time (in the depiction of overlapping histories) resounds with Mbembe's spatio-temporal understanding of the 'postcolony' as both a 'temporal formation' and a 'spatial geography'[18]. The film begins, importantly for its historical significance, with a scene of capture. An African American man is wandering at night on a darkened street in the suburbs. A white car begins to follow him, eerily blasting the 1939 song 'Run, Rabbit, Run' from its speakers; the man is then placed in a chokehold by a figure wearing a strange mask and forced into the trunk of the car. The viewer will encounter this kidnap victim later in the film, when the protagonist meets him at a garden party; but the man appears altered, vacant-eyed and formal, nearly unrecognisable in this 'depersonalised' state, a figure recalling various types of living death in cinema, as well as Orlando Patterson's description of the enslaved[19]. After the abduction scene at the beginning of the film, haunting music plays with lyrics in Swahili that translate to 'listen to your ancestors; run!' The film's second nondiegetic song, coming directly after the credit sequence, 'Redbone' by hip-hop artist

Childish Gambino, acknowledges the challenges faced by coloured people today: 'They gon' find you, / gon' catch you sleeping / . . . But stay woke!' The use of the phrase 'stay woke' is a direct call to political action associated with recent incidents of police brutality (since the shooting of Michael Brown by police in Ferguson, Missouri, in 2014). It is also one of the slogans of the Black Lives Matter movement, which places the previous song's appeal to the African ancestors on a single timeline[20].

Immediately after our introduction to Chris and Rose in his apartment, we see Chris in the passenger seat of a moving car. The woods previously shown in the film's credits are now reflected across his face as he makes the same journey as the kidnapped man. The shadow of police prejudice looms large when the couple hits a deer with their car. Sizing up the interracial couple, the police officer demands to see Chris's identification despite the fact that Rose was driving. Her outrage is juxtaposed to Chris's lack of surprise, a glimpse of the daily discrimination endured by African Americans of which white people are blissfully ignorant. Rose is enraged by police discrimination but the rest of the film reveals her agenda, much like it reveals similarities between Chris and the wounded deer. Alive but unable to move, Chris will be paralysed by hypnosis, the prey and potential trophy of his girlfriend's family. At first blush, the Armitage family seem like awkward white people: the dad infuses slang into his conversation—like 'thang' and 'my man'—stressing how much he loved President Obama and generally fetishising black culture, which (misleadingly) resembles a newer form of racism[21] until it becomes clear that Armitage's father had been a runner beaten by African American athlete Jesse Owens for a spot on the 1933 Olympic team. In the film, one racism is overturned for another; the black body's alleged athletic and sexual superiority is ceaselessly fetishised[22]. This is most directly shown during the garden party scene in a cringe-worthy montage of ignorant comments that the guests make to Chris, asking about his performance in sport and in bed. However, on display is more than ignorant banter because the guests are, in fact, sizing him up as a potential purchase, echoing the African's examination on the auction block. The doublings of this scene, which reads first as gaucherie but later as butchery, calls into question the role of micro-aggressions in the greater apparatus of oppression. On a first viewing one might suppose that the Armitages and their friends are representative of those who just 'don't get it' concerning the realities of racial injustice in America. But that they are also, directly, the mechanism of oppression illustrates the continuum from fetishisation to *dehumanisation*. In what is perhaps the most haunting scene in the film, Mr. Armitage auctions Chris off to the highest bidder. While Chris and Rose take a walk in the woods, the rest of the partygoers gather at the backyard gazebo to bid for Chris's body and his life. Silently raising bingo cards to signal their interest, the crowd of white faces is mostly expressionless, offering tepid and hushed applause to congratulate the winning bidder. The aesthetic choice to stage this scene outside (rather than, say, in the drawing room) conjures a vision of the wooden auction block in the village square. Just as the film references the traditional scene of the slave at auction, the plot alludes to the body snatching of Atlantic slavery, the soul stealing of the plantation, the social death of the slave *and* the devaluation of African Americans from emancipation to the present day. The film's use of space calls to mind the occupation of territory as well as the conquest of black people; there is a clear parallel between the house and the victim's body as he becomes 'occupied' by the new owner. The last name 'Armitage'—a corruption of 'hermitage'—conveys the significance of the house which, at first sight, seems gothic, inclusive of cupboards that open of their own accord, a strange groundskeeper and secret rooms containing evil doings. On the ground floor of the house, Mrs. Armitage's office is the location where the process of enslavement begins: she hypnotises her victims to render them physically powerless, conditioning them to fall into a state of paralysis at the sound of a spoon stirring in a teacup which she refers to as 'the sunken place'[23]. Mrs. Armitage asks her victims to 'sink into the floor', their journey carrying them metaphorically into their subconscious and literally to the basement of the house where they await the operation that will complete their transformation. Visually, space is used to emphasise the victim's removal from power: we see Chris floating helplessly in a dark void, a perspective rendered as a distant subjective shot framed in darkness, as if he were at the bottom of a deep well or an open grave. This, the viewer is later told, will be his permanent state if the process is completed: 'You won't be gone, not completely, a sliver of you will still be in there somewhere. . . . You'll be able to see and hear what your body is doing but your existence will be as a passenger, as an audience'.

This grim science fictional fantasy evokes Mbembe's description of the enslaved person as less-than-living: 'because the slave's life is a "thing," possessed by another person, the slave existence appears as a perfect figure of a shadow'[24]. Incarnated by dead white people, the film's victims literalise living-death; however, the film also parallels aspects of Mbembe's spatio-temporal description of the colony. The victims' bodies, invaded by the consciousness of another, represent geographic spaces that are physically occupied: Dre (the kidnap victim from the opening scene who has been purchased and incarnated by a wealthy white man), Georgina (the maid who is puppetted by the Armitages' late matriarch), and Walter (the groundskeeper, who is piloted by Roman Armitage, the deceased patriarch and founder of the process). These bodies also register as sites where sedimented temporalities are concretised[25]. In a manner similar to landforms, which illustrate geologic time, the film's victims can be read as 'spaces' in which the past is, quite literally, materially visible in the present. Crucially, the history of resistance is preserved in this cinematic translation of the necroscape of U.S. race relations. *Get Out* is tinged with the imagery of slave revolt, displaying a range of responses to oppression, most concretely visualised in the film's climax where Chris escapes capture as the house is set aflame. But the depiction of resistance in the film is also more nuanced. Recalling Brown's emphasis on the agency of the 'socially dead', the film abounds in struggles against metaphysical imprisonment. Taking our cue from Paul Gilroy's reading of Frederick Douglass's battle with the 'slave-breaker' Edward Covey, as an extension of G. W. F. Hegel's allegory, the film lends itself to the Hegelian master-slave dialectic[26]. Specifically, the 'trial by death' that features prominently in Hegel's articulation of the essential struggle for recognition is restaged in *Get Out* to illustrate a panoply of resistive potential—an internalised battle against ideology, an overt struggle to protect the community at large, suicide as rebellion, the choice to kill, and the choice to spare—representing the many historical strategies employed by so-called socially dead enslaved persons to combat their condition.

THE MASTER-SLAVE STRUGGLE

The usefulness of Hegel's master-slave (or lord and bondsman) dialectic and its significance is much disputed, but we can take as a given that it concerns subject formation and contains these parts or moments: 1) a need for the self-consciousness to find recognition in another self-consciousness, an other, outside him/herself; 2) a struggle between the two, a pivotal part of which is a confrontation with death—the master being the winner and the slave the loser because s/he chooses enslavement over death; 3) a revelation that the master, in being recognised by a nonentity—the slave—has not actually attained self-consciousness, while the slave, in confronting the master as well as death, has attained self-consciousness[27]. For Alexandre Kojève, Gilroy and others, the slave's confrontation of his/her own death is the key to ultimate 'victory'[28]. For example, in *Nietzsche and Philosophy*, which includes a discussion of the will to power, Gilles Deleuze writes: 'underneath the Hegelian image of the master we always find the slave'[29]. Kojève, by contrast, emphasises that 'mastery is an existential impasse' . . . [the master] cannot *live consciously* with the knowledge that he is satisfied by what he is', since, in Hegel, it is specifically the *acknowledgement of one's own mortality* that leads to the slave's self-consciousness, which means that, while the slave's work is key to this reversal, it is the fear of death that led to enslavement in the first place[30].

The continued relevance of the master-slave dialectic, for Gilroy, is that it 'correctly places slavery at the natal core of modern sociality'; his reading of Hegel, likewise, clearly states that in the struggle, the slave 'prefers his conqueror's version of reality to death and submits'[31]. But Gilroy proposes that we read Frederick Douglass's account of his physical fight with Covey as a revision to the master-slave dialectic: 'Douglass's version is quite different. For him, the slave actively prefers the possibility of death to the continuing condition of inhumanity on which plantation slavery depends'[32]. Gilroy connects this account to instances in which the enslaved committed suicide or infanticide as acts of resistance. Of these acts, he writes:

> The repeated choice of death rather than bondage articulates a principle of negativity that is opposed to the formal logic and rational calculation characteristic of modern western thinking and expressed in the Hegelian slave's preference for bondage rather than death.[33]

Gilroy reconceptualises the dialectic by recognising the embrace of death *as* an act of resistance. For me, Mbembe's gloss of this same passage in Hegel is telling: 'the human truly becomes a subject—that is, separated from the animal—in the struggle and the work through which he or she confronts death. . . . Becoming subject therefore supposes upholding the *work of death*'[34]. This might emphasise, after Kojève, the slave's *work*, but the phrase 'work of death' also echoes Nat Turner's voice in his 'Confessions', a document in which Thomas R. Gray purportedly transcribed Turner's prison testimonial regarding his role in the 1831 slave revolt that took the lives of fifty-five men, women and children[35]. I propose that we might consider as pivotal not only the slave's confrontation of his own death in the initial trial but of his capacity to kill; after all, Hegel emphasises as a part of the struggle that, 'just as each stakes his own life, *so each must seek the other's death . . .*'[36]. An acknowledgement of the slave's capacity for revenge is admitted in the historical context of the original text. Susan Buck-Morss's important essay 'Hegel and Haiti' emphasises the slave revolt that inspired the passage: Hegel was reading accounts of the Haitian Revolution in the newspaper *Minerva*. The bondsman accedes to historical agency, Buck-Morss demonstrates, because the enslaved of Saint Domingue had already done it. The German newspaper's objectivity—as opposed to the American and French presses' depictions of the revolt, which were animated by a fear that rebellion would spread—was a result of balanced articles. Buck-Morss mentions texts critical of the violence of the revolution and advocating for the rights of men[37]. And while they might not have included some of the goriest details of French accounts, like a rebel slave removing a colonist's eyes with a corkscrew, the deaths of white masters at the hands of their slaves were surely a feature of the articles Hegel was reading. If 'the slaves . . . achieve self-consciousness by demonstrating that they are not things, not objects, but subjects who transform material nature', a more historicised understanding of Hegel's dialectic insists upon the bondsman's capacity to kill[38].

Get Out uses a metaphor of living death to make visible that the hesitation on the part of some members of our society to avow without equivocation that Black Lives Matter *is* necropolitics in action. For Mbembe, 'sovereignty means the capacity to define *who matters* and who does not, who is disposable and who is not'[39]. *Get Out* effectively orchestrates an allegory with a purposeful sense of déjà-vu, suggesting simultaneously the devaluation of black lives in contemporary society and the history of slavery, thereby tracing a throughline between the social death of the enslaved and the theft of black lives allowed today under legalised injustice, in an illustration of what Baucom calls 'temporal accumulation'[40]. But to my mind, the film's most interesting feature is the focus on resistance even within death-worlds in which necropolitics is law, like the plantation. In fact, the film restages the master-slave confrontation, revealing a spectrum of resistive strategies from solidarity and rejection of internalised oppression to overt combat and violence, murder and suicide.

INTERNALISED OPPRESSION

At one point in the film, Chris and Georgina, the family's black maid, have an exchange. He has accused her of unplugging his phone and she has come to explain herself. By way of an awkward apology for the accusation, Chris says, 'All I know is sometimes, if there's too many white people I get nervous, you know?'[41]. This appeal to solidarity triggers an event. At first, her smile fades. We see Georgina physically struggle, giving a quick gasp that startles Chris and shaking as if she is trying to say something that won't come out. Her smile reappears but tears roll down her cheeks. The bewildering contrast in her facial expression, during which the camera holds a tight close-up on her face, reveals an internal conflict. The shot is intercut with close-ups of Chris, who is clearly confused and concerned by this display. Georgina's smile flickers as she cries, but then it is overmastered by a rising laughter, as if in an hysterical episode, and she says 'oh, no, no, no, no'. She repeats the word a dozen times, before averring that 'the Armitages are *so* good to us; they treat us like family'[42]. This is both a saw trotted out to justify the fantasy of benevolent enslavement and a key to the real nature of the servants' identities: Rose's grandparents have commandeered these bodies and live again through them, posing as servants. Directly after this incident, Chris rejoins the party only to encounter a similar scene. He attempts to document a strange character he had met previously, the only other black man at the party: the kidnap victim of the film's opening scene. An oddly old-fashioned outfit, together with his archaic formality of speech, his aged white wife and his unfamiliarity with the fist bump handshake prompt Chris to complain of the black people he has met at the house suggesting that it's like they 'missed the movement', which is both an accurate assessment (the victims are controlled by a generation of white folks born before the civil rights movement), and resounds with the sentiment that the colonised, which these occupied bodies also represent, are lost in time[43]. Wanting to capture this odd duck in a picture, Chris attempts to take a photograph of him surreptitiously with his cell phone, but the flash has an unintended effect. The cinematics here are oddly mechanical, perhaps to recall the trope of the robot as a stand-in for the slave, the machine man being one point on a spectrum of living death that includes the zombie. A faint electronic hum supersedes the diegetic sound as the man's wide, friendly smile falls, he begins to tremble slightly, and his irises reflect light[44]. Then, in a close-up on Dre, the camera rotates partially around him at eye level: his nose begins to bleed, and his expression changes. He awakens to agency. Furtively and almost under his breath, Dre utters 'get out'. Charging toward Chris, he cries, 'Get out of here! Get the fuck out of here!' before being subdued and dragged away[45].

Whereas Georgina's is an internal struggle unaided by outside forces, the camera flash has worked here to interrupt whatever mechanisms were in place and Dre temporarily regains control over his body. In that brief respite, he has time to take one action, and he tries to warn Chris of the imminent danger, a gesture of community instead of self-preservation. If we choose to read this example in line with the 'trial by death' Hegel describes, the combat between the intruder and the body's owner is internalised: we merely see the outward effects of this struggle but not the struggle itself. Such and similar scenes may symbolise not only the real-world effects of racial oppression but also the internalised operations of ideology. Although they do not depict a battle to the death, they nonetheless restage the essential features of Hegel's allegory about striving for recognition and agency within an oppressive framework. Taken as a recoding of the master-slave struggle, these battles against invisible invaders allude to the internal conflict that W. E. B. Dubois called 'double-consciousness', struggles against the dominant ideology or internalised oppression[46]. Dubois's concept of a struggle against an internal white oppressor, the master-slave dialectic of the twentieth-century 'American Negro', is suggested in the imagery of Georgina struggling with an internal occupier. For Dubois, double-consciousness is a dual sense of oneself and of the ideology with which one must align: 'two warring ideals in one dark body'[47]. The semiotic prolixity of this cinematic allegory engages the history of the colonial conquest and occupation, of necropolitics today, of double-consciousness and internalised oppression, the struggle for recognition by the other and finally, but perhaps most importantly, strategies of overt resistance. The film's climax concretely recalls the history of slave rebellion. In a scene coded as a scene of slave revolt, Chris stalks through the house as it burns, splattered with the blood of his captors, startling its inhabitants as he comes upon them. In the film's final scene Chris liberates Walter, the groundskeeper, by using his flash to break the spell. The same faint mechanical hum is heard as Walter blinks, the iridescent glow in his irises indicating that a change has taken place. Walter takes the rifle and fires on Rose, after which he puts the shotgun under his own chin. Evidently, he is not willing to wait to find out whether his release from enslavement is temporary or permanent but instead takes action to end his state, recalling the route that many enslaved persons also chose[48]. Despite the fact that Mbembe acknowledges that death can lead to freedom for the slave, or the end of 'the state of siege or occupation'[49] of the oppressed, his ambivalent treatment of resistance is perplexing. The survivor and the suicidal martyr are only treated briefly in Mbembe's article, which ends with the ambiguous assertion that 'whether read from the perspective of slavery or of colonial occupation, death and freedom are irrevocably interwoven'[50]. Like other scholars before me, such as Jeremy Weate and Moradewun Adejunmobi, I wonder about the place of resistance in Mbembe's articulation of necropolitics[51]. Of the suicide bomber, Mbembe writes that s/he is explicitly denied recognition under the Hegelian paradigm, for 'a dead person cannot recognize his or her killer, who is also dead'[52]. Surviving the death of the other is given short shrift in a few lines quoted from Elias Canetti, with a note that 'the lowest form of survival is killing'[53]. Indeed, Mbembe's codicil to the article rephrases this point in the following way: 'the essay has also outlined some of the repressed topographies of cruelty (the plantation and the colony in particular) and has suggested that under conditions of necropower, the lines between resistance and suicide, sacrifice and redemption, martyrdom and freedom are blurred'[54]. While I appreciate that some strategies of colonial resistance (such as terrorism) may end up creating alternative but equally destructive death-worlds, this is a flat ontology that risks negating resistance as violence. Reading Mbembe in the era of Trump truthism, it seems especially important not to equivocate between the violence of the oppressor and the counter-violence of the resistor. Simply put, I find it problematic when figurations of the living-dead elide the possibility of resistance: comparing the subjugated to the living-dead (from 'bare life' to zombies) risks effacing the lived, everyday agency of the oppressed. Further, failing to differentiate between the operations of necropower and the struggle against these mechanisms can lead to a nihilistic reduction or to 'a futile positivism'[55]. Shifting the emphasis to the Hegelian bondsman's exercise of agency more so than the other's recognition of him[56], and bearing in mind Brown's assertion that agency is 'an aspect of existence to be assumed even under conditions of "bare life"', the film's importance lies in the fact that it pushes against an acceptance of the oppressed's state as inherently powerless, even within a necroscape[57].

Stalking through the house, which is now aflame, Chris recalls Jean-Jacques Dessalines's injunction to the rebel slaves of Saint Domingue to '*koupe tet, boule kay,*' (cut the slave owners' heads off and burn their houses)[58]. Part of the way in which the scene maintains its resonances with slave revolt, I would argue, is that Chris is forced to kill the family members with his own brute force and whatever objects he finds immediately at hand, just as rebel slaves had to make use of whatever tools they had access to in carrying out their campaigns[59]. Chris attempts to kill Rose, his former lover, by strangling her to death, but his struggle here is not merely against his external opponent but also an internal one when, his hands wrapped around her throat, she begins to smile, knowing that he cannot bring himself to hurt her. That the film ends on this note, with Chris refusing to kill Rose, underlines the initial choice in the Hegelian 'trial by death' as one not merely about an unwillingness to die but equally concerning a refusal to kill. Chris has made a choice but here he walks away victorious; this is no less a resistive act than Walter's choice to shoot Rose and to kill himself. The point is the act and one's recognition of one's self in making a choice, not in the recognition of the other. If this is not a faithful translation of the master-slave dialectic as Hegel articulated it, it is nonetheless a more accurate depiction of its historical antecedent and the myriad choices made by the enslaved people of Saint Domingue as they liberated themselves. In this film, we see the apparition of Atlantic slaves' resistance: acts which could variously involve conspiracy, subterfuge and sabotage; self-defence or self-preservation; solidarity and sacrifice; suicide; overt rebellion, violence, destruction and murder. Simultaneously, contemporary concerns regarding police forces' prejudice are woven throughout the film; we see the struggle of the African American against ideology, for community, and still, after all these centuries, seeking what Dubois called 'a perfect and unlimited equality with any white man'[60]. It's a film haunted by the 'spectres of the Atlantic' in the sense meant by Baucom, in which the present state of affairs is predicated on *the past*. The challenge is threefold: to 'stay woke' to the persistence of the legacy of Atlantic slavery, to understand the many forms that struggle may take, and to not devalue death. The film may also serve as a reminder for scholars who study the necroscape not to neglect resistance, for sometimes the dead awaken.

NOTES

The author wishes to thank the organisers and participants of the Necrocapitalism panel at the 2017 session of the American Comparative Literature Association in Utrecht, where some of these ideas were first workshopped. Thanks also to my colleagues at the University of Tampa, Daniel Dooghan and Joshua Waggoner, for comments on drafts, and especially Natasha Lushetich for her generous guidance.

1. Achille Mbembe, 'Necropolitics', *Public Culture* 15, no. 1 (2003): 40.
2. Ibid., 21.
3. Ibid., 21. On slavery and social death, the key text is Orlando Patterson, *Slavery and Social Death: A Comparative Study* (Cambridge, MA: Harvard University Press, 1982), which focuses especially on the enslaved's cultural isolation from his ancestors.
4. Vincent Brown, *The Reaper's Garden* (Cambridge, MA: Harvard University Press, 2008), 127.
5. Vincent Brown, 'Social Death and Political Life in the Study of Slavery', *American Historical Review* (December 2009): 1236.
6. See, for example, Orlando Patterson's discussion of the master's right to murder his slaves, which often includes a prohibition against self-defense; most slaveholding societies, Patterson writes, 'forbade the slave to defend himself except at the order of his master' (*Slavery and Social Death*, 200), and Baucom's detailed study of the 1781 Zong massacre, *Specters of the Atlantic: Finance Capital, Slavery, and the Philosophy of History* (Durham, NC: Duke University Press, 2005), in which 133 slaves were thrown overboard so that the owners could collect an insurance payout.
7. Roxane Gay, 'On the Death of Sandra Bland and Our Vulnerable Bodies', *New York Times*, 24 July 2015.
8. The reference here is to Judith Butler's *Precarious Life: The Powers of Mourning and Violence* (London: Verso, 2004).
9. Ibid., 76. Although the focus of Butler's text is specifically on the treatment of Arab life in the United States after 9/11, her description of racism in action applies equally to the slayings of unarmed black men and children deemed a threat by the confronting police officer without recourse to a trial, as it does to the suspension of human rights in infinite deferment of a trial at Guantanamo, which is the actual context of this passage.
10. A scholarly treatment of this ilk is currently in production with Dawn Keetley at the helm; Adam Lowenstein is developing work on the film's connection to *The Stepford Wives*, based on Ira Levin's novel (pers. comm). Both *Stepford Wives* and *Invasion of the Body Snatchers* are based on novels and have been remade in film multiple times. Their commonality is a narrative in which townspeople begin to be replaced by beings that represent them physically but are vacant inside.
11. See on this point my book *The Transatlantic Zombie: Slavery, Rebellion, and Living Death* (New Brunswick, NJ: Rutgers University Press, 2015), and for a broader study of the reflection of the lived reality of slavery in Voudou and folklore, see Colin (Joan) Dayan's *Haiti, History, and the Gods* (Berkeley: University of California Press, 1998).

12. Jordan Peele tweeted '*Get Out* is a documentary' on 15 November 2017. See again Butler, *Precarious Life*.

13. Baucom, *Specters of the Atlantic*, 34.

14. Ibid., 325.

15. In my book *The Transatlantic Zombie*, I trace out the history of the myth and its resonances not only as an allegory of enslavement but one tinged with the history of slave revolt via its association with the Haiti, the site of what is called the world's most successful slave rebellion.

16. Although our hero is liberated at the end of the film rescued by a friend of his, a much darker and more pessimistic alternative ending was also turned. See Jacob Shamsian, 'The Alternative Ending to "Get Out" Shows the Movie Taking a Much More Horrifying Turn', *Business Insider*, 19 May 2017, http://www.businessinsider.com/get-out-alternative-ending-2017-5.

17. Susan Buck-Morss's influential article 'Hegel and Haiti', *Critical Inquiry* 26, no. 4 (Summer 2000): 821–65 posits that 'the Haitian Revolution was the crucible, the trial by fire for the ideals of the French Enlightenment' (837), but also that accounts of the slaves of Saint Domingue taking up arms against their masters were the real-world influence for Hegel's articulation of the master/slave dialectic.

18. Mbembe has said of this duality, 'as a temporal formation, the postcolony is definitely an era of dispersed entanglements, the unity of which is produced out of differences. From a spatial point of view, it is an overlapping of different, intersected and entwined threads in tension with one another'. Interview with Achille Mbembe by Christian Hoeller, https://www.laits.utexas.edu/africa/ads/1528.html.

19. Depersonalization is a concept invoked both by Orlando Patterson, in describing the slave's social death (Patterson, *Slavery and Social Death*, 38), and Peter Dendle's term for the central definitional characteristic of the zombie. Peter Dendle, *The Zombie Movie Encyclopedia* (Jefferson, NC: McFarland Press), 4.

20. An article on Merriam-Webster's website traces the most relevant uses of this phrase to Erykah Badu's 2008 song 'Master Preacher' and describes its application to issues of social justice: '*Stay woke* . . . and *woke* became part of a wider discussion in 2014, immediately following the shooting of Michael Brown in Ferguson, Missouri. The word *woke* became entwined with the Black Lives Matter movement; instead of just being a word that signaled awareness of injustice or racial tension, it became a word of action. Activists were *woke* and called on others to *stay woke*'. https://www.merriam-webster.com/words-at-play/woke-meaning-origin.

21. Eric Lott's important book *Love and Theft* illustrates the phenomenon in nineteenth-century blackface minstrelsy. Eric Lott, *Love and Theft: Blackface Minstrelsy and the American Working Class* (Oxford: Oxford University Press, 1995).

22. For one example, see Preston Mitchum's film review, which makes this point, in *The Root*, 4 February 2017, http://www.theroot.com/get-out-proves-that-nice-racism-and-white-liberalism-1792955235.

23. *Get Out*, dir. Jordan Peele (Universal Pictures, 2017).

24. Mbembe, 'Necropolitics', 22.

25. This resounds for me with Mbembe's language of the 'timescape' in *On the Postcolony*: 'The term "postcolony" indicates my desire to take very seriously the

intrinsic qualities and power of "contemporaneousness" while firmly keeping in mind the fact that the present itself is a concatenation of multiple temporalities'. Interview with Achille Mbembe by Christian Hoeller, https://www.laits.utexas.edu/africa/ads/1528.html.

26. Paul Gilroy, *The Black Atlantic and Double-Consciousness* (Cambridge, MA: Harvard University Press, 1993).

27. G. W. F. Hegel, *Phenomenology of Spirit*, trans. A. V. Miller. (Oxford: Oxford University Press, 1972), 114–19.

28. See Alexandre Kojève, *Introduction to the Reading of Hegel*, trans. James H. Nicolas Jr. (New York: Basic Books, 1969), 46–47, and Gilles Deleuze, *Nietzsche and Philosophy*, trans. Hugh Tomlinson (New York: Columbia University Press, 1983). For a comparative analysis of the different analyses of the dialectic, including differences of opinion in Habermas, Deleuze, Kojève and the social applications of theories like those of Franz Fanon, Patricia Hill Collins and David Brion, see Gilroy, *The Black Atlantic*, 50–54.

29. Deleuze, *Nietzsche*, 10.

30. Kojève, *Introduction*, 47–48.

31. Gilroy, *Black Atlantic*, 63.

32. Ibid., 63. Of course, Douglass himself doesn't perish in his fight with Covey, but he is nonetheless victorious in a manner in keeping with the original Hegelian dialectic. Gilroy writes that 'the two men were locked together in the Hegelian impasse. Each was able to contain the strength of the other without vanquishing him' (62). For Douglass, this is a moment of clarity, a turning point. As he writes, 'I was nothing before; I was a man now. . . . I had reached a point at which I was not afraid to die' (qtd. in Gilroy, *Black Atlantic*, 63).

33. Gilroy, *Black Atlantic*, 68. On suicide as an expression of resistance to slavery, see also Brown, *The Reaper's Garden*, and scholarship surrounding the tale of the 'flying Africans', an incident of mass slavery among captured Igbo peoples in 1803.

34. Mbembe, 'Necropolitics', 14; emphasis added.

35. See Herbert Aptheker's edited volume *Nat Turner's Slave Rebellion, Including the 1831 Confessions* (Mineola, NY: Dover, 1966): 'It was intended by us to have begun the *work of death* of the 4th of July last' (138; emphasis added). It should be noted that the text of Nat Turner's supposed 'Confessions' is a highly dubious document, likely created for the purposes of anti-abolitionist propaganda. See on this point Christopher Tomlins, 'Nat Turner's Confessions: A Paratextual Analysis', *Law & History* (2014): 1–28.

36. Hegel, *Phenomenology of the Spirit*, 114; emphasis added.

37. Buck-Morss, 'Hegel and Haiti', 838; n. 56, 57.

38. Buck-Morss, 'Hegel and Haiti', 848. The account of the corkscrew comes from Antoine Dalmas, *Histoire de la Revolution de Saint-Domingue* (Paris: Mame Frères, 1814), 209.

39. Mbembe, 'Necropolitics', 27; emphasis added. Here 'sovereignty' signifies the rule of a master class rather than a national identity, but Mbembe's attentions to plantation slavery and social death make plain that the model fits here as well.

40. Baucom, *Specters of the Atlantic*.

41. *Get Out.*

42. Ibid.

43. Here Chris may interpret this character as someone who has accepted his own oppression, or as Mbembe writes in *On the Postcolony* of the 'subjects of the *commandment*,' those who have 'internalized authoritarian epistemology to the point where they reproduce it themselves in all the minor circumstances of daily life', including dress and manners. Achille Mbembe, *On the Postcolony* (Berkeley: University of California Press, 2001), 128.

44. The reflection of light in their eyes may allude to the original *Blade Runner* film, in which the 'replicants' are nearly indistinguishable from the humans except for this trait, a reference that recalls the trope of the robot (a programmable drone) as a stand-in for the slave. The word 'robot' comes from the Czech word *robota*, which means forced labour, and has connotations of slavery and serfdom (228). For more on this theme, see Nicholas Anderson, '"Only We Have Perished": Karel Capek's R.U.R. and the Catastrophe of Mankind', *Journal of the Fantastic in the Arts* 25, nos. 2–3 (2014): 226–46.

45. *Get Out.*

46. Dubois writes, 'It is a peculiar sensation, this double-consciousness, this sense of always looking at one's self through the eyes of others, of measuring one's soul by the tape of a world that looks on in amused contempt and pity. One ever feels his two-ness, an American, a Negro; two souls, two thoughts, two unreconciled strivings; two warring ideals in one dark body, whose dogged strength alone keeps it from being torn asunder'. W. E. B. Dubois, *Souls of Black Folk* (New York: Dover Publications, 1994), 2–3.

47. Ibid., 2–3.

48. See, for example, Vincent Brown's discussion of suicide and the prohibitive measures slaveholders took to discourage it, such as the mutilation of corpses, in *The Reaper's Garden*, 132–35.

49. Mbembe, 'Necropolitics', 37.

50. Ibid., 38.

51. Other scholars have wrestled with Mbembe's 'ambivalence' towards resistance, especially as it is articulated in *On the Postcolony*. See, for a critique in this vein, Jeremy Weate's article 'Achille Mbembe and the Postcolony: Going beyond the Text', *Research in African Literatures* 34, no. 4 (Winter 2003): 27–41, and Moradewun Adejunmobi's chapter in *Writers and Social Thought in Africa*, ed. Wale Adebanwi (New York: Routledge, 2016).

52. Mbembe, 'Necropolitics', 38.

53. Ibid., 36.

54. In Jeremy Weate's detailed treatment of the failures of *On the Postcolony* to effectively address resistance, he writes, 'Mbembe tends to repeat the very "negative interpretation" [he] had sought to avoid, he summarizes this power complex as an "economy of death". . . For Mbembe, power that works against the state is essentially masochistic; the only way to avoid the destructive codification of the state the body is to will one's pain and to accept it as a form of enjoyment' (34).

55. Ibid. Jeremy Weate writes of Mbembe's *On the Postcolony* that his 'refusal to countenance any notion of resistance' is the result of various blindspots in his theory, as well as a dependence on poststructuralist frameworks and a neglect of everyday life (34).

56. This is true whether this agency be located in the choice of slavery in the initial struggle or more directly articulated as the 'will to freedom' in Hegel's Heidelberg lectures of 1817–1818 (qtd. Buck-Morss, 'Hegel and Haiti', 853) or from the work that comes afterwards, as in Kojève's interpretation.

57. Brown, 'Social Death and Political Life in the Study of Slavery', 1246.

58. See again Dayan, *Haiti, History, and the Gods*, 20; emphasis added.

59. See on this point sources on the Haitian Revolution such as those by Laurent Dubois, *Avengers of the New World* (Cambridge, MA: Harvard University Press, 2005), and Thomas Ott, *The Haitian Revolution* (Knoxville: University Press Tennessee, 1973).

60. W. E. B. Dubois, *Black Reconstruction in America* (New York: Atheneum, 1977), 703.

BIBLIOGRAPHY

Adebanwi, Wale, ed. *Writers and Social Thought in Africa.* New York: Routledge, 2016.

Anderson, Nicholas. '"Only We Have Perished": Karel Capek's R.U.R. and the Catastrophe of Mankind'. *Journal of the Fantastic in the Arts* 25, nos. 2–3 (2014): 226–46.

Aptheker, Herbert, ed. *Nat Turner's Slave Rebellion, Including the 1831 Confessions.* Mineola, NY: Dover, 1966.

Baucom, Ian. *Specters of the Atlantic: Finance Capital, Slavery, and the Philosophy of History.* Durham, NC: Duke University Press, 2005.

Brown, Vincent. *The Reaper's Garden.* Cambridge, MA: Harvard University Press, 2008.

Brown, Vincent. 'Social Death and Political Life in the Study of Slavery'. *American Historical Review* (December 2009).

Buck-Morss, Susan. 'Hegel and Haiti'. *Critical Inquiry* 26, no. 4 (Summer 2000): 821–65.

Butler, Judith. *Precarious Life: The Powers of Mourning and Violence.* London: Verso, 2004.

Dalmas, Antoine. *Histoire de la Revolution de Saint-Domingue.* Paris: Mame Frères, 1814.

Dayan, C. J. *Haiti, History, and the Gods.* Berkeley: University of California Press, 1998.

Deleuze, Gilles. *Nietzsche and Philosophy.* Translated by Hugh Tomlinson. New York: Columbia University Press, 1983.

Dendle, Peter. *The Zombie Movie Encyclopedia.* Jefferson, NC: McFarland Press, 2000.

Dubois, Laurent. *Avengers of the New World*. Cambridge, MA: Harvard University Press, 2005.
Dubois, W. E. B. *Black Reconstruction in America*. New York: Atheneum, 1977.
Dubois, W. E. B. *Souls of Black Folk*. New York: Dover Publications, 1994.
Gay, Roxane. 'On the Death of Sandra Bland and Our Vulnerable Bodies'. *New York Times*, 24 July 2015.
Gilroy, Paul. *The Black Atlantic and Double-Consciousness*. Cambridge, MA: Harvard University Press, 1993.
Hegel. G. W. F. *Phenomenology of Spirit*. Translated by A. V. Miller. Oxford: Oxford University Press, 1972.
Kojève, Alexandre. *Introduction to the Reading of Hegel*. Translated by James H. Nicolas Jr. New York: Basic Books, 1969.
Lauro, Sarah Juliet. *The Transatlantic Zombie: Slavery, Rebellion, and Living Death*. New Brunswick, NJ: Rutgers University Press, 2015.
Lott, Eric. *Love and Theft: Blackface Minstrelsy and the American Working Class*. Oxford: Oxford University Press, 1995.
Mbembe, Achille. 'Necropolitics'. *Public Culture* 15, no. 1 (2003): 11–40.
Mbembe, Achille. *On the Postcolony*. Berkeley: University of California Press, 2001.
Ott, Thomas. *The Haitian Revolution*. Knoxville: University Press Tennessee, 1973.
Patterson, Orlando. *Slavery and Social Death: A Comparative Study*. Cambridge, MA: Harvard University Press, 1982.
Shamsian, Jacob. 'The Alternative Ending to "Get Out" Shows the Movie Taking a Much More Horrifying Turn'. *Business Insider*, 19 May 2017, http://www.businessinsider.com/get-out-alternative-ending-2017-5.
Tomlins, Christopher. 'Nat Turner's Confessions: A Paratextual Analysis', *Law & History* (2014): 1–28.
Weate, Jeremy. 'Achille Mbembe and the Postcolony: Going beyond the Text'. *Research in African Literatures* 34, no. 4 (Winter 2003): 27–41.

Chapter Three

Aesthetic Autonomy at the Border

Notes on Necro-Art

Verónica Tello

In the Central Pavilion of the 57th Venice Biennale, Olafur Eliasson organises an iteration of his workshop series *Green Light* (2016–) through which asylum seekers and refugees collaborate on constructing lamps made from recycled materials; the lamps are sold for a minimum of €250, the proceeds of which support NGOs that work with refugees[1]. In Athens, Rick Lowe sets up his *Victoria Square Project* (2017–2018), a short-term community space hosting dialogues and skill-based workshops for/by refugees/migrants in collaboration with dozens of Greek NGOs and small businesses as part of documenta 14. In New York, Tania Bruguera initiates the *Immigrant Movement International* (2012–), a community space for, by and with undocumented Latina/o/x migrants which operates workshops on rights and the law, art practice and health in partnership with Queens Museum (Corona).

These three projects offer a glimpse into the recent instances of how contemporary art practice has unfolded with the ongoing aftermaths of draconian border policies affected by and affecting growing xenophobia towards migrants—the undocumented, the undeportable, asylum seekers and refugees—since the mid-to-late 1990s[2]. They broadly speak to the collaborative impulse driving much contemporary art, especially socially engaged art, in its attempts to dissolve boundaries between us/them, artist/community and contest the subjugation of migrants to the often-unlawful rule of nation-states and intergovernmental bodies such as the EU. Such works—and many others like them—embody, or at the very least critically gesture towards, the radical and/or remedial ambitions and capacities of art in the face of '*death-worlds*, new and unique forms of social existence in which vast populations are subjected to conditions of life conferring upon them the status of *living dead*'[3]. They seek to intervene in the decade-long management of the refugee as political problem rather than human life with legal rights. Questions such as 'what is to be done?' emerge within contemporary art discourse as nation-states fail to uphold the Universal Declaration of Human Rights or as existing infrastructures struggle to support refugees. In turn, terms such as 'solidarity' and 'hospitality' arise, suggesting the social role that contemporary art might play in such a context. As Eliasson states:

> In 2015, I was in Vienna working on an exhibition just as forced migration increased in Europe. It was clear at that moment that the EU was not going to come up with an adequate response, actually the EU was if anything falling apart, . . . the despair and the sense of tragedy, . . . it was hard to find out what to do. At the time, as I was in Vienna, I collaborated with TBA21 to find *a strategy from within (breathing the air of the cultural centre)* that we could apply [to the situation]. This is how the *Green Light* project started, [on the premise that] there must be tools, strategies, ways in which we [artists and art institutions] could come together, and come up with a solution.[4]

Eliasson's comments are not, at least on surface level, very different to those of the multiple artists and curators, including those mentioned earlier, who in working collaboratively with migrants and art institutions argue that art might offer a form of resistance to the imposition of necropolitics in Europe and other Western countries from '*within*'[5]. At the basis of such art's value—how it is valued by art-historical and critical discourse and/or how it generates support from funding bodies—is, I suggest, its operative and perceived *autonomy*. That is, its capacity to offer a space of critical distance from heteronomous forces (governments, the EU) and generate an *aesthetic* experience distinct from yet in critical dialogue with the border violence communicated and instituted by the nation-state and global corporations[6]. Autonomy, and more precisely aesthetic autonomy, is seen to offer a space for the temporary co-presence—or collectivity—of uneven subjects to advance a shift in thinking, doing and being in the world[7]. Autonomy is a category of resistance and of being *together* in time.

While the concept of autonomy in art may be intimate with ideas and practices of collective resistance, it has also historically been bound to individualism. Or, to put it another way, it has historically been contingent on and assumed the artist's distinctiveness or singularity, and more than this, the artist's *self-determination* (and distance from external social, economic and political forces). Indeed, this is revealed by the etymology of autonomy—*autos* signifies 'self' and *nomos* means 'law'; autonomy is thus the act of determining your own law for yourself. For Brian Holmes, this level of self-determination is always mediated by the social; humans only exist as an 'I' in relation to others—'they', 'us', 'we'—and shared languages and cultures[8]. Yet while this rings true, this does not negate that aesthetic autonomy has always been based on undeniable individualism. It assumes that the products of the artist's labour are unbound from other, more common, namely capitalist, modes of production and the production of the proletariat—however on their side the avant-garde may be[9]. As Karl Marx and Friedrich Engels argue, artistic autonomy is rooted in the artist's distinct social position that presupposes that their mental work (genius) is differentiated from that of the masses (and presumably the uneven social relations that underpin capital)[10]. This differentiation is in fact nothing more than the *division of labour*, which places the 'exclusive concentration of artistic talent in individuals and the suppression of it in the greater masses'[11]. Seen from this point of view, Eliasson's *Green Light* project appears to be founded on a fairly normative assumption of the politics of aesthetic autonomy. Collaborators, or migrant workers, labour to produce objects which gain their exchange value, and symbolic value, through the artist's name, reflecting and instituting a division of labour which ensures that the intellectual labour of the artist is inalienable from the object, even if the object is the labour of others.

I raise *Green Light* earlier as a means to set up the key questions that are the focus of this chapter on aesthetic autonomy: if autonomy is based on a division of labour—between the distinct labour of the artist and other kinds of labour (of assistants and participants)—then what kind of solidarity with those subjected to gendered and racialised bio- and necropolitically managed life is possible within and through art? To what extent can or should art be autonomous in the context of border and necropolitics? What modes of autonomy might be most robust within such a context? To answer these questions, I analyse a complex, long-term, collective art project, the *Silent University*. Initiated by Amsterdam-based Turkish artist Ahmet Ögüt in 2012, the *SU* is a self-identified 'autonomous' knowledge exchange platform founded in partnership with the Delfina Foundation and the Tate Education department (both in London)[12] that now has campuses in Stockholm (in partnership with Tensta Konsthall), Mülheim (with Ringlokschuppen Ruhr) and Athens (with a collective of artists, curators, students and activists). It was designed as a long-term initiative with the ambition of becoming 'self-determined' and led by migrants. The *SU*, as I show shortly, brings to the fore a set of problems around conceptions of aesthetic autonomy at the border of the art world (via social practice projects) and necropolitics. While I argue that the *SU* mobilises a fairly normative concept of aesthetic autonomy, which conceals the 'banal' labour that produces art, and prioritises the mental labour of the artist, through an engagement with emerging theories of autonomy, I offer a speculation as to how social practice, including the *SU*, can be rearticulated, and how our understanding of its autonomy—and its limits—may be questioned and expanded through an engagement with theories of contemporary art, contemporaneity and feminist aesthetics. The necropolitical conditions that create dispossession and migration give rise to the need for locating ways to collaborate across racialised, gendered and geo-economic divisions in forms that do not default to seemingly functional but structurally hierarchical stratifications. I begin with a critical overview of the ways in which aesthetic autonomy has been articulated in social practice discourse as a means to map its capacity and desires to expand its borders.

THEORIES OF SOCIAL PRACTICE

In social practice discourse, the concept of autonomy still often alludes to art contesting its instrumentalisation by heteronomous forces, on the one hand, and a commitment to maintaining artistic labour/authorship as a distinct form of labour that differentiates the artist from the rest, on the other[13]. For example, in her influential book *Artificial Hells* (after Schiller, Breton and Rancière), Claire Bishop argues that the politics of social practice's autonomy depends on its capacity to be ambiguous, that is, simultaneously removed from the real world and yet 'the only space from which it is possible to experiment'; she continues, 'art must paradoxically remain autonomous in order to initiate or achieve a model for social change'[14]. For Bishop, thus, the politics of socially engaged art reside in its capacity to offer prototypes for social change capable of opening up that which is otherwise impossible to see, say or do but not necessarily enacting it. That is, it may be in dialogue with heteronomous forces—community groups, social movements, politicians, governments—but it must remain within the boundaries of the artist's vision. Think, for example, of the early work of Santiago Sierra, which Bishop repeatedly uses as an example of the kinds of social practice she supports. In 2001, during the opening of that year's Venice Biennale, Sierra recruited 133 people—mostly undocumented migrants—to have their hair dyed blond and in exchange paid them 120,000 Italian lire. The procedure was undertaken en masse behind the closed doors of a warehouse, situated in the Biennale's Arsenale. The work, titled *133 Persons Paid to Have Their Hair Dyed Blond*, is typical of Sierra's early performances in which people were asked to undertake banal or humiliating tasks for minimum wage. Here, as Bishop has argued, Sierra's work seeks to bring to the fore the inequities of capitalism, and more specifically of globalisation, in which rich nations 'outsource' or 'offshore' labour to subjects from developing countries. Sierra's work does this through 'self-reflexive' and 'paradoxical' gestures which point to the problematics of exploitative labour and uneven global social relations, while embodying these 'themes' in the logic of the work. In being at once in dialogue with and suspended from heteronomous forces—if we can think of autonomy and heteronomy in such dichotomous terms—the work retains its aesthetic autonomy while engaging with politics on a thematic level. This is a fairly normative and, if I can be frank, conservative reading of autonomy, which seeks to promote art's critical capacities—its capacities to illuminate politics and economic concerns—without doing much to change or challenge the politics or economics underpinning art.

In the last few years, scholars Shannon Jackson and Sven Lütticken have made important contributions to critiquing normative conceptions of aesthetic autonomy, common not only in social practice discourse but in discourses of the nexus of art and politics more broadly. In tension with Bishop, they call on critics to challenge, even reject, the delineation between aesthetic autonomy and concepts of problematic compromise/collusion/heteronomy. Jackson, for example, asks what happens when we refuse the boundary between art and the sociopolitical realm. Social engagement necessarily engenders a stronger claim on art—its content and concern—than that of its critical autonomy (or aesthetics even). If this prioritisation is not necessarily always seen as a bad thing then the realm of the aesthetic is essentially broadened as 'we remember the contingency of any dividing line between autonomy and heteronomy'[15]. Jackson sees the continual insistence on criticising the external claims that particular groups (including audiences) may make on art's aesthetic form, or content, as being in opposition not only to established trajectories within art history (though perhaps not art criticism or historiography) and in denial of the 'usefulness' of social practice. In Jackson's writing there appears to be the tacit implication that such critiques are sacrificing the antagonistic or transformative/effective potential of socially engaged art in order to insist on autonomy. In a similar tone, Lütticken, following the work of feminist art historian Kerstin Stakemeier, argues that the Romantic conception of autonomy, of the distinction between art and the social and activism, has been part of 'the problem, not the solution'[16] and asks if we might not engage with the concept of *postautonomy*. By turning away from the autonomy of art and seeking to connect with fields outside its borders, art might side with more important ideas of autonomy than that of the autonomy of art[17]. The work of such critics amounts to an important intervention and generative framework through which to recast thinking of the politics of autonomy in social practice. The borders of aesthetic autonomy must be ignored and contested.

INSTITUENT OR POSTAUTONOMOUS PRACTICE

Over the past decade, a key strategy for contesting the limits of aesthetic autonomy has been to critically reengage with institutional critique—simply put, the critique of art institutions—as a means to expand the boundaries and politics of art[18]. This is distinct from the historical understanding of institutional critique, which emerged out of the conceptual art of the 1960s and 1970s. During this period, artists engaging with institutional critique deployed methodologies of 'immanent critique', seeking to understand and expose the politics and power of the art institution from within but never seeking to contest or undermine such an institution's autonomy[19]. As Alexandro Alberro and Blake Stimson argue, when artists such as Daniel Buren or Eduardo Favario called for boycotts or shut down galleries as part of their art or exhibition, they did so in the spirit of ensuring that art institutions would maintain or at least move closer to their ideal—of serving and representing the public in a transparent and egalitarian manner (concepts grounded in the Enlightenment)[20]. Such practice unfolded at a time when artists perceived art institutions as ethically or politically compromised by their affiliations with government or corporations. At the centre of earlier modes of institutional critique was both a recognition of art's collusion with heteronomous forces and an attempt to maintain their autonomy. While there is no facile dichotomy between autonomy and heteronomy, if we were to engage in relative thinking, contemporary models of institutional critique could be seen to be more on the side of opening art institutions up to heteronomous forces—or of being postautonomous (to borrow Lütticken's term)—than earlier models. Such a strategy basically reflects a shift from strengthening the autonomy of art institutions to aligning art institutions to and with social movements outside of the art world; such a strategy is born out of prioritising the autonomy of things other than art (postautonomy)[21]. It appears less within the art institution (as in the work of Buren or Favario) and more in the form of what Gerald Raunig has termed 'instituent practice', that is, the making of autonomous artist-led institutions that inherently critique institutional power and governance while simultaneously locating ways for publics and counter-publics to assemble and organise[22]. Instituent practice is characterised by its willingness and desire to leave art spaces behind, that is, to be extra- and anti-disciplinary, while rerouting and retooling art world resources to align with movements and actions that are beyond and that test the autonomy of art[23].

In the spirit of instituent practice, phenomena such as the *Silent University* arise. A prototypical, decolonial university led by a faculty of migrants through collaborative practice, the *SU* contests the politics of selective and exclusive knowledge production and distribution. It self-perceives as operating within the field of both border and educational politics more than art (I will address this in detail shortly). Another example of instituent practice is the highly regarded *New World Summit* (2012). Founded by Dutch artist Jonas Staal, the *Summit* is a mobile parliament that hosts and offers a platform to a range of stateless groups excluded from democratic processes at the national and international level (including the Kurdish Women's Movement and the We Are Here refugee collective in Amsterdam). It is funded by art institutions (for the most part) but conceptualises itself as working through international political matrices and hurdles, as evident by its recent collaborations with the Rojava administration. In the midst of the Syrian conflict, the *Summit* has been developing a parliament for the Rojava administration in support of the revolution[24]. Instituent practice is activist and instrumentalist or, as the artist Tania Bruguera argues, it is 'useful art' (*arte útil*). It mobilises the affirmative and generative dimensions of art to actively and materially enact new possibilities. It is not congruous with concepts of autonomy which would maintain art as somehow necessarily distinct from heteronomous forces. Instituent practice is built on the premise/promise that, to borrow Andrea Fraser's phrase, 'another artworld is possible' (echoing the decolonial World Social Forum's mantra 'another world is possible')[25].

THE SILENT UNIVERSITY: 'AUTONOMOUS KNOWLEDGE PLATFORM'

It is in the spirit of instituent practice that the *Silent University* manifests. As Ögüt argues, 'The Silent University is encouraged by necessity, urgency and need. It's both people's and institutions' concern to think and take action on this issue'[26]. The project addresses the negation of migrant knowledge as a result of systemic racism and correlative bureaucratic hurdles or neglectful policies. NGOs and policymakers have also been working toward activating migrant knowledge across educational and democratic systems, yet the *SU* has come to the fore as art. Ögüt argues, 'We often underestimate the potential of art, its capacity to achieve things'[27]. He continues, 'The Silent University can easily collaborate with an art institution or an NGO, as long as it's not described and understood as a "project" or a "workshop", but as an organisation that demands policy changing'[28]. Since its inception, the *SU* has come to consistently identify as a 'self-institutionalized, autonomous knowledge platform'[29]. It seeks to be autonomous from traditional educational institutions—like universities—but it also disidentifies as an artwork so that it may position itself as autonomous from art institutions too, all the while somehow still being connected to art (via its explicit partnerships with the art world, for example). Art institutions are seen as necessary hosts: '[The] Silent University is a challenging institution within different host institutions, which establishes its own adhocratic structure while being fully recognised by the hosting institution'[30]. For Ögüt, the question is: 'How can we place something like the *SU* inside an art institution?'[31]. In other words, how to maintain a concept of autonomy contingent on self-institutionalisation while leveraging the resources of cultural institutions in order create a space capable of contesting exclusivity? In embodying such a complex mode of postautonomy, the *SU* is almost always described as an organisation or institution in discourse, hardly ever as an *artwork*[32]. What are the implications of this? It is not that the *SU* is far removed from art. Ögüt is a highly respected artist[33]. And as the curator and theorist Florian Malzacher has observed, the *SU* has always collaborated with art institutions[34]. For Malzacher,

> This has advantages. For example: they [art institutions] are able to define their field of operations very broadly, they can make things possible and they can give a certain symbolic value to the people involved in The Silent University. However, the art world has the tendency to render things harmless. Everything it touches becomes 'art'. It is part of a certain market and it has the tendency to create mainly symbolic value for its own purposes.[35]

Echoing such critics as Lütticken, Malzacher recognises the potentiality of connecting the *SU* with art institutions in spite of its (stated) need for autonomy. Art offers the *SU* resources (which is key for instituent practice). Yet in being in proximity to art or even being art, the *SU* is also thought to have become 'tainted' (everything it touches becomes 'art'). Yet why resist the label of 'art', given that the *SU* is blatantly dependent on the artist and art institutions (as so many instituent practices are). What is at stake in such a rhetorical gesture, given that, as Andrea Fraser argues,

> there is no longer an outside to the art institution . . . just as art cannot exist outside the field of art, we cannot exist outside the field of art, at least not as artists, critics, curators, etc. . . . if there is no outside for us, it is not because the institution is perfectly closed, or exists as an apparatus in a 'totally administered society', or has grown all-encompassing in size and scope. It is because the institution is inside of us, and we can't get outside of ourselves.[36]

Everything can be turned into art by way if not of the artist then of the institution nominating it as art (after Duchamp and Fraser)[37]. The art institution is not a monolithic white cube in a metropolis; it is embodied in the discourses and values that define art, not least of which is the artist who is supported by art institutions to create instituent practice. To my mind, while the *SU* has rhetorically refused the category of 'art', it has failed to leave behind what is probably the key tenet of the idea of art, that is, the 'author'. The artist/author, as noted earlier, is founded on a division of labour—between the artist's mental work and the alienated, 'banal' labour of others (assistants, industry workers, domestic workers)—allowing the former a level of self-determination and autonomy to which the latter are not privy while it is the interrelated categories of autonomy, labour and authorship that reveal how and why racial hierarchies are maintained in and outside art.

AUTHORSHIP AND THE DIVISION OF LABOUR

The division of labour in industrialised society is characterised by the breaking down of specific tasks to be performed by individuals working together as part of a larger system for maximum efficiency. In art, the division of labour is contingent on something else. It is, as Theodor Adorno argued, dependent on concealing labour, so the artwork appears to be born out of virtuoso and genius[38]. This, of course, is not new. However, since the 1960s with the advent of conceptual art, de-skilling and dematerialisation the distinct 'mental labour' of artists, as divorced from other kinds of labour has only intensified. Delegated labour, or outsourcing and contracting work out to others in the name of conceptual art, has been a relatively common occurrence since then[39]. Within such an aesthetic regime, the artist's mental (and not physical) labour is the basis by which art accrues its value, symbolic or otherwise.

We do not think of artists as workers or labourers but rather as authors, as catalysts of unique ideas and visions. As Michel Foucault argued in his 1969 essay 'What Is an Author?' modern discourse had forged a concept of the author contingent not only on 'individuation' but also an irremovable 'ownership' over ideas[40]. Within such projects as the *SU*, however—though not by any means exclusive to it—one method to attempt to critique the category of the 'author'—and the division of labour it institutes—has been to deploy the term 'initiator'[41]. Such a term—used by Ögüt—is meant to connote 'founding' an institution that may have been conceptualised by an artist but which, ultimately, operates and is maintained as a collaborative entity with the faculty and the coordinators. Following André Lepecki (in his 2013 analysis of the politics of dance), we might think of 'initiation' as an attempt to energise, to set in motion, movements that elicit social ruptures—it could be a 'verb-event' which opens up space for responsive, dynamic movement between different subjects, rejecting both tokenistic participation *and* 'authoritative authorship' for the purposes of forming political assemblages and structures[42]. In this light, we might read the act of initiation and, more specifically, initiating long-term projects as a radical move—one that is attuned to expanding the boundaries/autonomy of art and its institutions for collaborating with social movements and subjects outside its usual purview (which is arguably the bourgeois public) in the spirit of 'postautonomy'.

Yet while promoted as a self-determined migrant social movement, there is a clear division of labour in the *SU*. It designates specific tasks and fixed roles for its members—'artist as initiator'/Ögüt, the 'faculty'/migrants and, last but not least, a category I have not yet clearly articulated, the female volunteers who perform the bulk of the administrative and affective labour to maintain the *SU*. They are called the 'coordinators' therein. Following the patterns of humanitarian volunteerism and unpaid work, the affective labour of coordinating—of organising lectures, forming support networks with/for the faculty, running social media for events—is performed by mostly white European women: students, activists, curators without or with little pay or social workers doing extra time. They represent what Andrea Francke and Ross Jardine have termed the 'administrator as infrastructure' allowing the 'hero/author' to maintain the semblance of working as a sole operator (a process contingent on concealing labour) while the administrator's labour is devalued, considered unauthored and unskilled[43]. If they appear, it is on the margins, much like the women in Daniela Ortiz's *97 House Maids* of 2016, a work composed of found photos posted by wealthy Peruvian families on Facebook. In the photos, housemaids appear in the background, in the margins and peripheries. While there are clearly distinctions between the housemaids and the coordinators, nonetheless they represent what feminist Marxist theorists have termed 'service or administrator as infrastructure'—commonly perceived as unskilled, devalued labour that art institutions—or domestic spaces—rely on[44].

If the coordinators' labour is rendered invisible, the faculty performing in front of a lectern or on a stage, usually accompanied by the *SU*'s logo, act as the key public interface of the *SU*. In turn, images of such events are heavily disseminated in the *SU*'s online communications. Such events and images work to evidence that the university is performing its task of circumventing the racialised division of labour that mutes the knowledge of migrants once they cross the border. Yet such events and images are also constituted by the labour conditions of the *SU*. In an act of what Claire Bishop has termed 'delegated performance', migrants are paid to perform themselves within the artwork[45]. Their presence offers the work a level of authenticity—and symbolic capital—that is otherwise unavailable through the body of the artist or coordinators. The artist delegates the authenticity of the work to the faculty of migrants while still remaining the 'artist', which gives the work its symbolic value. It's worth dwelling on the fact that in spite of being a self-proclaimed 'adhocratic' project, at every mention of the *Silent University*, the artist's name—as initiator—is uttered on promotional material, in art publications or lectures and public programmes, across *Frieze*, *e-flux*, Tensta Konsthall or the *SU*'s website. In a way, this reflects art business as usual. In today's art economy, the artist's persona is called on, valued and extended in multiple ways—not just by having shows or selling works on the art market but also by posting on social media or appearing in video interviews, in symposia, or publishing essays in art magazines. The artist as persona can and needs to perform all the time. As Lütticken argues, 'as an artist or writer or curator, you perform when you do your job, but your job also includes giving talks, going to openings, being in the right place at the right time. Transcending the limits of the specific domain of performance art, then, is what I would call "general performance as the basis of the new labor"'[46]. This new labour—or general performance—is seen as necessary to obtain resources for the *SU* to develop its symbolic value and keep the work going. However, this labour/performance also leaves us with an inevitable outcome: with the omnipresence of the artist's persona; everything that the *SU* does becomes an extension of it. The *SU*'s discourse—narrated by Ögüt—amounts to what I call the 'globally distributed aesthetics' of the *SU*: the signifiers that most reliably point to the conceptual scaffold, the mental work of the *SU*—able to be mined in the digitally and globally distributed artefacts that circulate across the art industry.

Indeed, critics invariably turn to the interviews and other statements uttered by the artist, including the *SU*'s manifesto, in their analysis of the project. Statements such as 'we act in solidarity with other refugee struggles and collectives around the world' or 'decentralized, participatory, horizontal and autonomous modality of education, instead of centralized, authoritatian, oppressive, and compulsory education' reflect the general tone and register in which the *SU* self-articulates. With the forceful polemical affect, these texts come to stand in as the art 'work'. They are the signifiers of authorship, of conceptualising the work. By circulating these signifiers within discourse of the *SU*, attribution, by which I mean the process of individualising the creator of the work and locating signs of an author (a unique idea), is at play. Within the discourse of the *SU*, the reiteration of the artist as initiator works to constantly contain the project within the borders of artistic, singular models of authorship.

While the term 'initiator' suggests a desire to abandon capitalist forms of art production under the banner of progressive politics—to form a new community—I posit this: the role of the artist here is closer to one of management (including delegation and negotiation) than to initiation. While not producing anything tangible themselves, managers are nonetheless unable to be alienated from the work they manage, (art)work in this case. The artist delegates the role of operating the *SU* to others, but the artist's autonomy (and ownership over the work) is nevertheless maintained because the artist's role has (through dematerialised conceptual art practice) expanded to the task of being a (de-skilled) 'service worker' or 'curator of social creativity'[47]. Artists now create experiences for people and communities or offer solutions for issues normally tackled by governments, NGOs or businesses. At the nexus of autonomous artistic practice and heteronomous forces, the artist's autonomy—*and their difference from government, NGOs or business*—is maintained by the robustness of the idea of authorship. Perhaps the question isn't what might be nonhierarchical or participatory about initiation, but rather: What are often highly precarious migrants being *initiated* into if not the fully functioning economy of contemporary global art markets in the name of collaboration?

NECRO-ART

The problematic, exploitative conditions of collaborative art are not new. As Stephen Wright argued in 2004 in his critique of 'relational aesthetics',

> Artists make forays into the outside world, [and] 'propose' (as artworlders like to say) usually very contrived services to people who never asked for them, or rope them into some frivolous interaction, then expropriate as the material for their work whatever minimal labour they have managed to extract from these more or less unwitting participants (whom they sometimes have the gall to describe as 'co-authors'). In so doing, they end up reproducing within the symbolic economy of art the sort of class-based relations of expropriation that Marx saw at work in the general economy: on the one hand, those who hold the symbolic capital (the artists), and on the other, those whose labour (such as it is) is used to foster the accumulation of more capital. And this is precisely what is usually passed off as 'collaboration'—making cynical mockery of the term—not just by such artists as Rirkrit Tiravanija, Maurizio Cattelan and all those whose names figure in all the almanacs of relational aesthetics, but by countless others besides.[48]

In the years since Wright wrote this apt, and still resonating, passage on relational aesthetics, correlative and interconnected discourse of collaborative practices, going under the rubrics of 'social practice' or 'socially engaged art', have tended to forego a materialist analysis of the social relations that ensue therein. In fact, the most prominent analyses of the socially engaged art (and I'm thinking here of Claire Bishop or Nato Thompson)[49] have preferred to focus their energies on the *potentiality* for such practice to offer a space for robust collectivity, or to think through the challenges and limits of collectivity, without expecting much in terms of material manifestations of nonhierarchical modes of being and working in time together[50]. Perhaps one of the strangest manifestations of such discourse has been Claire Bishop's concept of 'delegated performance', briefly mentioned earlier. As Bishop argues, delegated performance is characterised by the act of the artist hiring people to 'perform their own socio-economic category' (for example, migrant or refugee) and in turn delegating the 'authenticity' of performance to subjects other than the artist[51]. The category of delegated performance marks a shift between artists using their own bodies and identities as signs of authenticity in performance-based works from the 1970s toward artists hiring others (including migrants) to perform themselves within the logic of the work that they conceptualise (note the division between the mental and banal labour remains). Overall, Bishop is overly keen to praise the way in which such practices offer a 'self-reflexive', 'paradoxical' means to think through the politics of collaboration by deploying exploitative labour practices[52]. In other words, the use of exploitative practices in such works is valued by Bishop for the ability to critically *thematise* exploitation. For Bishop, the rules of capitalism are suspended therein for the sake of enabling a critical *reflection* of capitalism[53].

Bishop has been very quick to dismiss Marxist and postcolonial interpretations of delegated performance, which would attempt to think delegated performance in relation to other historical instances in which 'third-world' subjects have been asked to perform themselves in global exhibitions. While offering no substantive critique or citations, such approaches, she argues, reduce delegated performance to 'standard-issue questions of political correctness', condemning it as a 'reiteration of capitalist exploitation' in a 'seamless continuum with contemporary labour' rather than the more 'complicated' interpretation (hers) of 'offering a specific space of experience where those norms are suspended' (as represented by Sierra, to her mind)[54]. My concern here isn't so much with Bishop's theorisation of delegated performance in the work of Sierra. Rather, it's with her blunt refusal to think delegated performance in social practice projects as anything but an aesthetic experience that offers a means to think through the limits of collaboration amongst geo-economically disparate subjects within capitalism without acknowledging that the global art industry is also an extension of capital and relies on uneven social relations in order to create images of conviviality, community, collectivity, collaboration and so on (this is why a project like *Green Light* is brought to the Venice Biennale). Bishop's reading of delegated performance as a means to bring to the fore the paradoxes and limitations of collaboration within global capital bears little relevance to the *Silent University* or *Green Light.* Unlike Sierra's *133 Persons Paid to Have Their Hair Dyed Blond* (detailed earlier), the thematisation of exploitation is neither a concern nor a viable politics of the work here. Delegating authenticity to migrants is perhaps little more than a strategy for promoting an image of solidarity and collectivity while maintaining normative concepts of aesthetic autonomy. I'd like to propose that works like the *SU* are actually closer to what I term necro-art: art production underpinned by the exploitation and labour power of precarious subjects. In other words, art is in a position to extract capital (symbolic or actual) from those subjected to what Mbembe terms 'death-worlds'. The idea here is that communities affected by crisis—austerity, poverty and statelessness—attract artists to come and propel 'recovery' or elicit 'empowerment'. The community is put to work in a kind of nonpolitics of inclusion in which art, in lock step with business (and art institutions), gives the impression of empowerment but actually inhibits the capacity to question systemic structures (including those of the art world) that maintain inequity (including those of the art world). Necropolitics creates markets for artworks that offer images of solidarity and collectivity while being dependent on the exploitation and alienation of the labour of both volunteers (coordinators) and those subjected to and attempting to flee death-worlds. Necro-art is dependent on the autonomy of the artist in the most traditional sense, a division between their labour and capacity to 'extract' art world resources through their persona and the performance of volunteer and/or precarious subjects as willing participants in the development of a 'new world'.

REFRAMING AUTONOMY VIA REPRODUCTIVE LABOUR

Autonomy is operative because of the exploitation of human capital, of reserve armies of refugees, of reproductive labour and unwaged labour. Art has to register itself as an 'institution of reproduction—a service, an ambience, a deliberate dissolve between labour and signification'[55] (to borrow Marina Vishmidt's words) as a means to locate a viable concept of autonomy. Such a concept of autonomy would appear as 'problematic negativity in relation to capital' and would also refuse the division of labour that celebrates some and exploits others by seeing itself as nothing more than reproductive labour[56]. If social practice is repeatedly called on to perform remedial tasks in crisis, might it not be more appropriate to reveal this labour as *reproductive maintenance work* rather than frame it as the work of the hero/author, always contingent on individuation rather than the collective? This would require a recalibration of what is historically thought of as autonomous and heteronomous. Historically, art and (heteronomous) reproductive labour were excluded from normative capitalist categories and deemed 'unproductive'. Given the rise and demands of social practice, it may be time to better strategically align these distinct modes of production for a more radical concept of autonomy. That is, to forego what feminist conceptual artist Mierle Laderman Ukeles termed the 'death instinct' characterised by 'separation; individuality; Avant-Garde par excellence' and opt instead for 'the Life Instinct': 'unification; the eternal return; the perpetuation and MAINTENANCE of the species; survival systems and operations; equilibrium'[57]. As long as it isn't restricted purely to the symbolic realm, this aesthetic and political philosophy might offer an insight into a social practice that is better attuned to the spirit of being and working together in time, or of being contemporaries.

As Peter Osborne reminds us, the etymology of the term 'contemporary' denotes 'living, existing, or occurring together' in time[58]. Historically, within modernity, social interrelations have predominantly been imagined vis-à-vis the boundaries of the nation—of communities bound together by a deep if not also false sense of 'horizontal comradeship' as articulated by Benedict Anderson in his 1983 *Imagined Communities*. Post-globalisation, the idea of 'living together' can no longer convincingly be delimited (as was once the case) to the borders of the nation. Within today's geopolitically complex world, transnationalism occupies imaginations and shapes social interrelations. Contemporaneity, as Osborne argues, is constituted by the conjunction of multiple social subjects and diverse social experiences: the uneven co-presence of the diasporic, the settler-colonialist, the indigenous and the stateless. The many and diverging experiences of individuals across heterogeneous communities structure the heterogeneity of contemporaneity. At the same time, contemporaneity is not simply a field of difference. Contemporaneity is driven by critiques of who has the right to the means of production, of authorship, the questioning of whose histories matters and who has a right to visuality—to look and not just be looked at. As a process of delinking from modern narratives and systems, it is consonant with multiple decolonial movements working through the politics of epistemology in order to construct options for knowing and being in the world. With this mind, I would like to offer some speculations: if social practice, including instituent practice, is to be contemporary, it will form with the dialectical, sometimes overlapping subjectivities, energies and temporalities of the global Norths and Souths, acknowledging the complex and structural economic challenges this poses to co-presence. Social practice would animate the practical and antagonistic capacities of aesthetics to organise different ways of being and being together in the current period of both neoliberal hyperindividualism and intensified border politics/transnationalism. One could argue that the collectivity of contemporaneity—as made possible or manifested in contemporary art is speculative or futural, not empirical—it remains on the horizon as something to which to aspire. As Osborne argues, contemporary art is a privileged catalyst for exploring the 'geopolitically diverse forms of social experience that have only recently begun to be represented within the parameters of the common world[59]. Further, as a practice, labour and form of capital, contemporary art 'projects the utopian horizon of global social interconnectedness, in the ultimately dystopian form of the market'[60]. This means that it is simultaneously animating the spirit of a contemporaneity that aspires to the conviviality of the disjunctive unity of subjects, and working through the global art system which privileges subjects of the global North (it advances a dystopian market form which, to my mind, stubbornly holds onto the regime of modernity and authorship as opposed to the collectivity of contemporaneity). The question thus remains: How can art convincingly articulate or institute a space reflective of the speculative collectivity of contemporaneity, constituted by disjunctive social relations (and temporalities)? A collectivity built on recognising that we are all in it together—and that even if this 'togetherness' is never embodied by equivalent subjects, it's nonetheless important to utter a 'we' and not a 'they' or an 'I' when convenient or when profit (via surplus value and/or cultural capital) is on the horizon, or because of tradition and default modus operandi in art discourse and its non-articulation and vocabularies of collectivity. It may be less a matter of 'initiating' projects which pursue normative concepts of autonomy and which offer a rhetorical gesture to collectivity/collaboration and more a matter of creating a space through which both the 'author-function' is rigorously deconstructed and the *interdependencies* (rather than *division*) of labours are embraced as core to the advancement of collectivity (even if it is never constituted by equivalent subjects). Autonomy, as the feminist materialist theorists Marina Vishmidt and Kerstin Stakemeier argue, 'can only be achieved with the destruction of the system that denies autonomy to everyone who lives in it'[61].

NOTES

1. The two NGOs are Emergency and Georg Danzer Haus, both based in Copenhagen.
2. A note on the use of the word 'migrant': I use the term migrant, rather than differentiate between refugees, the stateless, asylum seekers, undocumented migrants, undeportable aliens and other categories. I do so as to not emphasise the different legal hierarchies of belonging that are often at play in the usage of these terms. And I also do so to emphasise the connectedness between migrants. Verónica Tello, *Counter-Memorial Aesthetics: Refugee Histories and the Politics of Contemporary Art* (New York: Bloomsbury, 2016), 10.
3. Achille Mbembe, 'Necropolitics', *Public Culture* 15, no. 1 (2003): 35.
4. Olafur Eliasson, 'Green Light', *Design Boom*, https://www.designboom.com/art/olafur-eliasson-green-light-venice-art-biennale-05-11-2017/.

5. See, for example, Rick Lowe, *Victoria Square Project*, http://victoriasquare project.gr.

6. This is not an unusual perception of the politics of aesthetics, as seen in Claire Bishop, *Artificial Hells: Participatory Art and the Politics of Spectatorship* (London and New York: Verso, 2012).

7. Such a conception of collectivity is drawn from Peter Osborne, 'The Fiction of the Contemporary: Speculative Collectivity and Transnationality in the Atlas Group', in *Aesthetics and Contemporary Art*, ed. Armen Avanessian and Luke Skrebowski (Berlin: Sternberg Press, 2011).

8. Brian Holmes, 'Artistic Autonomy and the Communication Society', *Third Text* 18, no. 6 (2004): 548.

9. Gavin Grindon, 'Surrealism, Dada and the Refusal of Work: Autonomy, Activism, and Social Participation in the Radical Avant-Garde', *Oxford Art Journal*, 34, no. 1 (2011): 79–96.

10. Karl Marx and Friedrich Engels, 'Saint Max', in *The German Ideology* (Amherst: Prometheus Press, 1932).

11. Ibid.

12. Ahmet Ögüt repeatedly frames *SU* as autonomous: 'This project is a self-institutionalized, autonomous knowledge platform that aims to challenge the idea of silence as a passive state'. The *SU* is 'an autonomous knowledge exchange platform by and for refugees, asylum seekers, and migrants'. See Ahmet Ögüt, 'New Schools: The Silent University', *Frieze* 149 (September 2012), https://frieze.com/article/new-schools; and Ahmet Ögüt, 'The Pitfalls of Institutional Pedagogy', *World Policy*, http://worldpolicy.org/blog/2013/06/13/pitfalls-institutional-pedagogy.

13. Beyond Bishop, discussed here, see Marc James Léger, 'Aesthetic Responsibility', *Third Text* 28, no. 4 (2014): 123–36.

14. Bishop, *Artificial Hells*, 27.

15. Shannon Jackson, *Social Works: Performing Art, Supporting Publics* (London: Routledge, 2011), 29.

16. Sven Lütticken, *Cultural Revolution: Aesthetic Practice After Autonomy* (Berlin: Sternberg, 2017), 14.

17. Ibid.

18. Gerald Raunig and Gene Ray, eds., *Art and Contemporary Critical Practice: Reinventing Institutional Critique* (London: Mayfly, 2009); Biljana Ciric and Nikita Yingqian Cai, eds., *Active Withdrawals: Life and Death of Institutional Critique* (London: Black Dog, 2016).

19. Andrea Fraser, 'Autonomy and Its Contradictions,' *open!* May 2012, https://www.onlineopen.org/download.php?id=363.

20. Alexander Alberro and Blake Stimson, eds., *Institutional Critique: An Anthology of Artists' Writings* (Cambridge, MA: MIT Press, 2009).

21. Gerald Raunig, 'Instituent Practice: Fleeing, Instituting, Transforming', in *Art and Contemporary Critical Practice: Reinventing Institutional Critique*, 3.

22. Ibid.

23. Simon Sheikh, 'Art After Trump', *e-flux conversations*, 2016, https://conversations.e-flux.com/t/simon-sheikh-art-after-trump/5325.

24. See, for example, Jonas Staal, 'IDEOLOGY = FORM', *e-flux journal* 69 (2016), http://www.e-flux.com/journal/69/60626/ideology-form.

25. Fraser, 'Autonomy and Its Contradictions'.

26. Ahmet Ögüt in conversation with Göksu Kunak, 'The Silent University', *Sleek* (2013), http://www.sleek-mag.com/2013/11/26/the-silent-university/.

27. Ibid.

28. Ibid.

29. Ögüt, 'New Schools'.

30. Ögüt, 'The Pitfalls of Institutional Pedagogy'.

31. Ahmet Ögüt and Florian Malzacher, 'How Can We Imagine a School Culture Based on Solidarity?', in *The Silent University: Transversal Pedagogy*, ed. Ahmet Ögüt et al. (Berlin and Ruhr: Sternberg and Impulse Theatre Festival, 2016), 12–23.

32. See, for example, *The Silent University*.

33. See Ögüt's website for details on his practice: http://www.ahmetogut.com.

34. Malzacher is involved in supporting the *SU* Mulheim via the Impulse Theatre Festival.

35. Ögüt and Malzacher, 'How Can We Imagine a School Culture Based on Solidarity?', 16.

36. Andrea Fraser, 'From the Critique of Institutions to an Institution of Critique,' *Artforum* 44, no. 1 (September 2005): 278.

37. With his 1917 work *Fountain*, a readymade urinal that he placed in an art context, Duchamp showed that anything can be art by way of the artist nominating it as such. With her practice, Andrea Fraser has revealed that it is increasingly the art museum that nominates what is art by including a range of artefacts therein which are not traditionally considered art, such as crafts or other non–fine art objects.

38. Theodor Adorno, *In Search of Wagner* (1952; London and New York: Verso, 2005), 72.

39. See Lucy Lippard, *Six Years: The Dematerialization of the Art Object from 1966 to 1972* (Chicago: Chicago University Press, 1997).

40. Michel Foucault, 'What Is an Author?' [1969], in *Aesthetics, Method, and Epistemology: Essential Works of Foucault, 1954-1984*, ed. James D. Faubion (New York: The New Press 1999), 205–33.

41. The term is also used in the abovementioned projects, *Immigrant Movement International*, *New World Summit* and the *Victoria Square Project.*

42. André Lepecki, 'From Partaking to Initiating: Leading Following as Dance's (a-personal) Political Singularity', in *Dance, Politics & Co-Immunity: Current Perspectives on Politics and Communities in the Arts*, ed. Gerald Siegmund and Stefan Hölscher (Zurich: Diaphanes, 2013), 21–38.

43. Andrea Francke and Ross Jardine, 'Bureaucracy's Labour: The Administrator as Subject', *Parse* 5 (Spring 2017): 24–33.

44. Ibid.

45. Bishop, *Artificial Hell*s, 219–40.

46. Sven Lütticken, "General Performance" *e-flux journal* 31 (2012), http://www.e-flux.com/journal/31/68212/general-performance/.

47. Marina Vishmidt, 'The Politics of Speculative Labour', *Transformative Art Production*, http://transformativeartproduction.net/the-politics-of-speculative-labour/.

48. Stephen Wright, 'The Delicate Essence of Artistic Collaboration', *Third Text* 18, no. 6 (2004): 533–45.

49. Thompson's discourse is overly celebratory of such practice, promoting its radicality and potentiality without much reserve. See Nat Thompson, *Seeing Power: Art and Activism in the Twenty-First Century* (Cambridge, MA: MIT Press, 2011).

50. Such a line of argument is even advanced by Bishop's theorisation of the antagonistic potentialities of social practice as a means for her to see it as vehicle to advance and critically reflect on the limitations of democratic, collective modes of being and art. See Claire Bishop, 'Antagonism and Relational Aesthetics,' *October* 110 (Fall 2004): 51–79.

51. Bishop, *Artificial Hells*, 219–40.

52. Ibid.

53. Such a conception of the politics of aesthetics is rooted in her normative understanding of autonomy, detailed earlier, which sees art as distinct from heteronomous fields. For Bishop, art's value stems from its capacity of triggering an aesthetic experience contingent on 'play'—a suspension of the way in which the world is and how it be differently felt, seen, heard, etc. (following Rancière).

54. Bishop, *Artificial Hells*, 238.

55. Marina Vishmidt, 'What Do We Mean by 'Autonomy' and 'Reproduction?,' in *Reproducing Autonomy. Work, Money, Crisis and Contemporary Art*, ed. Kerstin Stakemeier and Marina Vishmidt (London: Mute, 2016), 46.

56. Ibid.

57. Mierle Laderman Ukeles, *Manifesto of Maintenance Art*, 1969.

58. Verónica Tello, 'Rhetorical Gestures: The 18th Biennale of Sydney', *Afterall* (2012), https://www.aftrall.org/online/rhetoricla-gestures-the-18th-biennale-of-sydney.Wp3QPmZL3mI.

59. Peter Osborne, *Anywhere or Not at All: Philosophy of Contemporary Art* (London and New York: Verso, 2013), 15.

60. Ibid., 27.

61. Peter Osborne, 'The Fiction of the Contemporary: Speculative Collectivity and Transnationality in the Atlas Group', in *Aesthetics and Contemporary Art*, 115.

BIBLIOGRAPHY

Adorno, Theodor. *In Search of Wagner*. Translated by Rodney Livingstone. 1952; London and New York: Verso, 2005.

Alberro, Alexander, and Blake Stimson, eds. *Institutional Critique: An Anthology of Artists' Writings*. Cambridge, MA: MIT Press, 2009.

Avanessian, Armen, and Luke Skrebowski, eds. *Aesthetics and Contemporary Art*. Berlin: Sternberg Press, 2011.

Bishop, Claire. *Artificial Hells: Participatory Art and the Politics of Spectatorship*. London and New York: Verso, 2012.
Bishop, Claire. 'Antagonism and Relational Aesthetics'. *October* 110 (Fall 2004): 51–79.
Ciric, Biljana, and Nikita Yingqian Cai, eds. *Active Withdrawals: Life and Death of Institutional Critique*. London: Black Dog, 2016.
Eliasson, Olafur. 'Green Light'. *Design Boom*, https://www.designboom.com/art/olafur-eliasson-green-light-venice-art-bienalle-05-11-2017/.
Foucault, Michel. 'What Is an Author?' [1969], in *Aesthetics, Method, and Epistemology: Essential Works of Foucault 1965–1984*, edited by James D. Faubion, 205–33. New York: The New Press, 1999.
Francke, Andrea, and Ross Jardine. 'Bureaucracy's Labour: The Administrator as Subject'. *Parse* 5 (Spring 2017): 24–33.
Fraser, Andrea. 'Autonomy and Its Contradictions'. *open!* May 2012, http://www.onlineopen.irg/downolad.php?id=363.
———. 'From the Critique of Institutions to an Institution of Critique,' *Artforum* 44, no. 1 (September 2005).
Grindon, Gavin. 'Surrealism, Dada and the Refusal of Work: Autonomy, Activism and Social Participation in the Radical Avant-Garde'. *Oxford Art Journal* 34, no. 1 (2011): 79–106.
Holmes, Brian. 'Artistic Autonomy and the Communication Society,' *Third Text* 18. No 6, 2004: 548.
Jackson, Shannon. *Social Works: Performing Art, Supporting Publics*. London: Routledge, 2011.
Léger, Marc James. 'Aesthetic Responsibility'. *Third Text* 18, no. 4 (2014): 123–36.
Lepecki, André. 'From Partaking to Initiating: Leading Following as Dance's (a-personal) Political Singularity'. In *Dance, Politics & Co-Community: Current Perspectives on Politics and Communities in the Arts*, edited by Gerald Siegmund and Stefan Hölscher, 21–38. Zurich: Diaphanes, 2013.
Lippard, Lucy. *Six Years: The Dematerialization of the Art Object from 1966 to 1972*. Chicago: University of Chicago Press, 1997.
Lütticken, Sven. *Cultural Revolution: Aesthetic Practice after Autonomy*. Berlin: Sternberg, 2017.
Lütticken, Sven. 'General Performance'. *e-flux journal* 31 (2012), http://www.e-flux.com/journal/31/68212/general-performance/.
Marx, Karl, and Friedrich Engels. 'Saint Max'. *The German Ideology* [1845–1846]. Amherst: Prometheus Press, 1932.
Mbembe, Achille. 'Necropolitics'. *Public Culture* 15, no. 1 (2003): 11–40.
Osborne, Peter. *Anywhere or Not at All*. London and New York: Verso, 2013.
Ögüt, Ahmet. 'New Schools: The Silent University'. *Frieze* 149 (September 2012), http://frieze.com/article/new-schools/.
Ögüt, Ahmet, et al., eds. *The Silent University: Transversal Pedagogy*. Berlin and Ruhr: Sternberg and Impulse Theatre Festival, 2016.
Rauning, Gerald, and Gene Ray, eds. *Art and Contemporary Critical Practice: Reinventing Institutional Critique*. London: Mayfly, 2009.

Sheikh, Simon. 'Art After Trump'. *e-flux conversations*, 2016, https://conversations.e-flux.com/t/simon-sheikh-art-after-trump/5325.
Staal, Jonas. 'IDEOLOGY = FORM'. *e-flux journal* 69 (2016), http://www.e-flux.com/journal/69/60626/ideology-form.
Stekemeier, Kerstin, and Marina Vishmidt. *Reproducing Autonomy: Work, Money, Crisis and Contemporary Art*. London: Mute, 2016.
Tello, Verónica. *Counter-Memorial Aesthetics: Refugee Histories and the Politics of Contemporary Art*. New York: Bloomsbury, 2016.
———. 'Rhetorical Gestures: The 18th Biennale of Sydney'. *Afterall*, 2012, https://www.afterall.org/online/rhetorical-gestures-the-18th-biennale-of-sydney.Wp3QPmZL3mI.
Thompson, Nato. *Seeing Power: Art and Activism in the Twenty-First Century*. Cambridge, MA: MIT Press, 2011.
Vishmidt, Marina. 'The Politics of Speculative Labour'. *Transformative Art Production*, http://transformativeartproduction.net/the-politics-of-speculative-labour/.
Wright, Stephen. 'The Delicate Essence of Artistic Collaboration'. *Third Text* 18, no. 6 (2004): 533–45.

Part II

ABSTRACTIONS

Technological, Financial, Cultural, Scientific

Chapter Four

Inside the Corpse of Abstraction

(An Apotropaic Text)

Franco 'Bifo' Berardi

THE AUTOMATON

Capitalism has gained immortality—the immortality of abstraction. The result are living bodies encased in a corpse, frantically but vainly looking for a way out. During the course of the past two centuries, as the light of modernity grew brighter and brighter, a necropoetic foreboding infiltrated the psychosphere. Pools of darkness around the brightly lit stage—upon which the spectacle of technological advancement is enacted—were occasionally shot through with spasmodic flashes of consciousness. But then the automaton invaded the biosphere and the technosemiotic micro-engines penetrated all spheres of social life. Mobilised by the neuronetwork, the hyperconnected body finds itself in a digital necrosis. At the beginning of the twentieth century, which in *After the Future* I defined as 'the century that trusted in the future'[1], Futurism celebrated the machine as an external extension of human power, an object inseparable from urban experience. In the twenty-first century, which is much less confident in the future, the machine is internalised. Moreover, it is turning the living organism, and society itself, into bio-info mutation. While the 'info-machine' of our time is entwined with the social nervous system, the 'bio-machine' interferes in the genetic becoming of the human organism. As I suggested in *After the Future* (you must forgive me for quoting myself),

> Digital and bio-technologies have turned the external machine of iron and steel into the internalised and recombining machine of the bio-info era. The bio-info machine is no more separable from the body and the mind, because it is no more an external tool, but an internal transformer of the body and of the mind, a

linguistic and cognitive enhancer. Now the nanomachine is mutating the human brain and the linguistic ability to produce and communicate. The Machine is us.[2]

The *Futurist Manifesto* exalted the aesthetic virtues of speed. In the twenty-first century, however, speed has shifted from the sphere of external machines to the sphere of information and neurocognitive stimulation. Speed has become internalised, triggering a pathological working. As the cyberspace is expanding and accelerating the rhythm of info-neural stimulation, the ability of social attention to process information (that I have called cybertime) is collapsing. We no longer have the time for a rational and emotional elaboration of the content circulating in the infosphere. Subjected to the acceleration of the info-stimuli, the mind reacts with panic or it becomes desensitised. In the past few years, an awareness of necrosis has emerged in several social movements. In July 2017, during the Hamburg G-20 Summit, a thousand young actors, dressed in grey, with their faces painted white, marched like zombies in a *mise-en-scene* of urban life in hell[3]. During the protest against the financial dictatorship the crowd waved a banner with the words 'Welcome to hell' unequivocally stating that we are living in the rotting corpse of capitalism and that, as far as we know, there is no way out. The bitter irony of necropoetry seems to be the only way to mitigate despair.

In 1803, at Newgate in London, the Italian alchemist Giovanni Aldini gave a famous public demonstration of electrostimulation utilising the corpse of an executed criminal. *The Newgate Calendar* described the scene in the following way:

> Upon the first galvanisation the jaws of the deceased criminal began to quiver, and the adjoining muscles were horribly contorted, and one eye was actually opened. In the subsequent part of the process the right hand was raised and clenched, and the legs and thighs were set in motion.[4]

This episode echoed in the intellectual milieux of the time and seems to have reached Mary Shelley, the creator of Frankenstein, a fictional character, a prototype of the organic automaton and a corpse with an artificially reactivated brain. 'By the glimmer of the half-extinguished light', Shelley writes in her novel, 'I saw the dull yellow eye of the creature open; it breathed hard, and a convulsive motion agitated its limbs'[5]. Can zombies think or is their neural activity unconscious and devoid of intention? The cognitive automation has given way to the intelligent zombie that can be seen everywhere in the metropolitan landscape of our time. The two techno utopias of the twentieth century, the info and the bio, have given birth to the bio-automaton—an attempt to prevail over death. Mary Shelley's *Frankenstein*, like Gustav Meyrink and Isaac Bashevis Singer's *Golem*[6], is a literary anticipation of the postmodern digital automaton.

The process of automation, which is the result of applying intelligence to the process of production, has been steadily expanding and has infiltrated all spheres of daily life, including the sphere of cognition and language. It has also transformed knowledge into a mere execution of tasks replacing the activity of the conscious brain with mere (technical) performance.

The automaton transfers the cognitive activity of the human brain to the simulated brain of the digital machine. It animates the digital machine, lending it self-sufficiency while simultaneously reducing the cognitive activity of the conscious organism to passive dependence. Automation has played a positive role in reducing labour time; however, under the conditions of capitalist exploitation, it has gradually subsumed the workers' autonomy under the self-regulation of the automaton whose only function is profit increase. The automaton is the product of the conflict between living labour and capital, originally conceived as a tool for reducing the time of human labour. But the automaton has redesigned its purpose and its function; by subjugating living labour, dead labour (capital) has gained an independent life. The automaton may have been conceived, under the anthropological and economic conditions of capital accumulation, as an enhancer of human power. The problem, however, is that it has turned into a self-regulating power that subjugates human will, fosters impotence and abets the annihilation of social autonomy, one of the reasons for which is the automation of language. The automation of language and of cognitive behaviour—the result of inserting digital devices into the continuum of living experience and the accompanying intensification of neurostimulation—has induced a mutation that can be described as a spasmodic attempt to cope with the chaotic infosphere that surrounds us as well as an attempt to reframe the relationship between the infosphere and the brain. A spasm is a painful vibration that forces the organism into the extreme mobilisation of all its nervous energies. This painful vibration is the effect of the compulsively accelerated rhythm of social interaction and of exploitation of nervous energy. As semiocapitalist valorisation commands an increase in nervous productivity, the nervous system is increasingly subjected to exploitation. The spasm is the result of the violent penetration of the capitalist exploitation of info-technologies, which takes place in the sphere of cognition, sensibility and the unconscious alike. Not only is the psychological dimension of the unconscious disturbed, the fabric of the neuronal system itself is subjected to trauma, overload and disconnection. For the human brain, adapting to the new environment involves enormous suffering. It also unleashes violence and madness. The most prominent feature of the psychopathology that, for me, is the consequence of the technoneural mutation is the increase in suicide rates. Suicide is spreading epidemically as an effect of social stress, of emotional impoverishment and of the constant aggression on attention.

According to the World Health Organization, in the past forty-five years, suicide rates have increased by 60 percent worldwide[7]. Significantly, these have been the years of the worldwide implementation of the capitalist model, the years in which attention and time have become increasingly subjected to the rhythm of the economic machine. Note that these suicide figures do not include suicide attempts, which are up to twenty times more frequent than successful suicides. Particularly remarkable in this context is the increasing rate of suicides among the younger population. How can we explain this? In the past forty-five years, two new phenomena have pentetrated human bio-sociality: the neoliberal acceleration of the economic pace and the digital mutation of cognitive and emotional stimulation. It is these two trends that are at the root of the growing suicide epidemic. An epidemic of misery is spreading on the planet while the absolutism of financial capitalism asserts its right to total control over our lives. As bio-semiocapitalism infiltrates the conscious organisms' nervous cells, it simultaneously inoculates these very organisms with a necropolitical rationale—a morbid sentiment that is progressively infesting the collective unconscious, culture and sensibility at large. The biopolitical effect of semiocapitalism—or, better said, the thanato-political effect of semiocapitalism—consists of capturing cognitive activity and of subjecting the lingustic animal's faculty of expression to the sleepless, aggressive dynamics of the labour market. Exploitation, competition, mobbing, precariousness and layoffs are no longer perceived as a result of conflictual social relations. On the contrary, they are internalised as deficiencies of the self, as personal inadequacies. The unceasing restructuring and reorganisation of work is experienced as a brutality and humiliation, too.

IMMORTALITY

Capitalism is an attempt to overcome death and to fix time in a never-ending process of accumulation (the accumulation of dead labour). As labour is the source of valorisation, valorisation is the most accomplished and most successful attempt to achieve immortality, a sort of frozen immortality of dead labour that traps living labour. '*Le mort saisit le vif* [death captures life]', wrote Marx speaking of the relation between capital and living labour[8]. In fact, being dead labour (and dead nature), capital implies a steady expansion of death in the sphere of all living organisms: human beings and, more broadly, all sentient beings. The dead form of labour (capital) captures and codifies all forms of life and, finally, annihilates it. The current sixth extinction, the disappearance of 50 percent of the species living on the planet, is evidence of this process. Today, for the first time in history, the extinction of the human species is in the range of the possible. Necro-aesthetics in the spheres of art, fashion and media testifies to the emerging awareness of a trend that spreads from aesthetic perception to social imagination at large. Zje Zhangke's films are, in my opinion, a perfect example of this trend, in particular his 2006 *Still Life*, a film about a Chinese worker who returns to his native village where, until a few years ago, he had lived with his wife and daughter. His wife and his daughter are no longer there. The village is no longer there. A new landscape has arisen in place of the old one literally subsuming life, the village, its inabitants, their memories and affects to the triumph of economic innovation. The authorities of the recently-converted-to-capitalism Chinese state decided to build a dam and so they replaced life with a sort of hyperrealistic nothingness: still life. Replacing life with a technosimulation is the overall trend of our time, the background against which the contemporary necrosis is played out. Are we powerless to stop this trend? And should we, as individuals and as a collectivity, elaborate aesthetic forms of cultural adaptation to the ongoing suicide of the species? The only line of escape is to dismantle the capitalist trap. But capitalism has gained the immortality of abstraction, and we cannot break its spell. We are powerless. Capitalism is dead, but it has achieved immortal nonlife via financial and virtual transubstantiation. It has achieved immortality by replacing concrete life with mathematical abstraction. Given that the (financial) mathematisation of daily life is the source of immortalisation, we ought to be able to break free from the reign of mathematical ferocity. But thus far we have not found the key. Humankind is trapped in a necrotic condition that paves the way to suicide. In a book devoted to the subject of suicide and mass murder—*Heroes*—I proposed the concept of 'absolute capitalism' in order to pin down the nature of current financial dominance in the economic sphere. You must forgive me, once again, for quoting myself (for the last time, I promise):

> The rise of financial capitalism, the deterritorialization of production and exchange and finally the emergence of a virtual class without territorial identity go together with a general process of deregulation. The global dimension of corporations hindered and rendered impossible any legal control on their activity. The sovereignty of the national states lost effectiveness and the global corporations gained absolute freedom, not responding to the local authority and shifting their immaterial assets from a location to another. This is particularly evident in reference to the environmental crisis, as the legal limits to the exploitation of physical resources and the pollution of the environment are systematically (and ultimately, suicidally) ignored by corporations.
>
> This is why I believe that the contemporary, global system should be defined as Absolute Capitalism. The only effective regulations of this world are those of value-accumulation, profit-growth and economic competition.

> These are its all-encompassing priorities, and the almighty force at its core. Any other issue, including the survival of the planet or the future of the next generation, fades in comparison. Compared to the past of bourgeois industrial capitalism, the relation between social welfare and financial profit is now inverted. In the industrial economy, profits increased when citizens had enough money to buy goods produced in the factories. In the sphere of financial capitalism financial, indexes go up only if social welfare crumbles, and salaries fall.[9]

In the old days of industrial capitalism, the transformation of resources into physical objects was the main source of valorisation. This was followed by the boom of postindustrial technology, which enabled the immaterialisation of labour processes until, finally, digital language subsumed the physicality of the labour process. What is at stake here is a multidimensional reality dissolving into zero-dimensional information while the application of artificial intelligence to the Internet of Things lends a three-dimensional existence to the zero-dimension info-simulatory codes. Artificially intelligent micro-engines are increasingly built into the infrastructures of daily life. The digital is invading the biosphere and turning chaos into order: the order of abstraction. The Latin word *abstrahere* means 'to drag away, to divert from'. Abstraction is therefore the extraction of nihil from something: the extraction of a mathematical relation from a physical set of phenomena, of an informational algorithm from a material process. But this nihil is supremely operative. In the sphere of (capitalist) production, labour is abstracted from the concrete usefulness of any given activity. Further, capital continues to be abstracted from physical assets, which are turned into a purely mathematical relation: figures, algorithms, deductions.

MONEY

> When those who had been evicted went back where they came from, they found their villages had disappeared under . . . dusty quarries. Their homes were occupied by hunger and policemen. People returned to live on city streets and pavements, on hovels, on dusty construction sites, wondering which corner of this huge country was meant for them. . . . In the drive to beautify Delhi from Commonwealth games, laws were passed that made the poor vanish, like laundry stains. Street vendors disappeared, rickshaw pullers lost their licenses, small shops and businesses were shut down. Beggars were rounded up, tried by mobile magistrates in mobile courts, and dropped outside the city limits. The slums that remained were screened off, with vinyl billboards that said DELHIciously yours.[10]

In the 1990s, capitalist globalisation promised to create a future of prosperity for everybody, or at least for the majority of the world's population. It then became clear that the universal mobilisation of labour energies was not leading to prosperity for the majority but only to an agglomeration of wealth for a small minority and a life of precarious exploitation and marginalisation for the rest. Now that globalisation is failing, stagnation is the most likely prospect unless a large population is wiped out of the sphere of survival. What is going to happen to the 50 percent of the world population who have received none of the advantages of globalisation but are now exposed to the consequences of environmental devastation, to social immiseration that financial plundering continues to perpetrate? The years 2016–2017 were marked by a sudden awareness of the fact that the process of neoliberal globalisation is failing. A new alliance of neoliberal extremism and conservative nationalism began to emerge as a result. The worst of two worlds that, once upon a time, were opposed: aggressive neoliberal market and reactionary anti-globalism.

In November 2016, Narendra Modi, a Hindu nationalist and a neoliberal extremist currently governing India, began an experiment called demonetisation, the hoped result of which is a great leap forward in the implementation of a cashless economy and the digitalisation of money. In the past decades, steps have been taken towards the digitalisation of money (credit cards, digital payments), but so far the world economy has continued to use physical money alongside digital money, thus permitting the survival of those not partaking in the digital economy (or technology). This is no longer the case. Modi's goal seems to be to accelerate the pace of digitalisation in a country in which the digital divide still excludes the majority of the population from taking part in the digital economy. A significant proportion of the population has thus been pushed out of the national economy like those poor people hidden behind the 'DEHLIciously yours' billboards that Arundati Roy is talking about.

Are we witnessing the first glimpses of the expulsion of half of the planet's population from the cycle of economic exchange? Is this the beginning of an economic extermination? Is this the hidden mission of the rising Trump age? Reasons put forth by Modi seem quite weak: preventing tax evasion and financial crime, whereas, in actual fact, Modi has hit hard on average people, while tax evaders, who notoriously invest money abroad, have been spared (and do not seem to resent demonetisation). Comments in the Indian press, particularly in newspapers representing the pro-financial circles, are quite upbeat: demonetisation will accelerate India's growth enormously. How so? By getting rid of the dead weight, of the majority of the population unable to follow the pace, by forcing them out of the economic circulation, by throwing them off the racing train, so to speak. 'The problem for many is that they do not know how to do without cash. In the Chawri Bazar, generations of traders have bought and sold paper, from wedding cards to calendars to packing material, mostly in cash. Their customers paid cash, and they used it to pay their suppliers and workers'[11]. Modi's demonetisation of Rs 500 and Rs 1,000 banknotes—constituting over 86 percent of the total value of currency in circulation—does not follow the conventional logic of a currency 'stabilisation' measure but is instead a 'structural reform', targeted at promoting a cashless economy. The demonetisation triggered an increase in digital payments. Although it initially paralysed the economy, it subsequently catalysed a digital payment ecosystem. In India, most economic transactions take place in cash outside of the official market channels; hence they go largely untaxed. This practice has created a parallel 'black' economy; however, it has also allowed a large proportion of the Indian population to survive. The brutal transformation of the currency system has created panic and produced casualties. It has also redrawn the (digital) monetary sphere, while simultaneously expelling the majority from the economic circulation. The digital divide has here been turned into a *tool* for the elimination of the 'noncompetitive' human sector. It should not be forgotten that, fifteen years ago, Norendra Modi stepped into the limelight of international fame as the person responsible for the assassination of more than a thousand Muslims in the city of Ayodhya. Now his project is more ambitious; he seems to have set his mind on spearheading a (potential) monetary holocaust.

EXTERMINATION

There are signs in the current political and cultural environment that may be read as a return of the phenomenon we are accustomed to term 'Nazism': nationalist aggressiveness, racism, the massive enslavement of the *untermenschen* and extermination plans. The epidemic of violence and the explosion of fear, panic, depression and racist suprematism are the trend of the new century, which started with the shocking crumbling of the Twin Towers in New York City. Since that day, we have been obliged to acknowledge the reality of a global civil war that, sixteen years later, seems unstoppable and is gradually spreading to all corners of the planet as well as pervading all aspects of social life. Be that as it may, I do not think that the comparison with the historical experience of the twentieth century is well founded. Since the publication of Filippo Tommaso Marinetti's 1909 *Futurist Manifesto* and Benito Mussolini's rise to power in 1922, Fascism and Nazism have been expressions of an aggressive energy of young people returning from the trenches of World War I, rejoicing at the prospect of a territorial expansion and/or patriotic assertiveness.

The twentieth century really was the century that trusted in the future: despite the violence of the two world wars, and despite the social misery of the majority of people, the trust in the future was based on patriotic euphoria, on fertility, on high levels of reproduction, on the prevalence of young people among the population, on the growth of the industrial economy and on the ideological faith in the virtues of strong leaders. Nothing similar is happening today: aggressiveness has resurfaced but it is based on depression and a sense of impotence of a senescent population. There is no vision for a bright future. This contemporary trope of Fascism is the Fascism of the impotent and the frustrated, unable to stop financial plundering. It is the Nazism of people for whom there is no growth or expansion, a Fascism with no energy or euphoria. Might this imply that the present wave of darkness will perhaps ebb and fade away in a few years? Will the global civil war end soon? Will Fascism be defeated again? Is there a way out?

These questions sound empty; we should not fall into the trap (in the historical *trompe l'oeil*) of identifying the present apocalypse with the catastrophes of the past century. A hundred years ago it was possible to imagine a future beyond the wave of darkness. Right now, this vision is inert. Communism has been annulled, and the horizon is blank. Looking back to the past century, we are overwhelmed with a sense of tragedy, caused by the two world wars, and the suffering of countless victims of violence and terror. Despite this, a very different historical tone is easily detected. Even amidst destruction, in the mud and the blood of the battle of Stalingrad that claimed a million lives, people were optimistic. Beyond the darkness and the suffering of daily reality, they were able to look forward to a future of ideological fulfilment. They called this future variously democracy, Communism or Fascism depending on their political orientation or expectations. But no more. We do not live in the mud and the blood of Stalingrad; our daily life is not as hard as the lives of those who lived during Nazism and World War II, at least not for the majority of humankind. But the future is empty, unthinkable. The future is longer human. Indeed, necrosis is the chief feature of the aesthetic perception of the present. We should also consider the possibility that the very meaning of historical Nazism has been misunderstood. We have thought of Nazism as of a temporary explosion of barbarism destined to be rejected by humankind. This was the comforting vision created by the progressive culture of the second part of the twentieth century. The necro-aesthetic sentiment that has recently emerged tells a different story, a story reminiscent of Günther Anders's words in *We Sons of Eichmann*, first published in 1962:

> We can expect that the horrors of the Reich to come will vastly eclipse the horrors of yesterday's Reich. Doubtless, when one day our children or grandchildren, proud of their perfect 'co-mechanization', look down from the great heights of their thousand year Reich at yesterday's empire, at the so called 'third' Reich, it will seem to them merely a minor, provincial experiment.[12]

This appalling prediction is now becoming true. We may ignore it, we may close our eyes and ignore the spread of nationalism, racism, the proliferation of Hitler's imitators like the Modi of India, the Duarte of Manila, the Trump of America, the Kim of Korea, but denial will not help. Nazism seems to be back. According to Anders, Nazism was essentially about the perfection of extermination in a technological age. Afforded by industrial technology, inhuman tasks no longer required human operators. In much the same way, for Anders, the dropping of the atomic bomb on Hiroshima and Nagasaki was not the result of human action. It was the implementation of a technical procedure: at the touch of a button, hundreds of thousands of people were killed in just a few seconds. The automation of extermination is the essential contribution of the Nazi machinery. Worryingly, in our postmodern and postindustrial age, the project of automated extermination can be implemented on a much larger scale than in Hitler's age. Since Auschwitz and Hiroshima, the extermination machine has become automated, which has turned extermination into an institutional task to be completed by the ministries of finance, by the administrations of big corporations and banks, not only by military agencies that specialise in mass murder. For Anders, dropping the atomic bomb on Hiroshima and Nagasaki marked the beginning of a new era: 'from now on, all life stands under the sign of atomic self-annihilation. For the first time in human history, mankind is obliged to envisage the end of the human race as a real possibility. The "end time" has begun, an era that must anticipate the possibility of the "end of time"'[13].

The new era inaugurated by Auschwitz and Hiroshima has been suspended for several decades, however; the necro-aesthetic signs we see all around us suggest that the suspension has been suspended. What next? The convergence of automated extermination and the putrefaction of the social mind—depression, despair, aggression, fear and a massive Alzheimer—has turned the apocalypse into an unstoppable trend. Fascism will never reappear in its past historical form because something much more frightening is taking root: not the historical (criminal) Fascist leaders' *Wille zur Machte* [Will to Power] but automation of the process of extermination, which is already underway. Even if we decide to ignore this evident truth, 2017 showed that historical Nazism was only an experiment. Despite the failure of that particular historical attempt, the experiment is now returning, in a far more accomplished form.

In this text I have been using words 'Nazism' and 'Fascism' as if they were synonymous. They are not. It may be interesting to investigate their difference as, in my opinion, in the new century the two terms diverge much more than they did in the past century. For me, the essential meaning of Nazism resided in a sense of national and racial superiority and in a radical (and violent) opposition between the historial winners and losers. The cult of superiority returns in the neoliberal age in the guise of social Darwinist competition, which despises those who cannot survive the 'Natural Selection of the Market'. Fascism, on the other hand, may be seen as an aggressive resentment of the historical game's losers. In fact, Italian Fascism was a reaction of a nation that resented the humiliation of the 'maimed victory' of World War I and of the Treaty of Versailles, in which Italians were treated for what they were: a second-rate nation with a weak military apparatus and no colonial empire. I would say that while Nazism is an expression of suprematism, Fascism is the resentful and vengeful spirit of the historical losers, those marginalised in the economic game of competition whose reaction to this marginalisation took the form of cultural identification. The war that is raging in the new century may be described as a global civil war in which triumphant global capitalism and the resentful impotence of the immiserated and humiliated population fight along fragmentary and ever-changing lines. Financial capitalism is based on unrelenting deterritorialisation, which is the cause of fear among those who feel marginalised and humiliated by the precariousness of daily life and by the violence of the labour market. One of the consequences of this fear is the counter-effect of aggressive reterritorialisation: people clutch at (any form of) identity, as only belonging (to something or somewhere) seems to provide the much-needed shelter and protection. The problem, however, is that one's belonging can only be proven through aggression against the other. The combined effect of deterritorialisation in the sphere of financial capitalism, and of reterritorialisation in sphere of identity, is a permanent state of war.

The heart of darkness of contemporary necroculture emerged in the United States in the years 2016–2017 as a postmodern remake of the tradition of violence created by white suprematism in the course of two centuries of colonisation, extermination, massive enslavement and incarceration. In the past century, a minority of the American population attempted to counter the appalling legacy of the country's foundation by creating a democratic and civilised life. This attempt was provisionally successful; it led to the process of desegregation in the 1960s; later it led to the generous but failed attempt of Barack Obama, at which point the white majority, enraged by the immiseration brought on by the financial crash of 2008, humiliated by the disastrous Bush-Cheney wars and infuriated by the unpardonable offence of a black president, returned to the suprematist mindset. The true nature of white America has resurfaced. Could Trumpism be seen as a temporary error of the American mind, a surmountable fallacy of democracy? I do not think so. I think that Trumpism is the innermost core of white American history.

In his novels, Cormack McCarthy describes the sordid violence that flourishes in the brutal desert that is the anthropological ground of white American society. Novelist Jonathan Franzen discloses the connection between soulless brutality and digital culture. Digital mutation is the pinnacle of a history that began with the most perfect genocide in human memory: the elimination of the living and the replacement of life with the annihilating 'word of God': the binary code. Franzen speaks of the effect of the American annihilation experiment when describing the continent's physical landscape with the following words: 'a biotically desolate country-scape of the sort that America had come to specialise in'[14]. The transformation of the cultural landscape is not an exclusively American problem, although Trumpism is a U.S. phenomenon and the United States seems to be experiencing this pathology in a particularly severe form. People resort to racism, sexism and other forms of denigration—and aggression—as a form of revenge; racism is therefore both an identitarian stronghold and an exhaust valve. Contemporary racism, however, is not a mere return of 'old' racism, as theorised by Arthur de Gobineau in his 'Essay sur l'inegalité des races humaines' [An Essay on the Inequality of the Human Races][15].

Racism emerged in the European colonisers' cultures as a form of ideological justification for plundering; it was concurrent with the forming of the European colonial empires. 'Old racism' was an expression of the 'superiority' of the dominant race, based on technological advantage and on the weapons used to subjugate and exploit the coloured people of the so-called primitive South. In this day and age, weapons are available to everyone; no race distinction is made. Dispossessed white people are obliged to 'tolerate' the overcrowding of their living spaces as migrants 'invade' the suburbs of big cities. The new racism is the racism of the losers. Old racism was shared by the upper classes and the proletarians alike; it was a mark of white class 'superiority' vis-à-vis the colonised of the world. The new racism is the racism of the destitute and the ignorant. Upper classes are indignant against the (new) racism of the poor; from their rich, well-protected residential areas they look down on the slums where migrants mingle with the marginalised and the destitute. But the puritanical cancellation of history cannot erase the memory of violence inflicted on the indigenous population of the North American continent, on millions of deported black slaves, on the environment (that of the continent and, more broadly, of the entire planet). Consequently, the violated unconscious explodes in a chaotic manner, with no rational or political mediation. Stephen Paddock, the professional Las Vegas gambler who killed fifty-eight people from the window of his four-star hotel, is the hero of the American necrotic unconscious. 'This is the price of freedom', commented the Fox News anchorman (and sexual harasser) Bill O'Reilly after the massacre[16]. Indeed, freedom.

Here is what Franzen has to say about freedom:

> People came to this country for either money or freedom. If you don't have money, you cling to your freedoms all the more angrily. Even if smoking kills you, even if you can't afford to feed your kids, even if your kids are getting shot down by maniacs with assault rifles. You may be poor, but the one thing nobody can take away from you is the freedom to fuck up your life whatever way you want to.[17]

The dark American soul that Cormack McCarthy has described in his books has been going berserk since 9/11 and throughout the self-defeating wars of George Bush, the financial collapse and the recession, during the racist police violence preparing Trump's rise to power. Americans rejoiced in the devastation of Iraq and of millions of innocent lives; in an oblique way, this was a compensation for the humiliation of 9/11. It has been pointed out that Saddam Hussein had nothing to do with al-Qaida, but these kind of subtleties did not matter to people like Cheney and Bush.

SUBURBICON

The 2017 film *Suburbicon*, directed by George Clooney, begins with warm and fuzzy images reminiscent of the 1950s advertising rhetoric: a peaceful, idyllic suburban community with affordable homes and manicured lawns, a perfect place to raise a family, and in the summer of 1959, the Lodge family is doing just that. But this pleasant surface conceals a disturbing reality: the family's father Gardner Lodge (Matt Damon) betrays his (handicapped) wife with her sister, then murders his wife in order to collect life insurance and escape to a faraway, exotic island—Aruba. At the same time, an African American family moves into the neighbourhood, the perfect community's reaction to which is, in the first instance, bewilderment and protest, then blind rage. The fairytale of the perfect family living in a quiet suburb of the perfectly white Northern American continent all of a sudden appears tarnished: the ominous past resurfaces as soon as racial order is 'disturbed'. The horror of the past can be denied but it is forever imprinted on the white American unconscious. Imagine that Hitler had won World War II and perfected the project of extermination of the Jewish people. Imagine that the Third Reich had become the dominant worldwide media broadcaster and the centre for new technologies.

This is the United States of America: the perfect genocide of the indigenous people, the long-lasting enslavement of millions of blacks, the production of a bomb that killed hundreds of thousands of people in a few seconds. Is it not the United States? Is it not worse than the Third Reich? On 9/11, many people in the world, particularly those living in countries attacked and humiliated by the American bombings, overtly or covertly celebrated the unprecedented act of war on the American soil. Watching footage or images of people raving in the streets of Latin America and of the Arab world, there were journalists who wondered why so many people hated the United States. I don't think 'hate' is the right word. Horror is the word. The majority of the world population is horrified by the hyperexpensive, aggressive American lifestyle because we feel that the United States is the terminal illness of humankind. It therefore comes as little surprise that the United States is the homeland of necro-aesthetics. Heroin use has quintupled over the past decade in the United States; young, white males are the epidemic's most likely victims.

'We have a 9/11-scale loss every three weeks', Governor Christie said, adding that three-fourths of the losses are from opioid overdoses[18]. Psychosis and depression are haunting the American mind, which explains Trump's rise to power. The wave of mass murders that has befallen the world, but particularly North America, can be explained as a result of the easy access to lethal weapons; however, it is also a symptom of the putrefaction of the American psyche: the self-loathing of the people who have been persuaded that only winners deserve respect, and who are experiencing failure that engenders depression, psychosis and violent madness. Empathy is self-harming in hell. The door is open to the inflow of the surrounding suffering. In hell, people tend to seek solitude and close their doors so as not to be harmed by the suffering of others. In *The Parable of the Sower*, published in 1993, Octavia Butler outlines the dystopian premonition of a world full of violence, starvation and pain in which people are accustomed to the surrounding hell to the point of being emotionally indifferent and numb. In this world, a young girl is suffering from a rare disease that the doctors call 'organic delusional syndrome'[19]:

> My father has always pretended, or perhaps believed that my hyper-empathy syndrome was something I could shake off and forget about. The sharing is not real, after all. It's not some magic or ESP that allows me to share the pain or the pleasure of other people. It's delusional. . . . I can't do a thing about my hyper-empathy, no matter what Dad thinks or wants or wishes. I feel what I see others feeling or what I believe they feel. Hyper-empathy is what the doctors call an 'organic delusional syndrome'. Big shit. It hurts, that's all I know. Thanks to Paracetco, the small pill, the particular drug my mother chose to abuse before my birth killed her, I'm crazy. I get a lot of grief that doesn't belong to me, and that isn't real. But it hurts.
>
> I'm supposed to share pleasure and pain, but there is not much pleasure around these days.[20]

Empathy is a liability and an economic disadvantage in the time of all-pervading competition. The suffering of others is irrelevant from the point of view of the economic actor, who knows very well that *mors tua vita mea* [your death, my life].

THE END

The necro-aesthetic is the attunement of sensibility and of perceptual expectations to the current drift to extermination that is the key feature of the Trump age. It is not the political will (that can be countered and subverted by an opposed political will) but the *force of automated governance* that is pushing the human race towards extinction. This is evident in the huge transfer of economic resources from the majority to a restricted financial elite (1 percent of the world population possessing more or less 99 percent of the world resources). The tax reform of the Trump administration is the final step in this strangulatory trend. At the same time, monetary measures like the demonetisation imposed by Modi on the Indian economy and the forcing of a cashless economy indicate that the majority of society is likely to be denied access to the resources necessary for a decent life. The history of humankind is reaching its end. History is not going to finish, but it is no longer going to be human. The automaton will survive; human beings, however, will be asked not to be human.

Beauty is both an attempt to delay decomposition and an attempt to attune to decomposition. The algid beauty of mathematics is based on the absence of existence. But beauty is an unutterable passion for existence; it cannot be translated into ontological terms, as it is something that escapes the ontological grip. Necropoetic threads have traversed the history of modernity from Francisco Goya to Joseph Conrad. The sleep of reason gives birth to monsters, as Goya shows in *Pinturas Negras* [Black Paintings]. But if the sleep of reason gives birth to monsters, what about monsters borne of empathy's sleep? It's too late for action; we must rethink from scratch the relation between subjectivity and evolution and consequently reconsider and resize the importance of conscious action and political projects. Within the historical framework, action marks the relation between subjectivity and evolution. But as far as I understand, we are no longer living in a historical framework; we are dwelling in the posthistorical dimension of pure horror. Taoism suggests that nonaction (*wu wei*) is the only reasonable way of relating to evolution. Not a different action, but nonaction. This is the lesson that I have drawn from the years 2016–2017, when the lights went out.

NOTES

1. Franco 'Bifo' Berardi, *After the Future*, ed. Gary Genosko and Nicholas Thoburn, trans. Arianna Bove et al. (Oakland: AK Books, 2011), 8.
2. Ibid., 16.
3. Here the activist group Gestalten protested against the politics of the few.
4. See *The Newgate Calendar*: 'George Foster Executed at Newgate, 18 January 1803, for the Murder of his Wife and Child, by drowning them in the Paddington Canal; with a Curious Account of Galvanic Experiments on his Body', http://www.exclassics.com/newgate/ng464.htm, accessed 21 December 2017.
5. Mary Shelley quoted in Lorna Sage et al., *The Cambridge Guide to Women's Writing in English* (Cambridge: Cambridge University Press, 1999), 254.
6. The legend of the golem refers to an artificial man created to defend the Jews of Prague in the sixteenth century.
7. See http://www.who.int/mental_health/prevention/suicide/suicideprevent/en/, accessed 21 December 2017.
8. Karl Marx, *Capital*, trans. B. Brewster (London: New Left Review, 1976), 91.
9. Franco 'Bifo' Berardi, *Heroes* (London: Verso, 2014), 87.
10. Arundathi Roy, *Capitalism a Ghost Story* (Chicago: Haymarket Books, 2014), 13.
11. Geeta Anand and Hari Kumar, 'Indian Vendors see Empty Stores and Blame a Rupee Ban', *New York Times*, 24 November 2016.
12. Günther Anders, *We Sons of Eichmann: An Open Letter to Klaus Eichmann*, 1964, trans. Jordan Levinson, http://anticoncept.phpnet.us/eichmann.htm, accessed 17 December 2017.
13. Ibid.
14. Jonathan Franzen, *Purity* (New York: Farrar, Straus and Giroux, 2015), 255.
15. In this 1853–1855 work, Joseph Arthur, Comte de Gobineau argues that civilizations decline when races mix are mixed and that the white race is superior.
16. Chris D'Angelo, 'Bill O'Reilly on Las Vegas Massacre: "This is the Price of Freedom"', *Huffington Post*, 2 October 2017, http://www.latimes.com, accessed 3 October 2017.
17. Jonathan Franzen, *Freedom* (London: Picador, 2011), 361.
18. Governor Christie, 31 July 2017, https://edition.cnn.com/2017/07/31/politics/, accessed 3 August 2017.
19. Octavia Butler, *The Parable of the Sower* (New York: Four Walls Eight Windows, 1993), 22.
20. Ibid.

BIBLIOGRAPHY

Anand, Geeta and Kumar, Hari. 'Indian Vendors see Empty Stores and Blame a Rupee Ban', New York Times, 24 November 2016, https://www.nytimes.com/2016/11/24/world/asia/india-currency-narendra-modi.html.

Anders, Günther. *We Sons of Eichmann: An Open Letter to Klaus Eichmann*. Translated by Jordan Levinson, 1964. http://anticoncept.phpnet.us/eichmann.htm.
D'Angelo, Chris. 'Bill O'Reilly On Las Vegas Massacre: "This is the Price of Freedom"', *Huffington Post*, 2 October 2017, https://www.huffingtonpost.com/entry/bill-oreilly-las-vegas-shooting_us_59d29fa5e4b048a44324 81eb?guccounter=1.
Berardi, Franco 'Bifo'. *After the Future*. Edited by Gary Genosko and Nicholas Thoburn. Translated by Arianna Bove et al. Oakland: AK Books, 2011.
———. *Heroes: Mass Murder and Suicide*. London: Verso, 2014.
Butler, Octavia. *The Parable of the Sower*. New York: Four Walls Eight Windows, 1993.
Franzen, Jonathan. *Freedom*. London: Picador, 2011.
———. *Purity*. New York: Farrar, Straus and Giroux, 2015.
Marx, Karl. *Capital*. Translated by B. Brewster. London: New Left Review, 1976.
Roy, Arundathi. *Capitalism a Ghost Story*. Chicago: Haymarket Books, 2014.
Sage, Lorna, et al. *The Cambridge Guide to Women's Writing in English*. Cambridge: Cambridge University Press, 1999.

Chapter Five

Greenness

Sketching the Limits of a Normative Fetish

Jens Hauser

'The earth is sick', bemoans a group of extra-terrestrials as two 'naturally' green macrocephalous Selenites equipped with telescopes observe colossal yellow flames emanating from the only rudimentarily blue planet: 'these are, to me, great fires ignited by the Earthlings to delay the cooling of their planet'. This 1918 cartoon, created by French illustrator Auguste Roubille for *La Baïonnette*, depicted World War I 'as seen from other planets'[1] decades before Whole Earth images became available. While even after World War II humankind feared nuclear winters as a likely consequence of the use of atomic weapons, in 2018, in the greenhouse effect era in which increasing vegetal greening can, indeed, be seen from outer space, green aliens might well wonder about homo faber's need for climate engineering to actually cool the planet. Would they still feel alienated?

A morbid odour clings to the charm of the pervasive trope of greening everything, from mundane 'green burials'[2] to transcendental 'greening of the gods'[3], and even 'green warfare'[4], taught in military studies[5]. Despite its at first sight positive connotations of aliveness and naturalness, the term 'green' incrementally serves the uncritical, fetishistic desire to metaphorically hypercompensate for a systemic necropolitics that has variously taken the form of the increasing technical manipulation of living systems, ecologies, the biosphere and of very 'un-green' mechanisation which, according to Sigfried Giedion, has 'taken command' of life and death[6]. This resonates with Achille Mbembe's definition of necropolitics as the 'power and . . . capacity to dictate who may live and who must die'; Mbembe also draws attention to the less overt tendencies that concern 'the generalized instrumentalization of human existence' and 'the material destruction' of human and other-than-human populations, and the environment at large[7]. Paradoxically, I want to claim that

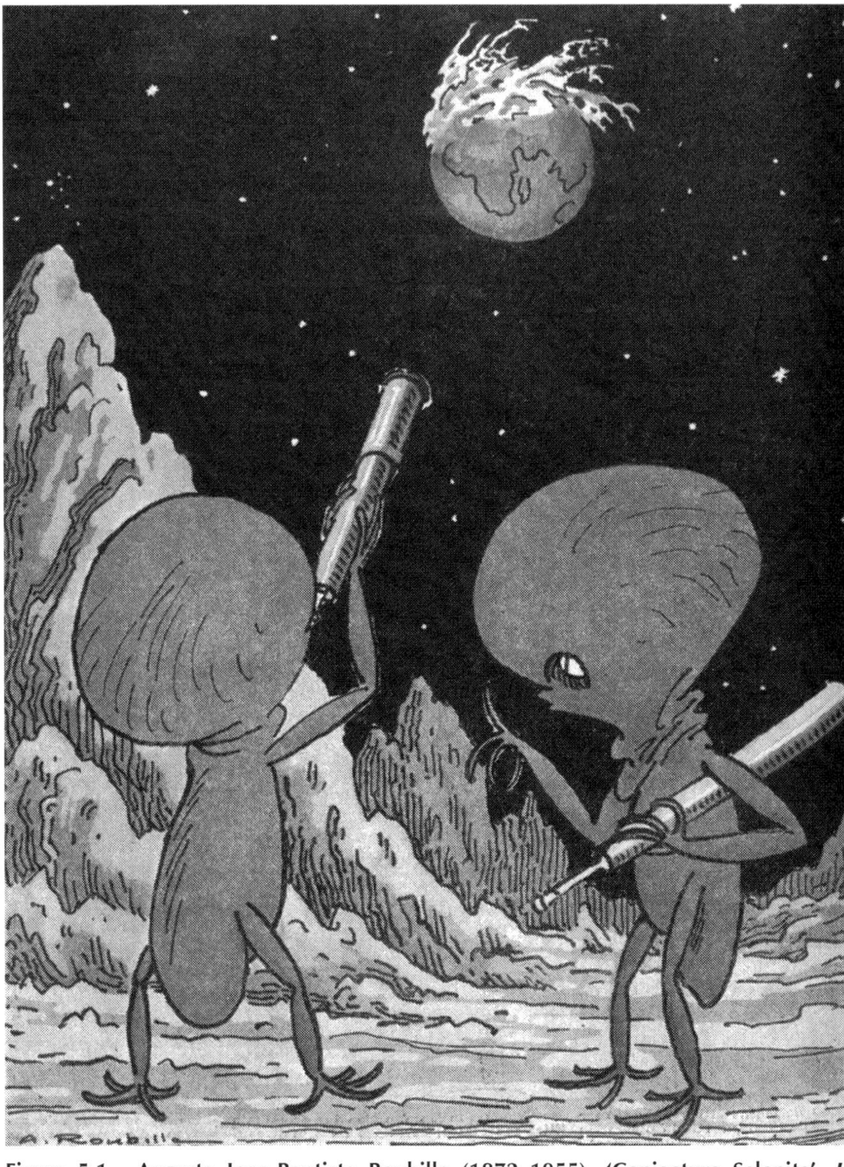

Figure 5.1. Auguste Jean-Baptiste Roubille (1872–1955), 'Conjecture Selenite', *La Baïonnette* Nov. 7, 1918.
Source: Public Domain.

green is both the most anthropocentric of all colours and, at the same time, the one that figures human's otherness. As such, it plays a central role in human evolution and self-understanding—as colour, percept, medium, material biological agency, semantic construct and ideology. In its inherent ambiguity, between alleged naturalness and artificiality, employed to reconcile humans with *otherness* as such, greenness urgently needs to be disentangled from terms—both putatively nontechnological—such as 'life' and 'nature'.

In the Western context, 'green' is rooted in Middle English and Latin and signifies growth or sprout. Across cultures, it is associated with vegetation, fertility, spring, youth, renewal, hope and aliveness[8]. However, in material practice, 'aliveness' and 'greenness' are increasingly connected to 'biofacticity'[9], to the idea that biological artefacts allow 'living material to grow as natural material' despite its technological condition. Growth, etymologically associated with greenness, suggests a self-governing dynamic, but veils that 'directed growth ensures from the beginning . . . technical control'[10] over such biofacts. Therefore, as Nicole Karafyllis claims, the concepts of 'life' and 'nature' need to be uncoupled[11]. Now, likewise, the concepts 'green' and 'nature' need to be disentangled as well. In the dominant cultural use, 'green' is increasingly reduced to its metaphorical value. More concept than colour, it is stripped of all material, epistemological and historical referents, which generates dramatic contradictions on the one hand and misplaced normativity on the other. Beyond the canonical combination of colour symbolism, colour categorisation[12], cultural history[13] and visual perception studies[14], an interdisciplinary investigation is needed to address the threefold trope *green—greenness—greening* as an increasingly complex political-social set of 'wicked problems'[15] that naturalise indirect and covert necropolitical tendencies. Unlike 'problems in the natural sciences, which are definable and separable and may have solutions that are findable'[16], 'wicked problems' require a change of mindset and behaviour. Problems that are ill defined cannot be solved with efficiency alone. Rather, such problems need to be considered as a 'symptom of still another, "higher level" problem'[17]. For example, the good intention to metaphorically use *green* as a proxy to defend ecologically sustainable policies has been superseded by an uncritical attitude which enables antagonistic capitalist mechanisms to appropriate the metaphor by *greening* everything. Greenness has become a 'metaphor we live by', one that 'in allowing us to focus on one aspect of a concept' keeps us from 'focusing on aspects inconsistent with that metaphor'[18]. Existing research has not clarified how *greenness* came to be perceived simultaneously as a natural and a technical colour—used in visualisations, lasers, GFP biomarkers or night vision devices—as well as an index of alarming perniciousness, which turns its ambivalent status into a powerful discursive and political tool. Greenness acts as a symbolic and composite *ou-vert*[19] chameleon colour[20], a medium *in and of itself*, a central cue in the evolution of cultural representations, including art. And yet there has been surprisingly little reflection on—and much abuse of—the term's migration across different cultures of knowledge, which increasingly obstructs, rather than enables, an interdisciplinary dialogue between the humanities and the natural sciences—a dialogue all the more urgently needed in the light of anthropogenic effects on climate and biodiversity—and their denial. Researchers, policymakers and citizens lack a common terminology for addressing real-world problems while simultaneously greenwashing greenhouse effects away. Given that 'green' is related both to the representation of natural phenomena and to technoscientific and social fabrication, in this chapter I discuss the colour's cultural fetishisation, symbolic overcoding and opportunistic appropriation in the context of a research agenda that examines the shift from biopolitics to necropolitics. My aim in performing an epistemic deconstruction is to, in the first place, articulate the glaring contradictions of this persisting cultural and technical abstraction and, in the second, to offer a methodological alternative.

UNDISCIPLINED METAPHORS

A short and potted history shows that far from having a universal meaning across cultures, languages and academic fields, *greenness* marks a knowledge gap open to systematic misunderstandings. On the one hand, engineers declare 'green chemistry' ecologically benign, claiming it as a 'worldwide term used to describe the development of more eco-friendly, sustainable chemical products and processes'[21]. 'Green biotechnology' promotes the engineering of chloroplast and the production of renewable bio-plastics. Often, even biologists committed to ecologically sustainable solutions discredit their outreach by the uncritical use of 'green' metaphors[22] amidst greenwashing scandals and toxic algae blooms that have done much to discredit the overused association of 'green' with ecological sustainability[23]. On the other hand, when climate researchers speak of the 'greening of the earth'[24], they mean something very different: the alarming effect of anthropogenic CO_2 emissions resulting in 'global greenness trends' that in the period from 1982 to 2009 increased from 25 percent to 50 percent. There are many 'drivers' of these trends: a high concentration of 'atmospheric CO_2, regional climate change, and the varying rates of nitrogen deposition'[25]. Within this context, *greening*, as action, literally means that the global environmental change is altering the dynamics of terrestrial vegetation growth. While biology and related sciences may not have an anthropocentric focus per se, explaining what 'green' means puts indeed human perception at the centre: the large cosmic electromagnetic spectrum is filtered by the earth's atmosphere, which blocks short-wave UV radiation and permits photosynthesis in the chloroplasts, visually perceived as green by humans whose physiology of the perceptual apparatus and post-receptoral mechanisms are then studied. However, green prompts a startling epistemological paradox: to humans a plant only *appears* green because its chlorophyll absorbs high-energy red and blue light photons for photosynthesis and reflects the middle spectrum as 'waste', so to speak. This spectrum with a wavelength between 490 and 565 nm, which cannot be used for the plant's photosynthesis, corresponds precisely to the largest spectrum visible to humankind. Humans are therefore tempted to take vegetal chaff for the vegetal green itself. While human perception depends on the reflection of this middle spectrum, 'colour perception and colour language give us anthropocentrically defined colours and not colours themselves'[26]. This prompts questions about a general human 'chlorophilia'[27] as related to evolutionary patterns that enabled trichromatic primates to distinguish chromatically between red and green, a relatively recent phenomenon. The assumed evolutionary advantage of being able to distinguish between more nutritious leaves or fruit and green foliage[28] may explain such an adaptation to specific light wave spectrums.

However, recent findings in paleogenomics suggest that humans, and primates in general, may have paid 'an eye for a nose'[29]. Analyses of defunct olfactory receptor genes that are the basis of the sense of smell seem to suggest that 'the deterioration of the olfactory repertoire occurred concomitantly with the acquisition of full trichromatic colour vision'[30]. More sophisticated red-green colour vision apparently means a less sensitive nose. This poses the bio-semiotic question of greenness' multimodality; it also calls occularcentrism into question while integrating hearing, gustation and olfaction into neuro-aesthetic perception patterns[31]. If, for different beings, greenness is more than the wavelength of the visual spectrum, what might be the information 'associated with green that we cannot visually observe'[32] lodged between the aromatope and sonotope[33]? The 'smell of greenness'[34] or 'green odour'[35] are often being ascribed different types of therapeutic effects. Scientific literature reveals cross-sensory phenomena that connect biological signalling components to the various pheromone-like substances that induce 'bioprotective responses in plants'[36] affecting sensorimotor function and nociception, thus reducing pain in mammals. In addition, in business and management psychology, it is thought that 'natural views, plants and the colour green increase visual creativity'[37]. In the quest for workplace enhancement with colour, it appears that 'no statistically relevant difference between plants and green wallpaper'[38] has been found. While as early as 1810 J. W. Goethe claimed that the combined effects of blue and yellow, mixed to produce green, give rise to sedative stimuli 'so that one most often choses green colours for the wallpaper in rooms where one sojourns usually'[39], it is nevertheless surprising that psychological tests suggest that an urban classroom painted green is an unproblematic replacement for green vegetation itself. What is at work here is abstraction; vegetation is abstracted to its alleged dominant hue.

THE PARADOX OF SYMBOLIC FETISHES

Such abstraction from indexical materiality is pushed even beyond the iconic relationship of greenness to 'nature' when green is used just as a shallow symbol. Numerous disciplines use green as a superficial metaphor, in particular economics and political sciences often use the greenness trope in a naively literal way. For example, 'green growth'[40] is supposed to reconcile ecologically sustainable development with market-based economic models[41]. While claiming to be remediating the widespread impact of necropolitical operations, it is turning the ecological crisis into business opportunities. 'Green growth' has come under critical scrutiny as a strategy, but not as a metaphor. It is being discussed whether it perpetuates 'the existing structures of inequality and socio-economic exclusion'[42]. Likewise, the 'post-growth economy's' definition of growth is questioned: 'does growth refer to increases in monetary value or does it refer to physical/resource measures?'[43]. Despite this, the fallacious metaphorical connection between the economic and vegetal growth is purposefully maintained to capitalise on the metaphor's positive connotations. In similar fashion, when the 'green paradox'[44] is addressed in economics, it does merely state that well-intended climate policies may, on occasion, even counterproductively accelerate global warming[45], but the 'green' metaphor remains untouched.

The paradox of green is a symbolic fetish, and fetishes are difficult to grapple with. While chronic drought fuels the dubious business of lawn painters in rich California neighbourhoods where emerald pigments are used to hide brown greenswards during watering restrictions—and, in this way, maintain the image of undisrupted individual wealth—such problematic fetishisation is more thoroughly examined in urbanism and anthropology. Here, these paradoxes are approached as *material* and *relational*, as 'a synecdoche for landscape' because 'the question is not if but how, and where the state will grow, and how green that growth will be [whereby] *growth* and *green* become ambiguous terms united conceptually in their ties to the rapacious appetite for development under capitalism'[46]. Taking the example of urban 'greening policies' in the Arabic city-state and 'green oasis' Bahrain, Gareth Doherty points to the contradictions between greenery in prosperous urban areas and its 'significant environmental costs in terms of the resources required to maintain it. To have and to be green is often presented as a moral imperative, yet the provision of urban greenery can be morally questionable especially in arid environments such as Bahrain'[47]. Green is also the symbolic colour of Islam. Islamophobia can therefore unfold as chlorophobia. Such a striking example is provided by philosopher Frederik Stjernfelt in 'The Green War Banners in Copenhagen'[48], in which he describes how a classic piece of military art in bronze was targeted by right-wing protesters apparently because it was seen as '"celebrat[ing] Islam", which was further interpreted as an "insult" to the Danish troops serving in Iraq and Afghanistan'[49]. The argument here was that the bronze flags would, over time, turn green and come to represent (the victorious) Islamic armies instead of the Royal Danish Life Guard. The example demonstrates that even the corrosion of metals may lead to unexpected emergence of meaning, constrained by the political context, notwithstanding the better known examples of Western ecologist green parties that have emerged over the last decades.

Given such performative semantics, it is necessary to establish a correlation between cultural fetishisation, symbolic overcoding and the etymological and cultural differences in the use of 'green'. Colour categorisation, in language and in cultural symbolism, varies according to the physical environment despite the fact that it is widely held that there are universal tendencies in colour terms across languages. However, colour terms deviate from Western language in the way boundaries between colour terms are being placed. And differences in colour terms, in turn, also correlate with differences in colour cognition[50]. A good example is the linguistic bundling of green and blue into 'grue' found around the equator ('yak' in Mexico or 'nol' in Papua New Guinea)[51]. If it is true that colour 'universalism makes itself felt through chemistry, mimesis, cognitive effects, and nomenclature'[52], it is, indeed, necessary to consider the complex patterns essential for the vegetation's economy[53] as well as ethnobotanic data that goes beyond colour optics, for example the taste and smell of green. According to Nelson Goodman's thoughts on world making, '"grue" and "bleen", rather than "green" and "blue" might mean to live in a different world'[54].

Artists sensitive to colonial legacies take these issues very seriously. The Colombian director Ciro Guerra shot his 2016 film *Embrace of the Serpent*, a film about Western explorers in the Amazonas, in black and white. For Guerra, 'Amazonian people have fifty words for what we call green', which indicates a sophisticated appreciation of their environment. Guerra also addresses the issue of how media apparatuses standardise human perception, because

> it would not be possible for any kind of film, any kind of video, any kind of representation, to give you a real idea of what the green of the Amazon is [like]. . . . With black-and-white images there was no difference between nature being

> green and us being something else. Every human, every bird, every drop of water is made up the same in black and white so it was perfectly coherent. . . . We had to overcome the expectations of a lot of people, but we stuck to it. If I had been forced to film in colour, I would have preferred not to do it.[55]

The Embrace of the Serpent emphasises not only how green is *perceived*, *measured*, *filtered*, *encoded* and *transmitted*, it also points to how colour is determined by analogue and digital technologies based on the increasing standardisation, modularisation and grammatisation that break the seemingly continuous range of colours into a small number of categories (red, green, blue/violet in the RGB system). Specifically designed to match human visual perception[56], these media devices correspond to the peaks in human cone spectral and rod brightness sensitivity, where green is seen as brighter than red or blue of equal intensity.

PRISMATIC MEDIATIONS

Media studies and media archaeology[57] appear to be well situated to trace the epistemological changes in and of 'greenness' by dissecting subjacent 'discourse networks'[58] and by revealing the entanglement of politics, techniques, apparatuses and semantics in different contexts. What is needed is an investigation into the materialities of communication[59], which calls for posthermeneutic literacy, including technoscientific knowledge, combined with, for example, French mediology with its more sociological focus. According to its founder, Régis Debray, the task of mediology is to investigate the relationship between social functions and technical structures. Here, media are seen as hybrids that enact 'technical, cultural and social mediations'[60]. It is precisely by combining discourse analysis and material media analysis that scholars have started to blame the phenomenon of 'greening the media'[61] used by information and communication technologies to dress up as ecologically benign, while downplaying the role of toxic ingredients sourced in toxic working conditions, hazardous waste and the greenhouse gases produced by large computing centres. Such analyses bear directly on necropolitical concerns. For example, one might well ask how many workers have been killed in the open mining industry as a logical consequence of the IT engineers' programming of built-in obsolescence of tools and equipment, not to mention the environmental harms that affect human and other-than-human life and ecosystems, which, since the 1990s, have been grouped under an appropriate—yet symbolic—name: 'green criminology'[62]. But it is only in recent years that the poststructuralist cultural and media studies have recognised that environmental destruction is related to technological materiality:

> The field remains enthralled by two largely distinct but eerily compatible discourses: first, the cult of humanism adores the cultural devolution afforded by consumer technologies that generate millions of texts and address viewers and users as empowered. Second, the cult of scientism adores the mathematisation of daily life afforded by the digital.[63]

The obscenity of environmental destruction caused by pervasive technologies in the Anthropocene age has been described as the 'anthrobscene'[64] by Jussi Parikka—who avoids the word 'green' in his entire book. It hardly comes as a surprise that greenness has become a much-contested trope in contemporary philosophy, too, which rejects the privileging of human over other-than-human existence and agency. A case in point is object-oriented ontology (OOO), which describes spatio-temporally distributed phenomena that escape human perception—such as the global warming—as hyperobjects[65]. Instead, OOO promotes 'ecology without nature'[66]—an ecology that is dark, not bright green[67]. In addition, 'prismatic ecology'[68] opposes the idea of the 'green Eden', proposing instead 'multihued contaminations, impurities, hybridity, monstrosity, contagion, interruption, hesitation, enmeshment, refraction, unexpected relations, and wonder. A swirl of colours, a torrent, a muddy river'[69] that is usually ignored because 'we humans see only a certain bandwidth of light'[70]. An important point, made by Timothy Morton, is that 'X-rays form part of the electromagnetic spectrum, but humans cannot see them. They see you. They see you so intensely that in sufficient quantities they kill you'[71]. What is problematised here is the alleged *neutrality of observation* in which 'perception [is] severed from causality' and which affirms the impossibility of seeing 'the world without having an effect on it'[72]. The very conception of our mesoscopic bubble as the supposedly central point of observation has tangible, material effects, an opinion shared by many post-anthropocentric philosophers, such as Michael Marder, who shifts the focus from the human to the plant as *phuton*, a growing being, thus engaging the performative phenomenology of photosynthesising beings that represent a 'synecdoche between a single natural entity—a plant—and all of nature'[73]. Marder describes this tendency as *phytocentrism to come*; however, 'phytocentrism does not reconstitute a more authentic center of existence' but 'names the immanent *implosion* of this center' in a 'critique of a centralized totality'[74]. Marder addresses phytocentrism as a chance 'for the "greening" of human consciousness brought back to its vegetal roots'[75]. But isn't *greening*, then, again indicative of an anthropocentric mindset? It seems to be difficult to avoid such fallacy in the argument, as recalls environmental philosopher Holmes Rolston III: 'Trees are not really green after we have learned about electromagnetic radiation and the optics of our eyes, though we all view the world that way'[76].

MEASURING GREENNESS

In an epistemological approach to greenness, and despite all efforts to 'green human consciousness' in a flattened ontology[77], technical mediation is, indeed, the critical question. As Morton suggests, 'the real thing, whatever it is, disappears beyond the glass screen of my measuring'[78]. Technical devices and colour codes are not neutral. The mediality of green—its *aesthetic rendering*—plays a central role in climate-related measurements, modelling and visualisations, such as in simulated photosynthetic activities of the global carbon cycle. This concerns both the parameters within which alleged greenness is technically registered and the translation of these parameters into colour codes that are indexical or symbolic. For example, the abstract measurements of the satellite-based normalised difference vegetation index (NDVI) scrutinise large pixels of more or less uniform greenery. Their task is to map the carbon exchange needed to assess impacts of the CO_2 sequestration strategies in living forests—the so-called negative emissions technologies (NETs). However, they often align technophilic positions with a managerial approach to environmental problems calling for a 'good anthropocene'[79], as articulated in the ecomodernist manifesto[80] which states that 're-greening and re-wildering' can be achieved by integrated human-technological action, that vegetation is no more than monotonous greenery while abstract *quantifiable* CO_2 neutralisers are, within 'the fetishisation of the global carbon budgets . . . the ultimate metrics of planetary health'[81]. As Natasha Myers points out, green beings may yet be seen as 'climate criminals' in a scenario in which old-growth forests are logged 'to make way for young, managed forests, which, according to models absorb more carbon from the atmosphere'[82]. Measurements can indeed concentrate on the *qualitatively relevant parameters* of biodiversity, not on abstract greenness indexes. For this, we need what Donna Haraway has described as 'situated knowledge', which consists of clear positioning:

> Vision requires instruments of vision; an optics is a politics of positioning. Instruments of vision mediate standpoints. . . . Positioning is, therefore, the key practice in grounding knowledge organized around the imagery of vision. . . . Situated knowledges are about communities, not about isolated individuals. The only way to find a larger vision is to be somewhere in particular. The science question in feminism is about objectivity as positioned rationality.[83]

The question here is how the current practices of measuring greenness, and the aesthetisation of the obtained data, define the cultural categories on which our understanding of the complexity of environmental diversity depends.

EPISTEMOLOGICAL DEBUNKING IN ARTISTIC PRACTICE

The entanglement between symbolic *green*, ontological *greenness* and performative *greening* is currently critiqued and applied as a *mise-en-abyme* strategy in the arts. While 'the arts' cover a whole set of 'wicked problems' themselves, they are nevertheless capable of transposing and condensing technoscientific, cultural and political notions, and are therefore well situated to serve as epistemic indicators. Although it is well known that Marcel Duchamp once famously played with a large range of 'green' homophones to create puns and unexpected symbolic associations between 'vert' (green), 'verre' (glass), 'ver' (worm), 'vers' (a line in a poem/towards) and 'envers' (reverse)[84], it is less in the (self-referential) world of contemporary art, dubbed 'the Duchamp Land' by Lev Manovich, and more in the 'Turing Land'[85]—the experimental media arts—that the ambiguity of greenness is being unpacked. Inspired by cybernetics, systems theory and ecology, such practices build on the history of green as an unstable and synthetic colour, far from 'technology's other' as 'the compensatory evocation of absent nature'[86]. A case in point is Heather Ackroyd and Dan Harvey's work with *stay-green* genetically modified grass[87], often used to produce spotless green surfaces for golf or football turfs. Here, the artists turn chlorophyll into pigment for growing and controlling green-scaled photographic images that 'concretise' ephemerality[88].

Green fluorescent protein biomarkers are frequently used by artists such as Eduardo Kac[89], whose works question why GFP is preferred both by 'chlorophile' artists and biologists to other readily available colours (RFP, YFP). Philippe Rahm and Jean-Gilles Décosterd, for their part, present 'meteorological architectures' in which visitor's melatonin production is stimulated to affect sleep rhythms with 509 nm wavelength green light[90], pointing both to the physiological and psychological dimensions of the electromagnetic spectrum of human perception as well as shifting the focus from visual to hormonal information, like Morton's earlier mentioned electromagnetic waves. The debunking of greenness represents a particularly dominant trope in artist duo HeHe's work[91], where it is revealed as a camouflage of the technological. *Planète Laboratoire*—or *Domestic Catastrophe*—is the aptly titled installation created by Helen Evans and Heiko Hansen in collaboration with the atmospheric physicist Jean-Marc Chomaz, in which a domestic globe rotates in an aquarium while a slow-release fluorescent green dye wraps itself around the sphere, enveloping it in a thin and fragile atmosphere that surrounds the formerly blue planet earth as seen from space: Gaia. Another miniaturised *son et lumière* show, *Fleur de Lys*, simulates a nuclear meltdown as a Disneyfied green atomic mushroom cloud. Dissipating like a slowly unfolding lily blossom (In French, *fleur de lys* has been a symbol of purity and of the French monarchy since the twelfth century), the seductive and sedative spectacle refers to the *Grande Nation*'s policy to draw 80 percent of its energy from nuclear reactors, advertised as clean and green. HeHe's work also complicates colour code standards that vary between disciplines when measuring, for example, vegetation indexes or pollution data. For instance, their chromatic installation *Champs d'Ozone* aesthetises current air contamination levels data. A double-pane window offers a view of the city, yet a cloudy mist of various colours, each of which represent different real-time contamination levels, blurs the view: clouds appear to be hanging over the city, continually changing colour according to the data that reflect the concentration of nitrogen dioxide, sulphur dioxide, ozone and particle dust. Trapped between two glass panes, the computer-generated clouds are both proverbially and materially in the air, creating a digital *sfumato*. Red, the colour of alarm and emergency, is used to indicate poor air quality. Blue, symbolically associated with the blue skies, is used to indicate low pollution levels. Green, however, is used to indicate mid-level contamination and is therefore more ambivalent. The object of representation (the particles in the air) and the mode of representation (the pollution data rendered as colourful clouds) are equivalent. Upon closer examination, however, the three-dimensional veil of clouds is revealed as a holographic effect of light projected through micro-prisms integrated into the glass pane. In this way, HeHe point to the illusionistic traps always at work in *modelling and representing* climate figures where their unfathomability escapes human comprehension and reveals hegemonic operations in the supposedly neutral media and modelling procedures. Finally, green is also the colour chosen for an intriguing DIY artwork that can be performed by depositing soluble tablets in the gutters of the Parisian drainage system, traditionally flooded on a daily basis. Apart from being an hommage to ecological land and eco-art projects, such as those of the Argentinean ecological artist Nicolás García Uriburu, who coloured large and often polluted waterways with fluorescein sodium salt, *My Green River* refers to the Parisian sewers, where a popular rat poison called Paris Green was used, a highly toxic copper aceto-arsenite identical to the deadly bright pigment pervasively used by painters in the eighteenth and nineteenth centuries and beyond[92].

TOXICITY REMEDIATED

It is not only the visual effect but materiality itself that is at stake here. While natural green pigments are easy to obtain, they are difficult to fix. They fade and degrade when exposed to sunlight, and even degrade their supports [93]. Despite the availability of plant-based materials, pigments stable enough to technically fix green are the most toxic in art history. It is, indeed, ironic that they have come to represent nature and vegetation. In 1775, Swedish chemist Scheele produced a green copper-arsenite pigment that enabled painters to go out 'into the green' with handy metal tubes. What is not known is how many painters and art lovers actually *died* in an effort to represent 'nature', given that 'in order to hide the substance's toxicity, all sorts of phantasy names'[94] were invented. The history of green in art is connected to the irony 'that green should be so prominent in the landscape and so hard to achieve with pigments and dyes'[95] while, at the same time, 'the humanistic concern to match colours to nature placed a greater demand on green than on any other colour'[96]. French medievalist and expert in Western symbology Michel Pastoureau argued that it has been only from the Romantic period onwards that art developed an explicit connection between green, nature and vegetation, whereas it was clear even before Romanticism that green was 'chemically unstable', which is the reason why 'it has come to symbolize everything changeable or capricious'[97]. This provocative thesis questions the *material-technological a priori* of green's metaphoricity and should be considered in light of Friedrich Kittler's argument about the material-technological infrastructures that always precede 'changes in symbolic and artistic systems, which are *medial a priori*'[98].

Taking into consideration perceptual, biological and ecological aspects, as well as the philosophical-political 'nature versus culture' debate, biotechnology, chemistry and digital media art may all benefit from *greenness studies*, which would include philosophy, sociology, art, art history, history of science and technology, the medical and cognitive sciences, environmental humanities and ethno-botany. The purpose of such an interdisciplinary field is not only to debunk or detourn the overt and covert necropolitical operations but also to establish a connection between any ecological phenomenon, its modalities of technical (re)production and its transhistorical metaphors. The technosciences of today have themselves become powerful producers of aestheticised images. But what we need are material, media-specific analyses of how 'green mediation' conceals its technological character and appears transparent while, in fact, camouflaging precisely those layers that *produce* what they pretend only to *mediate*—including the deadly worrisome spectacle the extra-terrestrial macrocephalous Selenites took for a temporary illness.

NOTES

1. *La Baïonnette*, 175, 7 November 1918.
2. Norman L. Cantor, *After We Die: The Life and Times of the Human Cadaver* (Washington, DC: Georgetown University Press, 2010), 102–3.

3. The Faraday Institute organised an academic conference titled 'Greening the Gods: Ecology and Theology in the Ancient World' in 2014.

4. NATO has adopted a Green Defence programme aiming at 'green solutions' such as reducing fuel costs consumption in military operations, minimising risk for soldiers and demonstrating environmental awareness in times of global climate change: https://www.nato.int/docu/review/2014/NATO-Energy-security-running-on-empty/NATO-energy-security-agenda/EN/index.htm.

5. http://cms.polsci.ku.dk/english/publications/greendefense/.

6. An indicator that biopolitics and necropolitics are genuinely linked through both generalised abstraction and instrumentalisation characteristic of capitalism can be found in what Swiss historian Sigfried Giedion, in *Mechanization Takes Command*, lamented to be the dominant cultural and economic development since the eighteenth century as mechanisation, automation, standardisation, interchangeability and hierarchisation of parts progressively transformed creatures into commodities. Among his examples are Réaumur's 'Artificial Mother' (1750) techniques for growth and fertilisation, slaughterhouse mechanisms and technocultural displays designed for the mechanisation of life and death demonstrating features later identified as bio- and necropolitics, especially within the *Zoe*-centric turn that treats the exploitation of 'other' bodies. Sigfried Giedion, *Mechanization Takes Command: A Contribution to Anonymous History* (Oxford/New York: Oxford University Press, 1948).

7. Achile Mbembe, 'Necropolitics', *Public Culture* 15, no. 1(2003): 14.

8. Eva Heller, *Wie Farben wirken. Farbpsychologie—Farbsymbolik—Kreative Farbgestaltung* (Hamburg: Rowohlt, 1989), 69–85.

9. Nicole C. Karafyllis, ed., *Biofakte. Versuch über den Menschen zwischen Artefakt und Lebewesen* (Paderborn: Mentis, 2003).

10. Nicole C. Karafyllis, *Endogenous Design of Biofacts: Tissues and Networks in Bio Art and Life Science*, in *sk-interfaces: Exploding Borders—Creating Membranes in Art, Technology and Society*, ed. Jens Hauser (Liverpool: Liverpool University Press, 2008), 47.

11. Nicole C. Karafyllis, 'Natur als Gegentechnik. Zur Notwendigkeit einer Technikphilosophie der Biofakte', in *Technikphilosophie im Aufbruch. Festschrift für Günter Ropohl*, ed. Nicole C. Karafyllis and Tilmann Haar (Berlin: Edition Sigma, 2004).

12. Brent Berlin and Paul Kay, *Basic Color Terms: Their Universality and Evolution* (Los Angeles: University of California Press, 1969).

13. John Cage, *Colour and Culture: Practice and Meaning from Antiquity to Abstraction* (London: Thames and Hudson, 1993); Bruce R. Smith, *The Key of Green: Passion and Perception in Renaissance Culture* (Chicago: University of Chicago Press, 2009); Michel Pastoureau, *Vert. Histoire d'une couleur* (Paris: Seuil, 2013).

14. Evan Thompson, *Colour Vision: A Study in Cognitive Science and the Philosophy of Perception* (London/New York: Routledge, 1995).

15. Horst Willhelm Jakob Rittel and Melvon M. Webber, 'Dilemmas in a General Theory of Planning', *Policy Sciences* 4 (1973): 155–69.

16. Ibid., 160.

17. Ibid., 165.

18. George Lakoff and Mark Johnson, *Metaphors We Live By* (Chicago: University of Chicago Press, 1980), 10.

19. This research project at the University of Copenhagen includes interdisciplinary art, cultural and media studies and natural sciences in investigating the exceptional role of *greenness* as colour, perceptible phenomenon, biological agency, material medium, semantic construct and ideology: http://ou-vert.ku.dk.

20. Jens Hauser, 'Atmosph-Air? Atmos-Faire!' in *Man Made Clouds*, ed. Heiko Hansen and Helen/Hehe Evans (Orléans: Éditions Hyx, 2016), 50.

21. James H. Clark, 'Introduction', in *Handbook of Green Chemistry and Technology*, ed. James Clark and Duncan Macquarrie (Oxford: Blackwell Science, 2002), 6.

22. Esa Väliverronen and Iina Hellsten, 'From "Burning Library" to "Green Medicine". The Role of Metaphors in Communicating Biodiversity', *Science Communication* 24, no. 2 (2002): 229–45.

23. Marilyn DeLong and Gozde Goncu-Berk, 'What Color Is Sustainability?' in *Color and Design*, ed. Marilyn DeLong and Barbara Martinson (London: Berg, 2012), 89–100.

24. Zaichun Zhu et al., 'Greening of the Earth and Its Drivers', *Nature Climate Change* 6 (April 2016): 791–95.

25. Ibid., 791.

26. David R. Hilbert, *Color and Color Perception: A Study in Anthropocentric Realism* (Stanford: CSLI, 1987).

27. David Lee, *Nature's Palette: The Science of Plant Color* (Chicago: University of Chicago Press, 2007), 296–318.

28. Jeremy Nathans, 'The Evolution and Physiology of Human Review Color Vision: Insights from Molecular Genetic Studies of Visual Pigments', *Neuron* 24 (October 1999): 299–312.

29. Yoav Gilad et al., 'Human Specific Loss of Olfactory Receptor Genes', *Proceedings of the National Academy of Sciences of the United States of America* 100, no. 6 (2003): 3324–27; and Yoav Gilad et al., 'Loss of Olfactory Receptor Genes Coincides with the Acquisition of Full Trichromatic Vision in Primates', *PLoS Biology* 2, no. 1 (2004): 120–25.

30. Gilad et al., 'Loss of Olfactory Receptor Genes Coincides with the Acquisition of Full Trichromatic Vision in Primates', 120.

31. S. Brown et al., 'Naturalizing Aesthetics: Brain Areas for Aesthetic Appraisal across Sensory Modalities', *NeuroImage* 58, no. 1 (2011): 250–58.

32. Judith van der Elst, 'Contemplating Greenness', *Noema*, online publication, 2016, https://noemalab.eu/ideas/contemplating-greenness/.

33. Almo Farina, *Soundscape Ecology: Principles, Patterns, Methods and Applications* (Dordrecht: Springer, 2014).

34. Diana Young, 'The Smell of Greenness: Cultural Synaesthesia in the Western Desert', *Etnofoor* 18, no. 1, 'Senses' (2005): 61–77.

35. Shuji Aou et al., 'Green Odor Reduces Pain Sensation and Fatigue-Like Responses without Affecting Sensorimotor Function', *Chem. Senses* 30 (2005): 262–63.

36. Ibid., 262.

37. Sylvie Studente et al., 'Facilitating Creative Thinking in the Classroom: Investigating the Effects of Plants and the Colour Green on Visual and Verbal Creativity', *Thinking Skills and Creativity* 19 (2016): 1.

38. Ibid., 6.

39. Johann Wolfgang von Goethe, *Zur Farbenlehre* (Tübingen, 1810), 331.

40. Gareth Dale et al., eds., *Green Growth: Ideology, Political Economy and the Alternatives* (London: Zed, 2016).

41. Robert Pollin, *Greening the Global Economy* (Cambridge, MA: MIT Press, 2015).

42. Anne Posthuma and Paulo Sergio Muçouçah, 'Green Jobs to Promote Sustainable Development: Creating a Value Chain of Solid Waste Recycling in Brazil', in *Green Growth: Ideology, Political Economy and the Alternatives,* edited by Gareth Dale et al. (London: Zed, 2016), 166.

43. John Barry and Peter Doran, 'Refining Green Political Economy: From Ecological Modernisation to Economic Security and Sufficiency', in *Analyse & Kritik* 28 (2006) (Stuttgart: Lucius & Lucius): 265.

44. Hans-Werner Sinn, *Das Grüne Paradoxon. Plädoyer für eine illusionsfreie Klimapolitik* (Berlin: Econ, 2008).

45. Frederick van der Ploeg and Cees Withagen, 'Global Warming and the Green Paradox: A Review of Adverse Effects of Climate Policies', in *Review of Environmental Economics and Policy Advance* 9, no. 2 (Summer 2015): 285–303.

46. Gareth Doherty, *Paradoxes of Green: Landscapes of a City-State* (Oakland: University of California Press, 2017), 5.

47. Ibid., 1.

48. Frederik Stjernfelt, 'Green War Banners in Central Copenhagen: A Recent Political Struggle Over Interpretation—And Some Implications for Art Interpretation as Such', in *Investigations into the Phenomenology and the Ontology of the Work of Art: What Are Artworks, and How Do We Experience Them?*, edited by Peer Bundgaard and Frederik Stjernfelt (Heidelberg/New York: Springer, 2015), 209–23.

49. Ibid., 211.

50. Debi Roberson et al., 'Color Categories: Evidence for the Cultural Relativity Hypothesis', *Cognitive Psychology* 50 (2005): 378–411.

51. Paul Kay and Terry Regier, 'Color Naming Universals: The Case of Berinmo', *Cognition* 102 (2007): 289–98.

52. Stephen Houston et al., *Veiled Brightness—A History of Ancient Maya Color* (Austin: University of Texas Press, 2002), 8.

53. Andrew S. Mathews, *Instituting Nature: Authority, Expertise, and Power in Mexican Forests* (Cambridge, MA: MIT Press, 2011).

54. Nelson Goodman, *Ways of Worldmaking* (Indianapolis: Hackett Publishing Company, 1978), 101.

55. Michael Guillén, 'Embrace of the Serpent: An Interview with Ciro Guerra', *Cineaste* (Spring 2016), https://www.cineaste.com/spring2016/embrace-of-the-serpent-ciro-guerra/.

56. Roy S. Berns, *Billmeyer and Saltzman's Principles of Color Technology*, 3rd edition (New York: John Wiley, 2000).

57. Erkki Huhtamo and Jussi Parikka, eds., *Media Archaeology: Approaches, Applications, and Implications* (Berkeley and Los Angeles: University of California Press, 2011).

58. Friedrich A. Kittler, *Aufschreibesysteme 1800/1900* (München: Fink, 1985).

59. Hans Ulrich Gumbrecht and Ludwig K. Pfeiffer, eds., *Materialities of Communication* (Stanford: Stanford University Press, 1994).

60. Régis Debray, *Manifestes Mediologiques* (Paris: Gallimard, 1994), 29; Régis Debray, *Transmitting Culture*, trans. Eric Rauth (New York: Columbia University Press, 2004).

61. Richard Maxwell and Toby Miller, *Greening the Media* (Oxford/New York: Oxford University Press, 2012).

62. Michael J. Lynch, 'The Greening of Criminology: A Perspective on the 1990s', *The Critical Criminologist* 2, no. 3 (1990): 1–4; Michael J. Lynch and Paul B. Stretsky, 'The Meaning of Green: Contrasting Criminological Perspectives', *Theoretical Criminology* 2, no. 7 (2003): 217–38.

63. Maxwell and Miller, *Greening the Media*, 11.

64. Jussi Parikka, *The Anthrobscene* (Minneapolis: University of Minnesota Press, 2014).

65. The concept of hyperobjects is used by Timothy Morton to describe objects that are so massively distributed in time and space, relative to humans, as to transcend spatiotemporal specificity. Such hyperobjects can be global warming, the biosphere or nuclear materials. Timothy Morton, *The Ecological Thought* (Cambridge, MA: Harvard University Press, 2010), 130–35.

66. Timothy Morton, *Ecology without Nature: Rethinking Environmental Aesthetics* (Cambridge, MA: Harvard University Press, 2007).

67. Timothy Morton, *Dark Ecology. For a Logic of Future Coexistence* (Cambridge, MA: Harvard University Press, 2016).

68. Jeffrey Jerome Cohen and Lawrence Buell, eds., *Prismatic Ecology: Ecotheory beyond Green* (Minneapolis: University of Minnesota Press, 2013).

69. Cohen and Buell, *Prismatic Ecology*, xxiv.

70. Timothy Morton, 'X-Ray', in Cohen and Buell, *Prismatic Ecology*, 311.

71. Ibid., 314.

72. Ibid., 316.

73. Michael Marder, 'For a Phytocentrism to Come'. *Environmental Philosophy* 11, no. 2 (2015): 243.

74. Ibid.

75. Ibid., 237.

76. Holmes Rolston III, 'Nature for Real: Is Nature a Social Construct?' In *The Philosophy of the Environment*, ed. T. D. J. Chappell (Edinburgh: University of Edinburgh Press, 1997), 38.

77. Flat ontology as a thought model supposes that all objects have the same degree of being-ness; it makes the ability of an object to affect another object the decisive criteria so that all subjects are also objects which have similar degrees of reality at different scales. The term is often ascribed to Manuel DeLanda, who opposes flat ontologies to hierarchical ontologies: 'While an ontology based on relations between general types and particular instances is hierarchical, each level representing a different ontological category (organism, species, genera), an approach in terms of interacting parts and emergent wholes leads to a flat ontology, one made exclusively of unique, singular individuals, differing in spatio-temporal scale but not in

ontological status'. See Manuel DeLanda, *Intensive Science and Virtual Philosophy* (London: Continuum, 2004), 58.

78. Morton, 'X-Ray', 317.

79. Clive Hamilton, 'The Theodicy of the "Good Anthropocene"', *Environmental Humanities* 7 (2015): 233–38.

80. John Asafu-Adjaye et al., *An Ecomodernist Manifesto*, 2015, http://www.ecomodernism.org/manifesto.

81. Natasha Myers, 'Photosynthesis, Lexicon for an Anthropocene Yet Unseen. Theorizing the Contemporary', *Cultural Anthropology*, 21 January 2016, https://culanth.org/fieldsights/790-photosynthesis.

82. Myers, 'Photosynthesis'; Natasha Myers, 'Amplifying the Gaps between Climate Science and Forest Policy: The Write2Know Project and Participatory Dissent', in *Canada Watch*, Special Issue on 'The Politics of Evidence', ed. Colin Coates, Jody Berland and Jennifer Dalton (Fall 2015): 18–21.

83. Donna Haraway, 'Situated Knowledges: The Science Question in Feminism and the Privilege of Partial Perspective', *Feminist Studies* 14, no. 3 (1988): 586 and 590.

84. Paola Magi, *Treasure Hunt with Marcel Duchamp* (Milano: Edizioni Archivio Dedalus, 2011), 38–42.

85. Lev Manovich, 'The Death of Computer Art', *Rhizome*, 23 October 1996, http://rhizome.org/community/41703/.

86. Hervé Fischer, 'Le symbolism du vert', in *Uriburu 1968–1978*, ed. Jacques Damase (Paris: Jacques Damase Éditeur, 1978), 75.

87. Howard Thomas and Helen Ougham, 'The Stay-Green Trait', *Journal of Experimental Botany* 65, no. 14 (2014): 3889–900.

88. Heather Ackroyd and Dan Harvey, 'Chlorophyll Apparitions', in *Signs of Life: Bio Art and Beyond*, ed. Eduardo Kac (Cambridge, MA: MIT Press, 2007), 199–210.

89. Eduardo Kac, 'Life Transformation—Art Mutation', in *Signs of Life*, 163–84.

90. Guy Tortosa, 'Décosterd & Rahm Associés, the sense(s) in the Senses', in *Physiological Architecture*, ed. Philippe Rahm and Jean-Gilles Décosterd (Basel: Birkhäuser, 2002), 56–64.

91. Heiko Hansen and Helen/Hehe Evans, eds., *Man Made Clouds* (Orléans: Éditions HYX, 2016).

92. James C. Whorton, *The Arsenic Century: How Victorian Britain Was Poisoned at Home, Work, and Play* (Oxford: Oxford University Press, 2010).

93. Franz Mairinger et al., 'The Destruction of Paper by Green Copper Pigments, Demonstrated by a Sample of Chinese Wallpaper', in *Conservation within Historic Buildings*, ed. Norman S. Brommelle, Garry Thomson and Perry Smith (London: International Institute for Conservation of Historic and Artistic Works, 1980), 180–85.

94. Max Doerner, *Malmaterial und seine Verwendung im Bilde*. Nachdruck der 6. Auflage von 1938 (Stuttgart: Ferdinand Enke Verlag, 1992), 64.

95. Smith, *The Key of Green*, 60.

96. Philip Ball, *Bright Earth: Art and the Invention of Color* (Chicago: Chicago University Press, 2001), 130.

97. Pastoureau, *Vert*, 89; emphasis in original.

98. Kittler, *Aufschreibesysteme*.

BIBLIOGRAPHY

Ackroyd, Heather, and Dan Harvey. 'Chlorophyll Apparitions'. *Signs of Life: Bio Art and Beyond*, edited by Eduardo Kac, 199–210. Cambridge, MA: MIT Press, 2007.

Aou, Shuji, et al. 'Green Odor Reduces Pain Sensation and Fatigue-Like Responses without Affecting Sensorimotor Function'. *Chem. Senses* 30 (2005): 262–63.

Asafu-Adjaye, John, et al. *An Ecomodernist Manifesto*, 2015. http://www.ecomodernism.org/manifesto.

Ball, Philip. *Bright Earth: Art and the Invention of Color*. Chicago: Chicago University Press, 2001.

Barry, John, and Peter Doran. 'Refining Green Political Economy: From Ecological Modernisation to Economic Security and Sufficiency'. In *Analyse & Kritik* 28 (2006) (Stuttgart: Lucius & Lucius): 250–75.

Berlin, Brent, and Pay Kay. *Basic Color Terms: Their Universality and Evolution*. Los Angeles: University of California Press, 1969.

Berns, Roy S. *Billmeyer and Saltzman's Principles of Color Technology*. 3rd edition. New York: John Wiley, 2000.

Brown, S., et al., 'Naturalizing Aesthetics: Brain Areas for Aesthetic Appraisal across Sensory Modalities'. *NeuroImage* 58, no. 1 (2011): 250–58.

Cage, John. *Colour and Culture: Practice and Meaning from Antiquity to Abstraction.* London: Thames and Hudson, 1993.

Cantor, Norman L. *After We Die: The Life and Times of the Human Cadaver*. Washington, DC: Georgetown University Press, 2010.

Cohen, Jeffrey Jerome. 'Ecology's Rainbow'. *Prismatic Ecology. Ecotheory beyond Green*, edited by Jeffrey Jerome Cohen and Lawrence Buell, xv–xxxv. Minneapolis: University of Minnesota Press, 2013.

Cohen, Jeffrey Jerome, and Buell, Lawrence, eds. *Prismatic Ecology. Ecotheory beyond Green*. Minneapolis: University of Minnesota Press, 2013.

Dale, Garth, et al., eds. *Green Growth: Ideology, Political Economy and the Alternatives*. London: Zed, 2016.

Debray, Régis. *Manifestes Mediologiques*. Paris: Gallimard, 1994.

———. *Transmitting Culture*. Translated by Eric Rauth. New York: Columbia University Press, 2004.

DeLanda, Manuel. *Intensive Science and Virtual Philosophy*. London: Continuum, 2004.

DeLong, Marilyn, and Gozde Goncu-Berk. 'What Color Is Sustainability?' In *Color and Design*, edited by Marilyn DeLong and Barbara Martinson, 89–100. London: Berg, 2012.

Doerner, Max. *Malmaterial und seine Verwendung im Bilde*. Nachdruck der 6. Auflage von 1938. Stuttgart: Ferdinand Enke Verlag, 1992.

Doherty, Gareth. *Paradoxes of Green: Landscapes of a City-State*. Oakland: University of California Press, 2017.

Farina, Almo. *Soundscape Ecology: Principles, Patterns, Methods and Applications*. Dordrecht: Springer, 2014.

Giedion, Sigfried, *Mechanization Takes Command: A Contribution to Anonymous History*. Oxford/New York: Oxford University Press, 1948.

Gilad, Yoav, et al. 'Human Specific Loss of Olfactory Receptor Genes', *Proceedings of the National Academy of Sciences of the United States of America* 100, no. 6 (2003): 3324–27.

———. 'Loss of Olfactory Receptor Genes Coincides with the Acquisition of Full Trichromatic Vision in Primates'. *PLoS Biology* 2, no. 1 (2004): 120–25.

Goodman, Nelson. *Ways of Worldmaking*. Indianapolis: Hackett Publishing Company, 1978.

Guillén, Michael. 'Embrace of the Serpent: An Interview with Ciro Guerra'. *Cineaste* (Spring 2016), https://www.cineaste.com/spring2016/embrace-of-the-serpent-ciro-guerra/.

Hamilton, Clive. 'The Theodicy of the "Good Anthropocene"'. *Environmental Humanities* 7 (2015): 233–38.

Hansen, Heiko, and Helen/Hehe Evans, eds. *Man Made Clouds*. Orléans: Éditions HYX, 2016.

Haraway, Donna. 'Situated Knowledges: The Science Question in Feminism and the Privilege of Partial Perspective'. *Feminist Studies* 14, no. 3 (1988): 575–99.

Hauser, Jens. 'Atmosph-Air? Atmos-Faire!' In *Man Made Clouds*, edited by Heiko Hansen and Helen/Hehe Evans, 39–59. Orléans: Éditions HYX, 2016.

———. 'Molekulartheater, Mikroperformativität und Plantamorphisierungen'. In *Wahrnehmung, Erfahrung, Experiment, Wissen. Objektivität und Subjektivität in den Künsten und den Wissenschaften*, edited by Susanne Stemmler, 173–89. Zürich: Diaphanes, 2014.

Hawksley, Lucinda. *Bitten by Witch Fever: Wallpaper & Arsenic in the Victorian Home*. London: Thames & Hudson, 2016.

Heller, Eva. *Wie Farben wirken. Farbpsychologie—Farbsymbolik—Kreative Farbgestaltung*. Hamburg: Rowohlt, 1989.

Hilbert, David R. *Color and Color Perception: A Study in Anthropocentric Realism*. Stanford: CSLI, 1987.

Houston, Stephen, et al. *Veiled Brightness—A History of Ancient Maya Color*. Austin: University of Texas Press, 2002.

Huhtamo, Erkki, and Jussi Parikka, eds. *Media Archaeology: Approaches, Applications, and Implications*. Berkeley and Los Angeles: University of California Press, 2011.

Kac, Eduardo. 'Life Transformation—Art Mutation'. In *Signs of Life: Bio Art and Beyond*, edited by Eduardo Kac, 163–84. Cambridge, MA: MIT Press, 2007.

Karafyllis, Nicole C., ed., *Biofakte. Versuch über den Menschen zwischen Artefakt und Lebewesen*. Paderborn: Mentis, 2003.

———. 'Endogenous Design of Biofacts: Tissues and Networks in Bio Art and Life Science'. In *sk-interfaces: Exploding Borders—Creating Membranes in Art, Technology and Society*, edited by Jens Hauser. Liverpool: Liverpool University Press, 2008.

———. 'Natur als Gegentechnik. Zur Notwendigkeit einer Technikphilosophie der Biofakte'. In *Technikphilosophie im Aufbruch. Festschrift für Günter Ropohl*, edited by Nicole C. Karafyllis and Tilmann Haar. Berlin: Edition Sigma, 2004.

Kittler, Friedrich A., *Aufschreibesysteme 1800/1900*. Munich: Fink, 1985.
La Baïonnette. 175, 7 November 1918.
Lakoff, George, and Mark Johnson. *Metaphors We Live By*. Chicago: University of Chicago Press, 1980.
Lee, David. *Nature's Palette: The Science of Plant Color*. Chicago: University of Chicago Press, 2007.
Lynch, Michael J. 'The Greening of Criminology: A Perspective on the 1990'. *The Critical Criminologist* 2, no. 3 (1990): 1–4.
Lynch, Michael J., and Paul B. Stretsky. 'The Meaning of Green: Contrasting Criminological Perspectives'. *Theoretical Criminology* 2, no. 7 (2003): 217–38.
Magi, Paola. *Treasure Hunt with Marcel Duchamp*. Milano: Edizioni Archivio Dedalus, 2011.
Mairinger, Franz, et al. 'The Destruction of Paper by Green Copper Pigments, Demonstrated by a Sample of Chinese Wallpaper'. In *Conservation within Historic Buildings*, edited by Norman S. Brommelle, Garry Thomson and Perry Smith, 180–85. London: International Institute for Conservation of Historic and Artistic Works, 1980.
Manovich, Lev. 'The Death of Computer Art'. *Rhizome*, 23 October 1996, http://rhizome.org/community/41703/.
Marder, Michael. 'For a Phytocentrism to Come'. *Environmental Philosophy* 11, no. 2 (2015): 237–52.
———. 'Vegetal Anti-Metaphysics: Learning from Plants'. *Continental Philosophi cal Review* 44 (2011): 469–89.
Mathews, Andrew S. *Instituting Nature: Authority, Expertise, and Power in Mexican Forests*. Cambridge, MA: MIT Press, 2011.
Mbembe, Achille. 'Necropolitics'. *Public Culture* 15, no. 1 (2003): 11–40.
Morton, Timothy. *Ecology without Nature: Rethinking Environmental Aesthetics*. Cambridge, MA: Harvard University Press, 2007.
———. *The Ecological Thought*. Cambridge, MA: Harvard University Press, 2010.
———. *Dark Ecology: For a Logic of Future Coexistence*. Cambridge, MA: Harvard University Press, 2016.
———. 'X-Ray'. In *Prismatic Ecology. Ecotheory beyond Green*, edited by Jeffrey Jerome Cohen and Lawrence Buell, 311–27. Minneapolis: University of Minnesota Press, 2013.
Myers, Natasha. 'Amplifying the Gaps between Climate Science and Forest Policy: The Write2Know Project and Participatory Dissent'. *Canada Watch*, Special Issue on 'The Politics of Evidence', edited by Colin Coates, Jody Berland and Jennifer Dalton (Fall 2015): 18–21.
———. 'Photosynthesis, Lexicon for an Anthropocene Yet Unseen. Theorizing the Contemporary'. *Cultural Anthropology*, 21 January 2016, https://culanth.org/fieldsights/790-photosynthesis.
Nathans, Jeremy. 'The Evolution and Physiology of Human Review Color Vision: Insights from Molecular Genetic Studies of Visual Pigments'. *Neuron* 24 (October 1999): 299–312.
Parikka, Jussi. *The Anthrobscene*. Minneapolis: University of Minnesota Press, 2014.

Pastoureau, Michel. *Vert. Histoire d'une couleur*. Paris: Seuil, 2013.

Pollin, Robert. *Greening the Global Economy.* Cambridge, MA: MIT Press, 2015.

Rittel, Horst Willhelm Jakob, and Melvon M. Webber, 'Dilemmas in a General Theory of Planning', *Policy Sciences* 4 (1973): 155–69

Roberson, Debi, et al. 'Color Categories: Evidence for the Cultural Relativity Hypothesis'. *Cognitive Psychology* 50 (2005): 378–411.

Rolston III, Holmes. 'Nature For Real: Is Nature a Social Construct?' In *The Philosophy of the Environment*, edited by T. D. J. Chappell, 38–64. Edinburgh: University of Edinburgh Press, 1997.

Sargent, Walter. *The Enjoyment and Use of Color.* New York: Charles Scribner's Sons, 1923.

Sinn, Hans-Werner. *Das Grüne Paradoxon. Plädoyer für eine illusionsfreie Klimapolitik*. Berlin: Econ, 2008.

Smith, Bruce R. *The Key of Green: Passion and Perception in Renaissance Culture*. Chicago: University of Chicago Press, 2009.

Stjernfelt, Frederik. 'Green War Banners in Central Copenhagen: A Recent Political Struggle Over Interpretation—And Some Implications for Art Interpretation as Such'. In *Investigations into the Phenomenology and the Ontology of the Work of Art: What Are Artworks, and How Do We Experience Them?* Contributions to Phenomenology 81, edited by Peer Bundgaard and Frederik Stjernfelt, 209–23. Heidelberg/New York: Springer, 2015.

Studente, Sylvie, et al. 'Facilitating Creative Thinking in the Classroom: Investigating the Effects of Plants and the Colour Green on Visual and Verbal Creativity'. *Thinking Skills and Creativity* 19 (2016): 1–8.

Thomas, Howard, and Helen Ougham. 'The Stay-Green Trait'. *Journal of Experimental Botany* 65, no. 14 (2014): 3889–900.

Thompson, Evan. *Colour Vision: A Study in Cognitive Science and the Philosophy of Perception*. London/New York: Routledge, 1995.

Tortosa, Guy. 'Décosterd & Rahm Associés, the Sense(s) in the Senses'. In *Physiological Architecture*, edited by Philippe Rahm and Jean-Gilles Décosterd, 56–64. Basel: Birkhäuser, 2002.

Väliverronen, Esa, and Iina Hellsten. 'From "Burning Library" to "Green Medicine". The Role of Metaphors in Communicating Biodiversity'. *Science Communication* 24, no. 2 (2002): 229–45.

Van der Elst, Judith. 'Contemplating Greenness'. *Noema*, online publication, 2016. https://noemalab.eu/ideas/contemplating-greenness/.

Von Goethe, Johann Wolfgang. *Zur Farbenlehre*. Tübingen, 1810. English version *Theory of Colours*. Translated by C. L. Eastlake. London: John Murray, 1840.

Whorton, James C. *The Arsenic Century: How Victorian Britain Was Poisoned at Home, Work, and Play.* Oxford: Oxford University Press, 2010.

Young, Diana. 'The Smell of Greenness: Cultural Synaesthesia in the Western Desert'. *Etnofoor* 18, no. 1, 'Senses' (2005): 61–77.

Zhu, Zaichun, et al. 'Greening of the Earth and Its Drivers'. *Nature Climate Change* 6 (April 2016): 791–95.

Chapter Six

Desire, DNA and Transgenetic Technology

Life after Necropolitics

Mi You

A darkly humorous opening teaser to this chapter, borrowed from the novel and film *The Hitchhiker's Guide to the Galaxy*: having taken 7.5 million years to ponder 'the ultimate answer to life, the universe, and everything', the super computer announces its final calculation to a large, impatient audience: '42'. Naturally, everyone is dazed, confused and disappointed. On registering this, the super computer explains that the question wasn't clear enough and that in order to provide an answer to the ultimate question, a computer infinitely more complex would be needed, one comprising organic life, and that, incidentally, this computer should be called 'Earth'[1]. The ultimate computer is the bio-chemico-physical sphere of the earth itself. This is, of course, an ironic take on computation: if a super computer were capable of simulating absolutely everything, it would have to be absolutely everything itself. The underlying cultural problematic here is our deep, posthuman belief that everything is information and that, as Katherine Hayles has pointed out, information circulates *unchanged* between the different material substrates[2], instead of the substrates both changing and being changed by the circulating information. With this in mind, in this chapter, I set out to examine the politics of the DNA codes and the transgenetic engineering technology as related to notions of life and death, the organic and the inorganic and the temporal and material strata of sex and reproduction. I do so through the prism of two artistic positions: Paul Vanouse's *Suspect Inversion Center* (2011) and Klaus Spiess and Lucie Strecker's *Hare's Blood +* (2014). Vanouse's work challenges the veracity of the DNA as evidence in crime investigation and reveals the biopolitical *overcodification* of the DNA's material strata, which takes control of life. Spiess/Strecker, for their part, stage an auction of transgenic chimera whose organic 'death' critiques the virtualisation of value in affect economy and the subsumption of life under biotechnology. What this means is that life is rendered in informational parameters, measured by energy expenditure and reproduction costs, heralding a desire for self-reproduction, or parthenogenesis. However, the capitalist desire for desire (Deleuze) points to a possible double folding of the so-called primitive sex that comes before two-parent sex, suggesting that the inorganic becoming of the chimera may, in fact, harbour subversive potential to undermine the necropolitical tendencies inherent in genetic engineering technologies.

OVERCODIFICATION AND DNA AS SIGNIFIER

Paul Vanouse's installations and live performances often turn on biopolitics and the epistemological limit of biotechnologies. In his 2002 installation *Relative Velocity Inscription Device*, Vanouse used the DNA imaging technology including gel electrophoresis to render visible the DNA segments of his partially Jamaican family members. Each of the samples passing through the gel electrophoresis made a moving banding pattern in which light and dark transversed fluorescent-coloured bands visible to the naked eye, while simultaneously producing a racing effect. The artist intervened in the visualisation of the DNA by coupling his family members with their respective moving banding patterns, effectively creating a racing game to test the 'fitness' of his family members, thus not only alluding to the cultural myth of the 'fitter' (Jamaican) race but also acting as a poignant reminder that DNA studies harken back to racial studies. In his 2007–2010 installation *Latent Figure Protocol*, Vanouse purposefully subverted the DNA imaging process by adding enzymes to manipulate the outcome of the banding pattern and crafting them into cultural symbols such as ☺or ©. This strange synthesis of 'nature' and 'culture' raised questions about the expressivity of the DNA itself, while taking the authenticity of the DNA imaging technology to issue.

In a similar vein, *Suspect Inversion Center* (2011) is a staged, fully functional laboratory and a live performance in which the audience witnesses the laboratory processes of constructing historical DNA fragments of the alleged murderer O. J. Simpson with the aid of the artist's own DNA. The constructed DNA is made visible through the imaging process based on the previously mentioned gel electrophoresis technique in which long chains of DNA are cut into smaller pieces using restriction enzymes. These DNA pieces contain sequences that vary greatly among unrelated individuals, making them the perfect base for DNA profiling. The obtained fragments are subsequently separated and run through the electrically charged agarose gel field with shorter sequences moving further away from the original spot and longer sequences remaining closer to the original spot, thus marking the DNA profile used in forensic studies or for parental clarification. Playing with the acronym of CSI (crime scene investigation), *Suspect Inversion Center*, or *SIC*, situates itself at the intersection of laboratory sciences and crime investigation. Using various probes and enzymes to modify the fragmentation of his own DNA material, Vanouse succeeded in creating a banding pattern identical to O. J. Simpson's, the notorious (or notoriously) acquitted murderer. Described as 'the most publicised trial in history' by *USA Today*, Simpson's trial was also one of the first trials in which DNA profiling played a prominent role. Discussing the motivation behind his practice, Vanouse draws on a statement made by an FBI science spokesman who equated DNA profiling with the use of fingerprints, so that during the trial, the jury could use the available evidence to identify 'one individual to the exclusion of all others'[3]. As Vanouse rightly points out, the FBI spokesperson did not care about the politics of the DNA analysis; instead, the 'jury's belief was their main concern'[4]. Vanouse undermines the seeming authenticity of DNA profiling through the meticulously staged, detailed enactment of the laboratory process and the fabrication of a fake signifier. In popular imagination, understanding DNA as a signifier of a particular reality, be it identity or disease, stands in contrast to notions of content and expression, which I will use in conjunction with Luciana Parisi's three-tiered construction of biophysical, biocultural and biodigital (also called abstract) sex to undermine the reductionist tendency of reading genes as signs and to trace the discursive movements around DNA and life.

ABSTRACT SEX AND META-STABLE BODIES

In investigating abstract sex, Parisi draws on the feminist politics of desire, or the micropolitics of becoming-woman. She situates the politics of desire in the biophysical, biocultural and biodigital strata through a careful reading of the history of biology and genetic technology. Her alternative conceptual frame of 'abstract sex' radically redefines sex and the body; it is based on a continuum among three levels of sex: the cellular level or biophysical sex (bacterial sex), human or biocultural sex (heterosexual mating) and biotechnological or biodigital sex (cloning)[5]. These three levels are linked through the manifestation of a nondischarge-based desire for becoming, in other words, by the proliferation of information exchanged via the (unnatural) mixtures of bodies and sexes. Different bodies-sexes coexist; they enfold to make up the human body—the bacterial body, the nucleic cell's bodies and the multicell organisms' bodies. Some of these replicate by themselves; others participate in genetic trading and mixtures. A body is defined by 'metastable relations between microcellular and multicellular bodies, the bodies of animals and humans, the bodies of society' as well as by the 'technological bodies merging and unleashing new mutating compositions'[6]. On each level, this meta-stable state that defines the composition and organisation of bodies depicts the body as *nonholistic*, as discussed by Gilles Deleuze:

> The logos is a huge Animal whose parts unite in a whole and are unified under a principle or a leading idea; but the pathos is a vegetal realm consisting of cellular elements that communicate only indirectly, only marginally, so that no totalisation, no unification, can unite this world of ultimate fragments.[7]

The logos informs the common understanding of the human body. For example, Aristotle saw living organisms as nothing more than assemblages of machines. Such a machinic and reductionist understanding of the human body feeds into popular media and contributes to the misleading view that with the Human Genome Project we can piece together the secret of our existence as in a puzzle. The figuration of the vegetal realm reminds us that the human body cannot be reduced to a unified organisation, to a sum of discrete parts, and certainly not a sum that can be explained through our genes, as poignantly noted by the super computer in *The Hitchhiker's Guide to the Galaxy*. The field of epigenetics, in which 'epi' stands for being 'on top of', has shown that many tangible and intangible factors co-determine inheritable characteristics that are beyond the changes in the DNA sequence[8]. Behind this privileged position occupied by the virtual DNA codes in popular imagination is the scientific rendering of the world in terms of *telos* and linearity, which Parisi interrogates by placing the emphasis on nonlinear developments across three strata, thereby challenging the supposedly linear evolution or progression from bacterial DNA trading to genetic recombination processes of animal and human reproduction and, finally, to transgenetic operations such as cloning. In an effort to account for a nonlinear development, Lynn Margulis and Dorion Sagan's theorisation of endosymbiosis offers an important insight: symbiotic and parasitic relations precede the appearance of nucleic DNA and sexual reproduction but *coexist with the latter* as a form of continuing the life of a cell. In other words, bacterial and cellular beings, though seemingly belonging to different stages in the linear progression of evolution, have a mutual interest in each other's continued existence[9]. Based on Margulis and Sagan's study, Parisi identifies the connection between the two states of cell separation—mitosis and meiosis—as 'an intensive extension of microbial sex and reproduction'[10]. Mitosis, through which most human cells and animal cells are produced, is the cell division by which chromosomes self-replicate in the parent cell so that each of the two daughter cells gets the same set of chromosomes. Meiosis is the process of cell division in which the chromosomes in the parent cell self-replicate once while the cell divides twice, resulting in four daughter cells, or haploid cells, each containing half the number of the parent cell chromosomes. Meiosis enables genetic variation in sexual reproduction when two haploid cells—sperm and eggs—mix the genetic materials from two parents.

Through the lens of mitosis and meiosis, we can trace a nonlinear history of biophysical sex and biocultural life. According to Margulis and Sagan's study, the ancient protists (eukaryotic cells) ate each other under harsh circumstances, incorporating each other's genetic material in a process like mitosis (biophysical sex). A new (re)balance is achieved only by the reduction of chromosomal duplicity in the process of meiosis, heralding later developments in sexed haploids (biocultural sex)[11]. Studies show that when meiotic sex first spread in protists, sexual patterns appeared nearly identical, suggesting that the way genetic materials duplicate and transmit through meiosis leads to the formation of sexed organisms in animals and plants rather than the other way around. Hence Parisi claims that meiosis as a cell operation gives rise to sexed forms of organism in plants and animals[12]. This instance of meiotic sex sheds light on the parallel yet connected modes of sex, or exchange and differentiation of genetic materials on both the biophysical and the biocultural strata. The implication of the cross-strata continuum of meiotic sex and the cultural notions of sex related to feminist desire will be explained shortly. For the moment, I will resort to the already mentioned content and expression to examine the linguistic structure used in the scientific organisation of sex that simplifies and reduces the aforementioned strata (in)to codes.

CONTENT AND EXPRESSION OR HOW DNA BECOME OVERCODIFIED

Linguist Louis Hjelmslev's proposition is important for Deleuze and Guattari because it positions expression and content on a plane of immanence. In an attempt to replace the dichotomy of the 'signifier' and the 'signified', Hjelmslev uses 'expression' and 'content' and further clarifies that *both terms* have the intrinsic properties of 'form' and 'substance'. Content refers to the visible states of things formed by complex power relations. Expression is the set of articulate statements and discourses arising from the field of social relations. In Hjelmslev's view, 'form' is nothing but the shadow of a grid work cast on the surface of unformed, undifferentiated matter. 'Substance' is matter contained in the now delineated surface grids. Similarly, 'expression' is but the shadow of a grid imposed on 'an amorphous "thought matter"'[13], which separates what could be called 'content' elements from the surface of thought matter. Their designation is 'quite arbitrary. Their functional definition provides no justification for calling one, and not the other, of these entities expression, or one, and not the other, content'[14]. This means that expression or content, their form or substance are not fundamentally different *in kind* but are only different designations of levels or degrees. Brian Massumi interprets Hjelmslev in the following way:

> There are any number of forms of content and forms of expression, each with their own substance or specific materiality; further, between a form of content and a form of expression there is only the process of their passing into each other: in other words, an immanence. In the gap between content and expression is the immanence of their mutual 'deterritorialisation'.[15]

To understand the dynamic relation between expression and content in the social field, Deleuze and Guattari draw on Michel Foucault's analysis of the production of delinquency, which points to the penal law as the form of expression, to delinquency as the substance of expression, to the prison as the form of content and to the prisoners as the substance of content[16]. The performativity in and of the social field—in this case, sentencing delinquents—is what binds the content and expression through their mutual deterritorialisation. This performativity underlies the operation of biopolitics in Foucault's study of how human beings are socialised into subject positions through the institutionalisation of discourses and how life is managed and governed through the operation of power. Extrapolating the notion of expression and content, Parisi suggests that a similar dynamism is present on the immanent plane of genetic materials. She locates the form of expression in genotypes, the substance of expression in phenotypes, the form of content in chromosomes and the substance of content in cytoplasmic and mitotic processes[17]. The expression, or the 'decoded' genotypes, characterise an organism's identity, which is in a perpetual process of deterritorialisation with regard to content, in other words, the chromosomes that carry them. Here, genotypes refer to the genetic composition or the DNA codes of eukaryotic cells of humans, animals and plants, commonly held as the sole key to the secret of our (human) being. Yet there are other, nonnucleus-based forms of heredity, for instance, through mitochondria in the cytoplasm, which also possess genomes passing through the maternal lineage, whose molecular mechanism has remained elusive to scientific studies. However, studies have suggested that the human mitochondria might have come from bacteria with an ancient history and was only later incorporated into the eukaryotic cells. In this sense, mitochondria are a very ancient form of being preceding many other forms of life yet living *in endosymbiosis* with us. This means that the distinction between nucleus/chromosome (form of content) and cytoplasm/mitochondria (substance of content) is 'not a boundary but a threshold between parallel networks of sex and reproduction (nucleic and mitochondrial)'[18]. What *overcodifies* the multicellular forms of content and expression (the chromosomes and the genotype) is a 'regime of signs' through which biophysical processes become linguistic signs on the biocultural stratum. Parisi puts it thus:

> Overcoding implies that the [f]orm of expression becomes linguistic rather than genetic. On this new level of organisation, expression no longer operates through genetic connections, but entails the emergence of a new order above the layers of the genotype. This new order of expression is constituted by comprehensible and transmittable symbols that convey a superlinearity: the capacity to synthesise all codes-milieus' relations into a sufficiently deterritorialised system of signs. In particular, this order defines the capacity of the scientific world to translate all particles, codes and territorialities of the organic strata into a new order of signs. . . . It involves an abstraction (virtualisation or potentialisation) of particle-signs on a new level of relations, producing a new organisation (decodification and deterritorialisation) of forms and substances of content and expression.[19]

This overcodification imposes a linguistic character on genotype and all its associated material processes, disregarding the mutual deterritorialisation between the content and expression and enforcing each to form its own organisation. It further transforms these immanent intensities into extendible entities—signifiers, so that on this new level of organisation, the abstracted entity of DNA sequences or genotypes is taken conceptually as a signifier for phenotypes, be it identity or a particular illness. As Deleuze and Guattari put it, the imperialism of the signifier 'challenges exegesis in the name of recitation, pure textuality, and superior "scientificity" (*scientificité*)'[20]. Furthermore, the consequence of overcodification is an extension of Western intellectual history—a certain bifurcational thinking, using genotype to access the realm beyond (phenotype) without seeing the difference between the two as form and substance of the same expression.

It is on this level of scientific overcodification that Vanouse's work critically intervenes. His aptly enacted performance/scientific process decodifies the overcodified view of DNA through the performativity of scientific processes and through a conceptual questioning of the linguistic view of genetics. In the performance, the laboratory settings organise bodies (technical and epistemic, organic and nonorganic) into new relations deterritorialised from the plain of immanence, which Hans-Jörg Rheinberger critiques as the scientists' tendency of effacing the means and media necessary to bring the phenomena of their scientific interest into being[21]. Vanouse performs exactly this new organisation of bodies that generate new sets of *abstracted* meanings by following meticulous laboratory procedures. The twist is that he produces a fake artefact—a manipulated result of the DNA imaging that shows exactly the same patterns as that of O. J. Simpson's. The artist has thus produced a misleading signifier, a misnomer for a misnomer, effectively decodifying the regime of signifiers from within. The temporary suspension of scientific epistemology (in the case of the DNA as signifier) allows the relation between the discursive multiplicities of expression and the nondiscursive multiplicities of content to reemerge as a mutual deterritorialisation of both. It also takes on renewed rigour in the negotiation of a truthful identity.

If the DNA as signifier points to the particularity of identity or pathology after the Human Genome Project, human genetics, as a discipline, has shifted to another level of engaging with 'life itself'. Here, the capture of life is rendered in the regime of necropolitics, which, following Achille Mbembe, refers to the contemporary forms of subjugation of life to the power of death[22]. For example, research into normalcy informs the decision about which lives are worthy of living and which are not; it further heralds a whole new era of biodesign, genetic engineering and, with that, a new synthesis between power and the capitalisation of life and death.

INORGANIC BECOMING AGAINST DEATH: SPIESS/STRECKER'S *HARE'S BLOOD* +

In their 2014 *Hare's Blood* +, artists Klaus Spiess and Lucie Strecker perform a 'ritual' in the form of an auction, in which they introduce a genetically modified organism made with the DNA segments of hare's blood used by Joseph Beuys in his 1974–1977 mixed media work *Hare's Blood*. The performance starts with a video documentation showing molecular scientists preparing scraps of the dried hare's blood shrink-wrapped in Beuys's original mixed media work. The video documentation also features an art historian discussing the symbolism in Beuys's work. This is followed by the artists inserting the acquired DNA into a genetically modified organism with a standardised genetic sequence—or biobrick—creating a living organism encased in a triangular container (that resembles the plastic envelope used by Beuys). The audience is invited to participate in the auction by placing bids as to which the living organism responds. As the bids raise, the amount of injected enzyme—which protects the organism from ageing and, ultimately, death—decreases, thus allowing the organism to decompose. Beuys's original *Hare's Blood* is loaded with symbolic meaning; the hare features prominently in his earlier works, such as his 1965 performance *How to Explain Pictures to a Dead*

Hare, in which Beuys walked around the gallery explaining his drawings to a dead hare nestled in his arms. For Beuys, the hare 'has a strong affinity to women, to birth and to menstruation, and generally to chemical transformation of blood'; in carving out from earth a habitat to fit its own body shape, the hare demonstrates 'the movement of incarnation'; it is radically different from human's rationalising tendency and presents a thinking that is 'sharpened, then transformed, and [that] becomes revolutionary'[23].

DESIRE, DEATH AND CAPITALISM

In contrast to the overcodification of meiotic reproduction in systems of signs critiqued in Vanouse's work, Spiess/Strecker's work offers a critical perspective on the double fold of genetic engineering/biophysical sex under the condition of capitalism. Their work engages the three strata described by Parisi: the biophysical bodies that present an ancient form of bacterial reproduction preceding two-parent sex; the gendered/racialised body and its reproduction on the biocultural level, which is itself a site of biopolitical and sociosymbolic interplay; and the body in the biodigital age, which is constantly reshaped by biotechnologies begging a critical engagement with their political and ethical implications. Parisi stresses the nonlinear nature of the relation between the three strata as they define the meta-stable states of bodies and organise sex and reproduction[24]. This nonlinear continuum (from the variation of bacterial bodies to bioengineered bodies) sets in motion on each stratum 'a micro level of difference proliferating through the symbiotic engineering of information crossing not only species and sexes, but also humans and machines'[25]. As shown earlier, the organic level of meiotic sex is *overcodified* by the sociocultural organisation of sex. Similarly, the biodigital stratum of the organisation of sex involves the overcodification of other strata. Deleuze and Guattari's notion of desire and the three stages of history is particularly useful in charting these relations.

In Deleuze and Guattari's philosophy of history, the precapitalist societies code desire through inscription while the capitalist machine frees the decoded flow of desire[26]. Inscription entails marking bodies (human, nonhuman as well as abstract bodies) so as to create representations of things and to attribute meanings to them, which, in turn, represses the flux of desire. This process lies underneath the development of social formations, in other words, desire is socialised by coding. Deleuze and Guattari write: 'the primitive territorial sign is self-validating; it is a position of desire in a state of multiple connections. It is not a sign of a sign nor a desire of a desire'[27]. This position of desire meets a new destiny under the despotic regime in the next stage of Deleuze and Guattari's philosophy of history. The despot imposes a new alliance system placing himself in direct filiation with the deity. This can be observed in the rise of new spiritual empires or in cases in which a new empire comes to replace an old one. With this new system of alliance comes an absolute structure of hierarchy, 'a fictitious voice from beyond that expresses itself in the flow of writing as direct filiation'[28]. The biochemical complexity beyond the nucleic DNA can be likened to the primitive territorial sign—a 'position of desire', in which the coexisting cytoplasmic (somaline) and nucleic (germline) reproductions, exchanges of matter, communication, information and the proliferation of differences, all pertain to the activity of desire in a state of multiple connections. What disrupts this primary position of desire is the process of inscription, analogous to the overcodification of meiotic reproduction and the making of the two-parent sex, which is then turned into a disciplinary norm informing sex in the context of social production. Furthermore, the direct filiation in the new alliance system implies the cultural image of two-parent sex and the organic preservation of the germline, in tandem with the 'death' of the half chromosomes—the haploids not recombined in the two-parent sex and henceforth not preserved in the next generation figuring as organic death. In contrast, reproduction in cytoplasm and mitochondria does not involve sexed chromosomes; it presents an order beyond the question of organic life and death. In this way, the two-parent sex introduces 'the constancy of pleasure, stopping the dissipation towards the inorganic, [which] deploys the disciplinary link between sex and death of the organic composition of capital and human body'[29]. Sex and death are brought together in a despotic disciplinary state, which dreads the flow of production and of exchange from the primitive position of desire.

What decodes biocultural sex is the stratum of biodigital sex, which, in a strange motion, folds back to the earlier order of biophysical sex and detaches 'from organic death through an autonomous assemblage of desire-power of reproduction'[30]. Taking the model of cytoplasm and mitochondria reproduction, this parthenogenesis is a *decoded desire to desire*, a power to self-reproduce, devoid of two-parent sex. In a similar conceptual movement, in the Deleuzian-Guattarian philosophy of history, what overcomes the despot state is the capitalist machine that captures flows of desire by making them into a structural element of its own operation through the appropriation of production and conjuring the decoded flows of desire. Capital begets capital, bypassing the production of commodities. Parisi suggests 'escaping the law of filiation, the commodity interrupts energy-forces from being channeled towards genital reproduction, intensifying reproducibility without discharge: feminine parthenogenesis (cytoplasmic sex)'[31]. Reflected in the contemporary technological advancements as a means and an end of production, this parthenogenesis desire can be traced in cloning, in transgenetic and other genetic engineering experiments. As exemplified by Dolly the sheep, the only higher organism reproduced without reproduction to date, cloning entails inserting the nucleus of an adult organism with all its genes into an empty egg in order to reproduce a perfectly functioning offspring with the same set of genes. In theory, this process could be repeated ad infinitum: clones made from clones, made from clones—reproduction without reproduction[32].

Recent inventions in genetic engineering technology manifest this parthenogenesis desire ever more clearly. In 2012, Jennifer Doudna and Emmanuelle Charpentier deployed a decoy technique called CRISPR/Cas9 to effectively cut the DNA at targeted positions on genes within organisms. This made it possible to add a new genetic code to the genome, which could combat genetically governed diseases, or even cure them. However, the wish for 'enhancement surgeries', such as changing the eye colour or the level of alcohol tolerance of one's offspring, is on the rise[33]. As more DNA sequences are found correlating to particular characteristics, we are closer to targeted evolution. Some scientists are optimistic that the technological challenges such as establishing a reliable human embryonic stem cell, perfecting the precision of the genomic editing or finding ways to permanently modify the genome in human organisms are on the verge of being solved. Backed by technological advancement, genetics research crosses the threshold of pathological research and steps into normalcy research—the genetics of race, gender, sexuality, intelligence, temperament and personality. Yet as Siddharta Mukherjee emphatically puts it in the closing statement in his book *The Gene*, 'mutants would be eliminated but so would human variation. Infirmities might disappear, but so might vulnerability. Chance would become mitigated, but so, inevitably, would choice'[34]. The desire for desire manifested in transgenetic engineering emerges out of a masochist assemblage. Following Deleuze, masochism is an intensity of desire that separates the autonomy of desire from the libido of sexual genitality, sexual reproduction and pleasure and can be witnessed in other forms of reproduction, for example, capitalist reproduction and technical reproduction[35]. As such, it conveys 'a feminine intensive desire'[36]. Death figures differently in the masochist assemblage of intensive reproduction and sex: 'death exposes the potential of a body to become rather than the finitude of the organism'[37]. Therefore, the proliferation of cytoplasmic reproduction, characterised by the autonomy from two-parent sex and nucleic reproduction, passes through the threshold of organic death and exposes the potential of the inorganic becoming—that is, becoming no longer overcodified in the anthropocentric image and ruled by the coupling of sex/pleasure and death

We have seen the nonlinear continuum and the organisation of sex through the flow of desire in the three strata. It should be noted that this model of abstract desire does not pass moral judgement on the feminine intensive desire. Because 'artifice is fully a part of Nature'[38], the task is not to go back to a pretransgenetic-engineering past but to pose questions such as: How can feminine intensive desire challenge or subvert the existing and future technologies? In inorganic becoming—the 'ancient' and the biodigital form of reproduction—we will see potential for a new, nonhuman life.

HYPERNATURE

This grand return to inorganic becoming by way of genetic engineering takes us back to *Hare's Blood +*, a chimera not in the image of the hare itself but something minoritarian, akin to the inorganic becoming of an indeterminate body. The resurrection of advanced living forms through DNA engineering is technically impossible in complex organisms such as humans, due, perhaps, to histones, a protein wrapped around the DNA that etches permanent marks on genes so that an aged gene cannot revert to an earlier, pluripotent developmental stage as if governed by 'molecular memory'[39]. The revival of a full body would also fall into the biopolitical and late capitalist capture of life on the biodigital stratum. Yet the capitalist desire for desire is already infused in biotechnology. A history of patenting and privatising the gene points to the way in which capitalism passes from the formal subsumption of labour to the real subsumption of life. The former is defined by the implication of human labour in capitalist machines of production. The latter is indicated by the internal rearrangement and reorganisation of labour processes to meet the demand of capital, hence moving beyond human labour to include machinic labour and ultimately turning the body itself into a site of production. The complex interlocking of capitalism, biotechnology and necropolitical power—the power to exploit, redesign, even annihilate—takes full control of the body. The patenting of genetic data is one among many forms of capitalising on life, as seen in the synthetically produced DNA for medical use or in genetically modified crops. Not only are 'pathological bodies' subjected to medical research and/or gene therapy, 'healthy bodies', too, are increasingly monitored with the purpose of creating an expansive pool of genetic information. Accompanying genetic-specific medication is a large-scale adoption of diagnostic genetic testing, which creates a loop that turns 'the recirculation of products (pills, testing technologies) back into information (databases, test results, marketing and media campaign)'[40]. In real subsumption, capital achieves an abstraction of life into 'life itself', 'an abstraction which reduces life to a new unit for negotiating an equivalency between the cost of energy expenditure and its reproduction or replacement'[41]. Capitalism seeks a reduction of energy and resources in the informational substrate of the human body and 'life itself'. Patricia T. Clough puts it succinctly: 'in this passage from formal to real subsumption, the tendencies of capitalism are moved by the techno-ontological postbiological threshold'[42]. If Mbembe traces necropolitical domination in the racialised, economically and politically disenfranchised bodies that are kept in a form of death-in-life[43], then the dematerialisation of human bodies offers an updated image of necropolitics: decoded, depersonalised and exchangeable organs or 'organs without bodies' as Rosi Braidotti, following Slavoj Žižek's critique of Deleuze's inconsistency in locating the virtual and becoming, calls it[44]. Imbricated in capitalism, human bodies are subsumed into the production and consumption of genetic data in order to reproduce (to be disease-free), ruled by fear and always in debt to the self-realising loop of capital circulation.

Spiess/Strecker have created a scenario whereby the hare becomes subject to subsumption as both the means and the end of (value) production, as opposed to being only the means of (artistic) production in Beuys's original *Hare's Blood.* Precisely at this point of *real subsumption*, the physical, full-bodied reality of the hare is effaced by the logic of self-perpetuating production of value, attached to virtualised value creation processes through energy-information. In coupling the organism's decomposition with the art prosumer's confidence in it, the artists reveal how confidence, as an essential part of affect economy, configures the organism on the informatic level, thereby making a deft illustration of the commodification and virtualisation of life itself and the underlying mechanism that sustains it. Typically, an auction renders tangible the importance of confidence as a form of affect in capitalist economy: more confidence, more value, decoupled from the (real) use value of the commodity. On the one hand, we are reminded of the powerful synergy between the virtualisation of capital accumulation in the financial market, on the other, of the (proliferation of the) biotechnological capture of the body that marks an era in which 'life itself' is at stake. At first sight, the design of Spiess/Strecker's auction subverts the virtualisation of value creation/capital accumulation by inserting the correlation of bid value and the decomposition of the bid item. As prosumer confidence rises, the decomposition of the organism leads to its organic death. Or does it? Isn't the organic death of the organism always already based on our anthropocentric projection of organic life and death?

Deleuze and Guattari hold that the ultimate destination of the conjunctive desire of late capitalism is death itself: 'death is felt rising from within and desire itself becomes the death instinct, latency, but it also passes over into these flows that carry the seeds of a new life'[45]. What could the new life look like? And more importantly, who is the new life for? Would we experiment to see, as Claire Colebrook urges, 'what "we" might be like if we diminished our consumptions and productions, if we reduced—perhaps to the point of non-being—all those forces that we have, until now, taken to be human?'[46] What life does *Hare's Blood +* hint at, if not at the anthropomorphised and overcodified organic death? From a multiperspectivist point of view, the artists write, 'the subsequent rhizomatic burst of the GMO yeast may be experienced by the spectators as bodily decomposition, but by the GMO as a satisfying reproduction'[47]. Based on his anthropological research of Amazonian cultures, Eduardo Viveiros de Castro's multispectivism proposes that nonhuman beings such as animals and spirits are humans and continue to be humans 'behind their everyday appearance'[48]. Nonhuman agents and humans both perceive the world in the same way; what varies is the world which they see, effectively redeeming relationality rather than substantiality as the primary way of relating to the world[49]. Based on this principle of 'one culture, many natures', the artists explore performance as ritual, in which the GMO functions as a sacrificial element going through organic death, not to invite audience identification but to make the audience realise that they are indeed in the same culture as the GMO[50]. Here I'd like to expand on the notion of shared 'culture', which not only implies organic death but also channels an other-than-human desire, in other words, the desire of multiplication/decomposition or inorganic becoming.

As mentioned earlier, nucleic DNA is relatively inert, archival, while non-nucleic recombination such as mitochondrial recombination makes up the forces of inorganic becoming[51]. The latter doesn't pass through the two-parent regime of chromosomal sex and death, hence preceding and exceeding the chromosomal hierarchies of genetic filiation[52]. In a strange way corresponding to the forces of inorganic becoming on the biophysical stratum, the capitalisation of life itself via the bio-informatic technology proliferates the rate of variation, mutation and emergence of new biological organisms. Hence the biodigital sex machines' 'double fold', the biophysical machines of unpredictable differentiations[53]. Yet as promising as the future may seem to those who can afford it, or as dire as it might be for the rest, under the threat of biotechnical capture, this double fold does not come without cost. In the projected scenario of mammal cloning, or gene therapy, it is important to note that the technique does not just intervene at the nucleic level but involves mitochondria and cytoplasm in the cell as the organism grows, giving rise to possible intensifications of mitochondrial recombination and, potentially, triggering mutations hitherto unknown and unimaginable elsewhere in the organism. The risk rises exponentially as we deal with the complexity of genetics, given that most phenomes are co-determined by many genes. In contrast to conservative stances on genetic engineering such as the 'culture of life' movement[54], this scenario of inorganic becoming is firmly placed on the planes of abstract sex, of which humans are made yet do not fully control. Indeed, it entails 'a symbiotic association of bodies of all sorts unleashing the potential of a body to mutate on a hypernature of contagious encounters'[55]. As such, it offers the possibility of a nonlinear overflow of the biopolitical and necropolitical machines, which, for Parisi, is 'a reversible relation between absolute control or virtual subsumption (the capture of the interval between states) and absolute deterritorialisation or molecular recombination of all machines of sex and reproduction (biophysical, biocultural and bio-technical machines)'[56].

HYPERNATURAL FUTURE

If artifice is fully part of nature, then we have seen how the endosymbiotic relation manifests 'hypernatural capacities of a body to become'[57]. The works of Vanouse and Spiess/Strecker offer different critical approaches to this hypernature. Discursive scientific and cultural organisation recodes indeterminate body-sexes in meiotic reproduction into a filiative two-parent sex relation. The study of linguistics, firmly situated in a philosophy of immanence, sheds light on the mutual relation between the complex state of things/content and the discursive construct/expression, which, in the case of the DNA, translates into a mutual deterritorialisation of cytoplasmic realities/chromosomes and phenotypes/genotypes. In this light, the DNA fingerprint artifice crafted in Vanouse's *Suspect Inversion Center* challenges the process of overcodification that imposes on the DNA a top-down signifier function 'beyond reasonable doubt' in the juridical context, as evident from the previously mentioned FBI spokesperson's statement.

On the biodigital stratum, overcodification renders everything as information, coinciding with the capitalist machine's tendency to subsume life itself as labour and to reduce energy expenditure in increasingly virtualised production and reproduction. Biopolitics thus becomes necropolitics. However, the definition of organic death is once again challenged by the intensive feminine desire at the micro level of mitochondrial reproduction and in complex chain reactions that are unforeseeable in transgenetic operations. Spiess/Strecker's organism does not go through organic death; instead, its life is manifested through its indeterminate biodigital/biophysical becoming that exhibits a feminine intensive desire at the biophysical level, a desire that harbours the hypernatural potential to escape the capitalist desire of auto-reproduction and of the total capture of life through information. It is a manmade artefact that nevertheless reminds us of our own potential for becoming within the hypernature we co-inhabit with other beings.

NOTES

1. Douglas Adams, *The Hitchhiker's Guide to the Galaxy* (London: Pan Books, 1979).

2. N. Katerine Hayles, *How We Became Posthuman: Virtual Bodies in Cybernetics, Literature and Informatics* (Chicago: University of Chicago Press, 1999), 1.

3. Paul Vanouse, 'Counter Laboratories, Inverted Suspects and Latent Signs', in *Paul Vanouse: Fingerprints . . .*, ed. Jens Hauser (Berlin: argobooks, 2011), 61.

4. Ibid.

5. Luciana Parisi, *Abstract Sex: Philosophy, Technology, and the Mutation of Desire* (London and New York: Continuum, 2004), 12.

6. Ibid., 27.

7. Gilles Deleuze, *Proust and Signs*, trans. R. Howard (New York: Allen Lane The Penguin Press, 1972), 174–75. Quoted in Parisi, *Abstract Sex*, 13.

8. It should be noted, however, that the potential of epigenetics to rescue life from DNA determinism is subject to a new kind of determinism, that of social and behavioural circumstances. See, for example, how campaigns like "Begin Before Birth" (http://www.beginbeforebirth.org) from the Imperial College London portray stress and anxiety during pregnancy are correlated to troublesome behaviours in the kids later, implying a new correlation and determinism between social class and social behaviours and the well-being of one's offspring.

9. Lynn Margulis and Dorion Sagan, *Origins of Sex* (New Haven, CT: Yale University Press, 1986).

10. Parisi, *Abstract Sex*, 79.

11. Margulis and Sagan, *Origins of Sex*, 152. In Parisi, *Abstract Sex*, 70.

12. Parisi, *Abstract Sex*, 80.

13. Roland Bogue, *Deleuze and Guattari* (London and New York: Routledge, 1989), 126.

14. Louis Hjelmslev, *Prolegomena to a Theory of Language*, trans. Francis J. Whitfield (Madison: University of Wisconsin Press, 1969), 126.

15. Brian Massumi, 'Introduction: Like a Thought', in *A Shock to Thought: Expression after Deleuze and Guattari*, ed. Brian Massumi (London and New York: Routledge, 2002), xviii.

16. Eugene B. Young, *The Deleuze and Guattari Dictionary* (New York: Bloomsbury Academic, 2013), 140.

17. Parisi, *Abstract Sex*, 88.

18. Ibid., 78.

19. Ibid., 89.

20. Gilles Deleuze and Félix Guattari, *Anti-Oedipus* (Minneapolis: University of Minnesota Press, 1983), 208.

21. Hans-Jörg Rheinberger, 'Risking Reason: The Productive Tension of Art and Science in the Work of Paul Vanouse', in *Paul Vanouse: Fingerprints . . .*, 95–99.

22. Achille Mbembe, 'Necropolitics', *Public Culture* 15, no. 1 (2003): 11–40.

23. 'Why Joseph Beuys and His Dead Hare Live On', *Phaidon*, http://www.phaidon.com/agenda/art/articles/2014/march/03/why-joseph-beuys-and-his-dead-hare-live-on/ (accessed 17 September 2017).
24. Parisi, *Abstract Sex*, 11.
25. Ibid., 17.
26. See Deleuze and Guattari, *Anti-Oedipus*, chapter 3, 'Savages, Barbarians, Civilised Men'.
27. Ibid., 203.
28. Ibid., 205.
29. Parisi, *Abstract Sex*, 111.
30. Ibid., 99.
31. Ibid., 120.
32. Siddhartha Mukherjee, *The Gene: An Intimate History* (New York: Scribner, 2016), Kindle edition.
33. See, for example, David Cyranoski, 'Ethics of Embryo Editing Divides Scientists', *Nature* 519 (2015).
34. Ibid.
35. Gilles Deleuze, *Coldness and Cruelty* (New York: Zone Books, 1991).
36. Parisi, *Abstract Sex*, 100.
37. Ibid., 98–99.
38. Gilles Deleuze, *Spinoza: Practical Philosophy* (San Francisco: City Lights Books, 1988), 124.
39. Mukherjee, *The Gene*.
40. Eugene Thacker, *The Global Genome, Biotechnology, Politics and Culture* (Cambridge, MA: MIT Press, 2005), 85.
41. Patricia T. Clough, 'The Affective Turn: Political Economy, Biomedia and Bodies', *Theory Culture Society* 25 (2008): 14.
42. Ibid., 17.
43. Mbembe, 'Necropolitics', 21.
44. Rosi Braidotti, *Nomadic Subjects* (New York: Columbia University Press, 2011).
45. Deleuze and Guattari, *Anti-Oedipus*, 223.
46. Claire Colebrook, 'Introduction', in *Deleuze and History*, ed. Jeffrey A. Bell et al. (Edinburgh: Edinburgh University Press, 2009), 10.
47. Klaus Spiess and Lucie Strecker, 'In/Valuable Hare's Blood', *Performance Research* 22 (2017): 120.
48. Eduardo Viveiros de Castro, 'EXCHANGING PERSPECTIVES: The Transformation of Objects into Subjects in Amerindian Ontologies', *Common Knowledge* 10 (2004): 466.
49. Ibid., 471–72.
50. Ibid., 119.
51. Parisi, *Abstract Sex*, 155.
52. Ibid., 155.
53. Ibid.,159.

54. See chapter 6 in Bennett, *Vibrant Matter: A Political Ecology of Things* (Durham: Duke University Press, 2009) for a careful study of how the people behind 'culture of life' are against mechanistic metaphysics like the vitalists, but how they differ from the vitalists as they draw on a divine spirit that supposedly animate the matter of the embryo, thereby appealing to conservative Christians.

55. Parisi, *Abstract Sex*, 201.

56. Ibid., 159.

57. Ibid., 196.

BIBLIOGRAPHY

Adams, Douglas. *The Hitchhiker's Guide to the Galaxy.* London: Pan Books, 1979.

Bennett, Jane. *Vibrant Matter: A Political Ecology of Things*. Durham: Duke University Press, 2009.

Bergson, Henri. *Creative Evolution*. Translated by Arthur Mitchell. Mineola: Dover, 1998.

Bogue, Roland. *Deleuze and Guattari*. London and New York: Routledge, 1989.

Braidotti, Rosi. *Nomadic Subjects*. New York: Columbia University Press, 2011.

Buchanan, Ian. *Deleuze and Guattari's Anti-Oedipus: A Reader's Guide*. London and New York: Continuum, 2008.

Clough, Patricia T. 'The Affective Turn: Political Economy, Biomedia and Bodies'. *Theory Culture Society* 25 (2008): 1–22.

Colebrook, Claire. 'Introduction'. In *Deleuze and History*, edited by Jeffery A. Bell and Claire Colebrook, 1–32. Edinburgh: Edinburgh University Press, 2009.

Cyranoski, David. 'Ethics of Embryo-Editing Divides Scientists'. *Nature* 519 (2015).

Deleuze, Gilles. *Coldness and Cruelty*. Translated by Jean McNeil. New York: Zone Books, 1991.

———. *Proust and Signs*. Translated by R. Howard. New York: Allen Lane The Penguin Press, 1972.

———. *Spinoza: Practical Philosophy*. Translated by Robert Hurley. San Francisco: City Lights Books, 1988.

Deleuze, Gilles, and Félix Guattari. *Anti-Oedipus*. Translated by Robert Hurley et al. Minneapolis: University of Minnesota Press, 1983.

Hayles, N. Katherine. *How We Became Posthuman: Virtual Bodies in Cybernetics, Literature and Informatics*. Chicago: University of Chicago Press, 1999.

Hjelmslev, Louis. *Prolegomena to a Theory of Language*. Translated by Francis J. Whitfield. Madison: University of Wisconsin Press, 1969.

Margulis, Lynn, and Dorion Sagan. *Origins of Sex*. New Haven, CT: Yale University Press, 1986.

Martin, Randy. *Knowledge LTD: Toward a Social Logic of the Derivative*. Philadelphia: Temple University Press, 2015.

Massumi, Brian. 'Introduction: Like a Thought'. In *A Shock to Thought: Expression after Deleuze and Guattari*, edited by Brian Massumi, xiii–xxxix. London and New York: Routledge, 2002.

Mbembe, Achille. 'Necropolitics'. *Public Culture* 15, no. 1 (2003): 11–40.
Mukherjee, Siddhartha. *The Gene: An Intimate History*. New York: Scribner, 2016. Kindle edition.
Rheinberger, Hans-Jörg. 'Risking Reason: The Productive Tension of Art and Science in the Work of Paul Vanouse'. In *Paul Vanouse: Fingerprints . . .*, edited by Jens Hauser, 89–103. Berlin: argobooks, 2011.
Parisi, Luciana. *Abstract Sex: Philosophy, Technology, and the Mutation of Desire*. London and New York: Continuum, 2004.
Simondon, Gilbert. 'The Genesis of the Individual'. In *Incorporation*, edited by Jonathan Crary and Sanford Kwinter, 296–319. New York: Zone Books, 1992.
Spiess, Klaus, and Lucie Strecker. 'In/Valuable Hare's Blood'. *Performance Research* 22 (2017): 115–22.
Thacker, Eugene. *The Global Genome, Biotechnology, Politics and Culture*. Cambridge, MA: MIT Press, 2005.
Vanouse, Paul. 'Counter Laboratories, Inverted Suspects and Latent Signs'. In *Paul Vanouse: Fingerprints . . .*, edited by Jens Hauser, 49–65. Berlin: argobooks, 2011.
Viveiros de Castro, Eduardo. 'EXCHANGING PERSPECTIVES: The Transformation of Objects into Subjects in Amerindian Ontologies'. *Common Knowledge* 10 (2004): 463–84.
'Why Joseph Beuys and His Dead Hare Live On'. *Phaidon*, http://www.phaidon.com/agenda/art/articles/2014/march/03/why-joseph-beuys-and-his-dead-hare-live-on/ (accessed 17 September 2017).
Young, Eugene, B. *The Deleuze And Guattari Dictionary*. New York: Bloomsbury Academic, 2013.

Part III

TACTICS

Detourning the Limit, Overbidding, Mourning

Chapter Seven

Necropolitics and the Dark Comedy of the Posthuman*

Critical Art Ensemble

Twenty years ago, Critical Art Ensemble (CAE) wrote its first essay on the posthuman ('Posthuman Development in the Age of Pancapitalism'), and now we are back grappling with this topic once again. The upside is that very little has changed over the past two decades. The posthuman fantasy is still just that, but the fact that this fantasy remains so entrenched in the collective imagination of technocrats, engineers, solutionists and digital enthusiasts speaks to the power of nihilistic desire in humans—a desire for the end of humanity. This desire is what truly distinguishes those who champion the posthuman. The posthumanists are not pretenders or reformers. They have no interest in panhumanism like the so-called postmodern antihumanists[1] (a very poor choice of words), nor are they promoting some newly revised philosophy of humanism. They are revolutionaries dedicated to creating an explosive movement in evolution in which a new creature specialising in intelligence is formed and/or to eliminating humans from much or all of the earth.

HUMANS

Unfortunately, for the purposes of this essay, a model of what a human is is necessary so that it might function as a point of contrast to the posthuman. What CAE is about to offer is meant neither as a universal nor as a philosophically robust definition. We are only offering an imperfect, operational model that consists of eight points of tremendous elasticity. We are speaking

*CAE does not use references.

of tendencies that, when bundled in various configurations, could represent many human variations.

1. Flesh. Humans are tied to the organic.
2. Consciousness. Humans are not only conscious of objects in the world but are also conscious of themselves as objects.
3. Cognition. Humans are generally beyond stimulus/response and have the ability to think and even, at times, reason in the gap between the two.
4. Language. Humans can manipulate signs and symbols, and through this manipulation can communicate to one another in complex ways, which allows for the manufacture and accumulation of knowledge.
5. Sociality. As Aristotle profoundly stated, humans are social animals[2].
6. Technical proficiency. Humans can extend their bodies and minds through the use of technical objects.
7. Mortality. Humans die and are aware that they will die.
8. Biological reproduction. Humans have the ability to reproduce their population.

These tendencies can be placed into concrete situations, and in those situations different assemblies of the human can be made. The situation could be very simple, such as a person in a deep coma that may just be living flesh, or it could be a very complex interrelationship that would be more typical of life experience.

CYBORGS

One distinguishing characteristic of humans is their ability to radically enhance their capabilities and manipulate their environments through the use of technical objects. Consequently, humans who are at the more utopian and complex end of the technosphere are forever flirting with the idea of their technologies becoming integrated with their bodies and brains to an extent of complete interdependence. Conversely, those at the more apocalyptic end of the spectrum have a dread and fear of being fully integrated with their machines and becoming slaves to them and/or to the masters of the machines. Humans who have the power to do so appear to be more than willing to walk up to the line but generally do not cross it. In the 'happier' places within the complex technosphere, we see endless populations of digital zombies armed with phones, pads and laptops, permanently at work—either intentionally and directly working in the virtual marketplace in order to survive or working unintentionally by doing 'recreational' personal and social data entry for corporations and security agencies. Fortunately for them, they can still unplug at the end of the day. Those caught in the manufacturing and service hells of the global order such as call centres, data entry centres and digital sweatshops also remain attached to their machines but are recognized less as humans and more as necessary parts of a greater machine.

Full integration of human and machine to a point of complete interdependence seems to be the pivotal point here. Preparations are of course being made. Soldiers are now weapon systems, and under combat conditions probably relieved by the prospect. On the civilian side of the digital empire, as indicated earlier, classes of technocrats are filled with anxiety at the prospect of being without their devices. Of course the anxiety itself can be tracked and recorded by devices that measure blood pressure and heart rate. Some humans have entered a time in which even sleep management needs a device. Data must always be produced, with biodata rapidly becoming as important a category as demographic and purchase information. For the past twenty years, CAE has heard the constant argument that to have a pacemaker is a life-and-death integration of flesh and technology, so cyborgs already exist. If we use a flexible definition of a cyborg, perhaps. What holds CAE back from endorsing this position is that a cyborg as described here is not posthuman—in fact, it helps to explain why humans have not taken the next evolutionary step into full cyborgian existence. If we examine the popular fictional cyborgs that CAE would call posthuman (DC Comics's Cyborg, Darth Vader, and the like), not only was the technology fully integrated with its organic platform but it also enhanced the power of the individual to move far beyond human limits. A person with a pacemaker is only being returned to a human range of physical health and normality. CAE does emphasise the word 'human' in this case. The earlier narratives guiding the fictional examples of the posthuman centre on the urge either to 'improve' human abilities (move faster, radically elevate intelligence, be indestructible) and use those improvements to better the world (Cyborg is a member of the Justice League) or to enhance oneself in order to release a contained inner evil (or, to be less metaphysical, a maliciousness that will yield power in the form of domination)[3]. Both narratives are quite intriguing, and clearly so given the global fascination with superheroes and supervillains who surpass the boundaries of human norms. The question then becomes: Why is research not being poured into transplantable technologies and the techniques of organic/synthetic integration that will propel humans into the posthuman? Why isn't the market demanding these products of science fiction at once?

While humans can figuratively, and at times literally, love their devices and long for full integration, they also have millennia of purity myth constantly telling them that recombination is either evil or bad. This myth is so pervasive that it makes its way into many laws and norms and severely retards any evolution towards cyborg existence. In this myth in its many, many forms, the creation of life is not in the domain of humans. It is either in God's domain or in nature's. When humans interfere in this process, bad things happen, and the person or persons who do the interference are generally severely punished. Whether it is Icarus trying to fly or Dr. Frankenstein trying to create a human, the consequences are disastrous. Most of the monsters that populate stories and myths are recombinant creatures (which may in fact be the definition of the monstrous). Vampires, werewolves, demons and devils are part of ungodly combinations of the Creator's work or a deep perversion of nature. In turn, this piece of ideology has been used to maintain all manner of secular purity. Social and economic separations and hierarchies are reinforced and maintained though the appeal to purity and through the fear of the recombinant.

The mixing of human and machine, the organic and the inorganic, violates these categories of separation, and with this comes very deep skepticism about the morality of cyborg existence beyond that of normal human function. Two quick examples: first, one of the bulwarks stopping cyborg evolution is that medicine sees intervention into the human body for any purpose other than improving the health of the individual as frivolous and/or unethical/immoral. Admittedly, this line can be quite fuzzy. The cosmetic surgery industry has successfully argued that their services and products improve the mental health of their clients. In Holland, a sex worker can get breast augmentation with no out-of-pocket costs. Using this latter example, why couldn't a soldier have weapons implanted? At the moment, that appears to be over the line. Risking the dangers of medical intervention to satisfy a desire unproven to help a patient is not going to commonly occur. Moreover, in countries where private medical insurance still exists, the doctor's and patient's insurance companies will reinforce this idea, as will the patient's insurance provider.

Second example: In 2010, the artist Wafaa Bilal had a titanium plate implanted in the back of his head, to which a camera was attached that constantly took photos. CAE will let Bilal explain his reasons. What is important to this discussion is the reaction. Some of Bilal's students at New York University and the university itself objected, and he had to cover the camera while on campus. Why did this camera have to go? The argument from the university was that the camera had to be covered up or turned off for privacy reasons. Such an argument is patently absurd in an age of ubiquitous surveillance. For any resident of New York City, or for anyone who carries a cell phone for that matter, surveillance is simply a fact of everyday life. Not only is the university, as well as NYC, awash in cameras monitoring the vast majority of public space, but every student and faculty member is carrying one or more cameras at all times, and it is more than likely that these devices are tracking and gathering other data on each individual throughout the day. Something else must be at stake. The problem was not the act of surveillance; rather, it was the *form* of surveillance. CAE would argue that the camera's embeddedness in flesh was too unnerving. It constituted a form of surveillance that was too far beyond the norm by calling attention not just to itself but to a future flesh-and-technology integration that appeared perverse. We might say a similar thing about the failure of Google Glass. Even that simple level of flesh/machine integration for the purpose of superior performance was too unnerving.

It will be very difficult to change these norms. This is why the cyborgian posthuman is not emerging. Corporations in the business of recombinant life (particularly those in the food supply industry) are finding this out as well. These corporations have no problem with the purity myth for purposes of social exploitation but need to build in an exception so people will perceive their products with something other than suspicion and disgust. Cyborgs share this problem. We are no closer to this posthuman form than we were five decades ago. At present, cyborgs are nothing more than a compelling fiction.

TRANSHUMANISTS AND EXTROPIANS[4]

Happily, this thought fad among the STEM (science, technology, engineering and math) professions remains in the previous century, although some harmful residue still exists. That it is of any interest at all is due to the fact that it does present a variety of ideas about how to end humanity and transcend into a new kind of being with fewer 'limitations'. Pundits such as Max More, Ray Kurzweil, Aubrey de Grey and Hans Moravec believe that this transition could happen in their lifetime. Of course, such thinking could only occur in a bunker so isolated from the rest of the world and the daily life of most humans that boundaries between unbridled speculation and material reality could be ignored—a place where science fiction could be taken as reasoned reflection on the near future and mixed with the wild optimism of rapid progress. This loosely knit alliance of ideas regarding the advancement of technology in relation to the advancement and ending of humans is an odd form of right-wing accelerationism[5]. The faster STEM professionals can end humans, the more interesting the world will become. It is not that these believers are hoping for the worst; they are not. They are just done with being human and find the Faustian bargain to be a smart way to relieve their boredom and frustration over species limitations.

What also seems to help their optimism is their belief in capitalism. The question, 'Are you attracted to innovative, market-oriented solutions to social problems?' posed by More to help interested individuals decide if they might be an extropian is telling. For More and his extropian compatriots, the market is the means to solve social problems (it doesn't make them), and it will act as an extra line of defence against the deployment of new technology that could be construed as antihuman. Unfortunately for us in the twenty-first-century present, solutionism (market-driven technical fixes for all our problems) has not gone away. That element of the transhuman gospel still remains a fixture in the ideology of STEM. Where might technological development lead us? Humans could become cyborgs (as Moravec believes), or we could upload consciousness and live within the wires and circuits in the disembodiment of pure thought. And if we want to return to our former human selves, we can cryogenically preserve our bodies (or at least some cells), and technocrats will recall us when there is a cure for whatever damaged us. We can live the best of both worlds. If disembodiment does not sound attractive, then immortality might be a more appropriate selection. There are two ways this could be achieved. One is through nanotechnology, as popularised by Eric Drexler in *Engines of Creation* (1986), in which nanobots programmed to maintain or even morph our bodies keep us healthy and our identities flowing. The second path to immortality is through biological intervention, of which there are two primary possibilities. This may occur, on the one hand, as genomic manipulation that turns humans into recombinant creatures of our own design[6]. The other biological possibility, usually associated with de Grey, is that biologists will find a way to circumvent that which causes humans bodily damage unto death. Quite rightly, the processes that kill humans are known: mutations in chromosomes, mutations in mitochondria, junk inside and outside of cells that the body cannot eliminate, cell loss, extracellular protein cross-links and cellular senescence. De Grey is convinced that therapies to address these problems will be created in his lifetime, and they will allow him a long enough life span that he will see these therapies perfected, enabling him to become immortal. Strangely enough, this hope has made its way into the twenty-first century[7].

The technocratic solution to necropolitics is one of transformation—an avoidance in which humans can at least pretend to be beyond death. This refusal, combined with a belief that the market and accelerated technological development will also provide protection from human misdeeds and public policy errors, allows questions over the environment to be avoided. STEM will take care of it. The world will be a better place the sooner it becomes a fully engineered and managed environment. CAE would prefer that madcap ideas about nanobots and uploading were all that survived of transhumanism, but unfortunately it is the transhumanist philosophy of solutionism that has continued to sustain its relevance. This is a position that lacks any regard for necropolitics in that it refuses to confront human finitude as a fundamental reality or to admit that mass extinction continues unabated and that the human species is among the contemporary contenders for this possibility of extermination. At the other end of the political spectrum, we can find a posthuman future that also thrives on acceleration. This vision rests on sustaining the current environment without humans or with minimal, decentred human presence in limited areas. As with the transhumanists, there is no language for necropolitics, so while mass death is often implied in this discourse, it is never directly addressed.

GREEN POSTHUMANS

The relationship between the conservationists, necropolitics and the posthuman became problematic in the United States as soon as the frontier ran out[8]. Once environmental resources went from abundant and free of cost to a zero-sum finite resource, preserving the wilds as parks and monuments became even more contested and difficult, but this original preservationist model continued in a manner that calls for posthuman environments. For example, take the *Deep Ecology Platform* (1984), written by two luminaries of the environmental movement, Arne Naess and George Sessions, as a condensation of fifteen years of environmentalist thinking:

1. *The well-being and flourishing of human and nonhuman life on earth have value in themselves (synonyms: inherent worth, intrinsic value, inherent value). These values are independent of the usefulness of the nonhuman world for human purposes.*
2. *Richness and diversity of life forms contribute to the realization of these values and are also values in themselves.*
3. *Humans have no right to reduce this richness and diversity except to satisfy vital needs.*
4. *Present human interference with the nonhuman world is excessive, and the situation is rapidly worsening.*
5. *The flourishing of human life and cultures is compatible with a substantial decrease of the human population. The flourishing of nonhuman life requires such a decrease.*
6. *Policies must therefore be changed. The changes in policies affect basic economic, technological and ideological structures. The resulting state of affairs will be deeply different from the present.*

7. *The ideological change is mainly that of appreciating life quality (dwelling in situations of inherent worth) rather than adhering to an increasingly higher standard of living. There will be a profound awareness of the difference between big and great.*
8. *Those who subscribe to the foregoing points have an obligation directly or indirectly to participate in the attempt to implement the necessary changes.*

CAE would think that anyone with a heart would enjoy the poetic elegance of these statements and sympathise with the affect they induce—but do they make sense? For us the text is problematic. We know that humans, in any concentrated form, have never been good for a healthy environment for humans or for most nonhuman creatures (with exceptions such as our microbiomes). Not since pre-agrarian social formations, and with a total of 250 million humans or fewer on the planet, have we, by accident of circumstance, not harmed the environment, which makes CAE a little worried when we read principle five.

CAE also has to ask, what is meant by 'well-being and flourishing?' Other than associating it with utility (which lends itself poorly to poetry), it appears that the reader is invited to project any meaning that suits his or her interests or desires. The same could be said for 'vital needs', which apparently give humans some necropolitical rights in regard to the treatment of the nonhuman. The fantasy engine of consciousness is invited to rev up and complete this open-ended text.

The next phrase, the declaration that human and nonhuman life have 'value in themselves', is also a problem. Values are hierarchical conceptual constructions produced by humans and shared by humans (or imposed on them). They are not objects waiting to be discovered.

'Diversity' is the next overaestheticised word within this manifesto. Diversity in *social* and *cultural* formations is certainly a characteristic to be desired, as it enriches human experience and opens new possibilities and potentials in those who participate in these diverse formations. But do we need an ecosystem that maximises diversity? The perspective necessary for the answer to be yes is an anthropocentric one (just as with culture). If the world were once again populated by nothing more than single-celled creatures, neither they nor the earth nor the universe would care one bit. Diversity in the natural world appears to CAE as an aesthetic and/or economic value. Because only humans care for economy and aesthetics, negative views of anthropocentrism (a spillover from science) need to be reconsidered. In other words, there is no *scientific* reason why biodiversity is valuable, as such judgements are beyond the limits of science. But soon we get to what this platform is really about: a substantial decrease in the human population, which is presented as an ideological adjustment rather than the massive material cataclysm that such an imperative would entail! How do you eliminate billions of people from the planet? Who has to kill their germline, and who gets to reproduce? Which cultures are eliminated? Does accepting these principles necessitate participation in econihilism? Various forms of econihilism such as that suggested here are becoming givens among radical environmentalists. The one element this drastic proposal does bring to light is that producing life and producing death—biopolitics[9] and necropolitics—are indivisible opposites. The real challenge lies in balancing the critique of the two. Currently, discourse is skewed towards biopolitics in both its negative and positive forms, while necropolitics remains rather neglected. After all, promoting life is so much easier than taking a stand on what should die and how death should be operationalised. Moreover, once necropolitics is more than just acknowledged but made visible, the company in which we find ourselves is quite unpleasant. Moving into active planning within the parameters of a zero-sum game puts a person at the table with Malthusians, Spencerians, colonialists, fascists, corporatists, developers of total war and, most worrisome of all in its unexpectedness, a variety of everyday bureaucrats, technocrats and policymakers just doing their jobs. If nothing else, CAE has to admire the courage of Naess and Sessions to say that humans are the problem and that we need to rid ourselves of as many as possible. Unfortunately, they do not have the courage to explain how we should do this. Other radical greens do, as we shall see—but they leave the tactical choices up to the revolutionaries involved.

In the earlier paragraphs, we met the first of the posthuman deep greens and their poetic musings on saving the environment. They set the tone for the belief that the human experiment has been an unfortunate development for the natural world. Humans need to drastically slow, if not halt, their reengineering of the planet and bring about a vast reduction of their numbers. As we shall see with later deep green radicals, this applies to attendant species as well. Domestic animals and plants, those that have thrown their evolutionary lot in with humans and are thus a part, however unwittingly, of the current 'biotic cleansing', are deserving of the same fate of rapid reduction if not elimination. Yet in all the present-day environmental discourse, death is never directly addressed. It is always only implied and left to be the elephant standing in the room. We can take the examples of moderate to centre-right environmentalist and biologist Edward O. Wilson and radical green thinker and activist Lierre Keith. CAE has tremendous respect for the work of both to the extent of considering them proven friends of environmental struggle. We are looking at their work here only to illustrate a problem that plagues the entire movement across its political continuum, and not as an individualised accusatory complaint. CAE is asking the question: What does an environmentalist necropolitics look like?

Because until one explicitly emerges, the movement is doomed, if for no other reason than an inability to even discuss achievable, strategic objectives.

In 2016, Wilson published *Half-Earth: Our Planet's Fight for Life*. In it, he paints a picture of what is at stake in the current environmental struggle by indicating what humans will lose and what we have already lost in regard to biodiversity. The book is a compelling figurative call to arms and describes the sense of alarm that people should feel regarding the current ecological crisis of mass extinction.

> The only hope for the species still living is a human effort commensurate with the magnitude of the problem. The ongoing mass extinction of species, and with it the extinction of genes and ecosystems, ranks with pandemics, world war, and climate change as among the deadliest threats that humanity has imposed on itself.

CAE could not agree more with this description. The problem is when Wilson gets to the solution, and the solution is hinted in the title of the book: half of the earth's lands and oceans should become a posthuman environment. One would think that the majority of the book would be an explanation of how this could be done without the employment of outright atrocity. That is not the case. Only a very small portion of the book is dedicated to how this will occur, and most of this portion is marked by an exhaustingly Pollyannaish optimism generally reserved for the transhumanists.

Wilson argues that the population problem will solve itself because future citizens will choose not to overreproduce. They will reproduce only their own numbers or fewer, or not at all. The facts that he presents to promote his position seem to undermine it, in CAE's reading. Yes, there has been a slight deceleration in population growth. And yes, the United States and Europe are at zero population growth. And yes, in countries in which women have greater economic and political power fertility has dropped. However, Wilson goes on to admit that population growth is not going to stop and that by the end of the century the population will be somewhere between 9.6 billion and 12.3 billion. On a planet already strapped for resources, once half of them are off limits, the population rate is indeed going to go down, but not because women are choosing to reproduce less—starvation, malnutrition, inadequate health care and conflict over limited resources will be more likely causes. Wilson also seems to think that most of the world's women will share in the power status of European and North American women by the end of the century, thus lowering the population growth even further. CAE fails to see any evidence to justify this belief, and, regardless, if the population problem is not solved, it does not seem that the extinction crisis will be either.

Wilson goes on to tell us that fewer resources will be needed because the free market guided by high technology will accelerate a shift from extensive economic growth to intensive economic growth. We will have an economy of quality over quantity in which twentieth-century conspicuous mass consumption will be shunned. Extrapolating from the text, the Wilsonian future will be in dense cities in which people stay in their luxury pods and connect, consume, do business and so on using ever-improving high technology. Fewer resources will be used and less pollution generated. GM crops will improve crop yields for abundant food. Apparently, humans will still go outside, as Wilson mentions in an offhand remark that anyone will be able to visit any reserve. This is odd because reserves require human intervention such as management and policing, meaning that half the earth would *not* be left in a posthuman condition.

Here we find ourselves back in league with the transhumanists. Solutionism has made its way into neoliberal environmental discourse, resulting in the great faith that the free market and technological fixes will save the planet, humans and the diversity of the natural world. Leaving aside the fact that the world described earlier sounds closer to a prison than a utopia to CAE, what of all the problems that technology and the free market cannot solve? Sure, they can give us faster computers at lower prices for better shopping, but can they stop natural disasters? Can they eliminate water shortages? Can they keep free market greed from destroying economies and facilitating depressions? Can they stop military adventurism? They have failed to do anything of the kind so far. Moreover, the assumption that the free market works best for all would seem to conflict with historical events. In fact, what the global free market has brought is a misery for the majority so vast that the philosopher of misery himself, Arthur Schopenhauer[10], would be shocked.

This kind of whitewashing of such a difficult problem is to be expected. After all, Wilson is writing a semi-popular book, the audience for which is not interested in chapters on land-use law and administration or resource management and conservation. At the same time, part of the reason for *Half Earth*'s poverty of language is the human tendency to pretend that necropolitics does not exist, short of ethnic cleansing or genocide. For example, U.S. congressional committees are considering repealing the Affordable Care Act[11]. Should they succeed, the result will be near or immediate death for tens of thousands and shorter life spans for those who are denied medical coverage (which will be in the millions). Congressional committees are essentially deciding who will live (wealthy people) and who will die (poor people), and doing so in a legitimised manner, as they were seemingly fairly elected to make such decisions, much to the surprise of a benighted electorate. The current necropolitical system, as reflected in this example of the bureaucratic order of death, is a Malthusian form in which excess populations are designated by implication and left to die through malevolent neglect. This is the form of necropolitics in which we are all implicated but can pretend that we are not. One reason the Malthusian form of necropolitics continues ever onwards is because it is the easiest to ignore. Unfortunately for many Americans, necropolitics has come out of its dark world and is demanding attention.

The radical answer to reform, education and market solutions that is latent in extremist environmental discourse is that civilisation must be destroyed. In the 2013 conference anthology *Earth at Risk: Building a Resistance Movement to Save the Planet*, Lierre Keith lays out a plan and gives her literal call to arms (Keith's and other conference lectures are available on YouTube). Keith appears certain about two principles. First, that any complex division of labour from agrarian society forward is devastating to the environment and hence unacceptable. (She gives agriculture a necropolitical name: 'biotic cleansing'.) Second, the current system of global neoliberalism will hit a crisis point and implode. Given these principles, she takes an accelerationist position and argues that eco-warriors everywhere should do whatever they can to hurry this implosion, which most significantly includes an asymmetrical war against civilisation. The endgame of this activity is to eliminate humans from large portions of the planet and reduce their numbers and capabilities so that humanity is returned to a sustainable hunter-gatherer form of community. The goals, in her own words, are:

> Part 1: To disrupt and dismantle industrial civilization; to thereby remove the ability of the rich to steal from the poor and the powerful to destroy the planet.
>
> Part 2: To defend and rebuild just, sustainable and autonomous human communities; and as part of that, to assist in the recovery of the land.

With regard to the first goal, Keith explains:

> We aim for coordinated, *multiple attacks* using surprise; what we are ultimately after is cascading systems failure.
>
> The point is not to make a statement. The point is to make a decisive material impact. In other words: we bring it down.

Keith advocates this type of military adventurism with true passion and seriousness. Her example of how such a plan is already being operationalised is the Movement for Emancipation of the Niger Delta (MEND). From 2006 to 2009, this native resistance movement attempted to expel Royal Dutch Shell, Chevron and Exxon from the Delta region and see the oil wealth divided among the region's people (despite an amnesty deal with the government, there continue to be flare-ups). However, it's very difficult to see how the area could be recuperated because it is so badly polluted that the ecosystem has crashed. These are experienced fighters who understand guerrilla tactics and strategy and have managed to make their enemies pay in blood and assets for their continued occupation of the region. They also have popular support in the area, which contributes to the success of their operations. Using this model of fighting, Keith hopes to attack high-value targets that will lead to maximum damage to the system. She is not thinking, like Earth Liberation Front, of attacking logging camps or universities. She wants to sabotage sites like power stations and water systems. Hers is a plan of major destruction. The plan seems to be to end civilisation through mass sabotage. She does not explicitly advocate killing people directly, although CAE does not see how that could be avoided given the targets that interest her. As CAE reads her, Keith believes that her movement would be popular enough to get a critical mass of above-ground support in the way of aid and good will, but at the same time knows that this will be a tiny portion of the population, and unlike with MEND, the overwhelming majority of the population will be against the activity.

Admittedly, CAE has never heard of something like this before in a secular context. Keith's plan is a milestone in necropolitics. It is biblical, an Antichrist level of death and destruction. To get to the magic hunter-gatherer number of less than 250 million, around seven billion people need to die. This makes Wilson's half-earth strategy look modest in its death toll (although they are both equally unlikely, which is to say not in the realm of possibility). CAE cannot even begin to imagine the kind of fanatical commitment to the aesthetic of biodiversity that could lead a person to stand before an audience and advocate creating an apocalypse that would kill almost every person now on the planet. As if this doctrine could not get more unfathomable, two other unusual points are thrown into the plan. First, Keith claims to want to facilitate this final solution out of love. Second, she is a utopian who believes that once the dust clears, the survivors, if any, will live in hunter-gatherer peace and harmony organised around a progressive identity politics and environmental stewardship. Given the current political climate of antiterrorism and the sophistication of contemporary surveillance and tracking, CAE cannot see a campaign like this lasting even as long as the Symbionese Liberation Army, Red Army Faction or Black Liberation Army. And we would not be the least bit surprised to see, if there were to be any planned mission, a preemptive strike by security forces. After all, if one is going to be a leader in the destruction of civilisation, it is probably best not to talk about it in public forums and publish books and videos about it.

Ideas on the posthuman are remarkable only in the level of fantasy they engage. Clearly they provide excellent fodder for science fiction, where they can provide hours of amusement, but as human strategy to solve problems in the world they are far less useful. What would be helpful, as CAE hopes this analysis shows, is an emergent necropolitics—a popular means to speak about death in an organised manner and in relation to policy. Such activities are happening among various bureaucrats and officials and, of course, the militaries of the world on a daily basis as they make decisions about who lives and dies, but no one else has legitimate claim to do so. For a common citizen to do so is to be at best callous and uncaring and at worst monstrous. Unfortunately, full-spectrum democracy is not possible without it, and how it emerges if neglected is in fantasies like the ones we have been examining in this essay. CAE believes it's time to pull necropolitics out of the abyss of the inhuman.

NOTES

1. Antihumanism was a late twentieth-century self-proclaimed designation for arts and humanities theorists who criticised the Enlightenment model of humanism for not recognizing the vast majority of people in the world as human. In this Enlightenment model, humans were implicitly, and at times explicitly, European and male.
2. CAE means this statement as Aristotle meant it. We are not referring to robots, androids or other learning-capable machines with social programming.
3. Cyborg supervillains like Dr. Doom and Dr. Octopus both have the goal of 'world domination' and will kill or destroy anything that stands in their path to this form of rulership.
4. Transhumanism is a movement that seeks to transcend physical and psychological limitations of human beings through technological means.
5. In the United States, accelerationism has become quite common on the right, even though it historically is a concept associated with left-wing entities typically on the periphery of Marxism. As of late, the accelerationist creed has been accepted by the extreme right—the so-called alt.right and the neoconservatives. The alt.right notion of the deconstruction of the administrative state is a kamikaze mission to eliminate as many bureaucracies as can be eliminated and to push the rest into dysfunction. The sooner this happens, the sooner the next chapter of American history can be birthed. The neocons, on the other hand, used accelerationism as a strategy for mission management. This is what they did in Iraq—accelerated the crisis in the hope that as more and more states and actors were pulled into the conflict, and as more and more interests became compromised, something would have to give (as with left accelerationists, what will 'give' is never stated because it is an unknown). In the case of the Iraq war, this unknown moment was ostensibly when meaningful negotiations or total war would happen and a new Middle East would be created.

6. Given the transhumanists' libertarian biases, they view one's flesh as personal property. Property should be unregulated by government, and said owners should be able to do as they please with it. If people want to modify their bodies in any way, for ornamental or utilitarian reasons, even at the genetic or molecular levels, they have the *right* to do so. Further, they believe that the ability to produce such modifications is in the near future. This is one reason why morphological freedom and reproductive freedom have been defended by transhumanists as civil liberties.

7. When confronted with the problem of population in regard to immortality, de Grey dodges it by saying that population policy will adjust to the new development—an odd position for a transhumanist, as that would mean the regulation of reproduction.

8. In the United States, early understanding of land use emerged out of Lockean social and political philosophy. Given that the nation was then a frontier country, it embraced an aggressive policy in regard to 'wilderness'. Wilderness had a negative connotation. It was similar to waste. God demanded that his divine work be completed by human labour in order to bring forth its true value and potential. In practicality, this meant that all land should be exploited to the maximum extent. During a time of frontier abundance in the eighteenth and nineteenth centuries, this notion made sense, but as quality land and other resources began to be in shorter supply, this type of land use led to environmental disaster. In 1864, George Perkins Marsh (1801–1882) published an influential book, *Man and Nature*, that contained an early conception of environmental sustainability. In it, he argued that the conservation of resources allowed for greater value to be extracted from them by taking smaller amounts over a longer period of time. In other words, the beginning of an economic argument for environmentalism was introduced into the public sphere. This was followed by John Muir's (1838–1914) aesthetic argument for the preservation of scenic wilderness (thought of in a romantic sense). And in turn, this was the beginning of a radical and bitter split between the Lockean libertarians, who wanted to keep frontier land-use policies, and those who embraced the new economic and aesthetic arguments. This split directly impacts the necropolitics of environmental management on every level to this day.

9. When CAE uses the term 'biopolitics', our tendency is to use it in light of Michael Hardt and Antonio Negri's use. For CAE, both biopolitics and necropolitics can lead to just forms of social, economic and environmental management and administration. We realise that this notion is aspirational and a poor description of what has happened historically; we do not believe that humans are locked into apocalypse or dystopia.

10. Arthur Schopenhauer was an early nineteenth-century German Idealist philosopher who is known as the father of pessimistic philosophy. His major work *The World as Will and Representation*, translated by E. F. J. Payne (New York: Dover, 1969), chronicled physiological, psychological and sociological reasons for the sufferings of humankind, which he believed to be representative of existence and, for the most part, inescapable.

11. The Affordable Care Act was President Obama's key legislative act and a major step in the progressive attempt to see that all U.S. residents have health insurance and

access to healthcare. It contains a mandate for everyone to buy health insurance with government support in the form of subsidies and an expansion of the government-run program Medicaid, for those who cannot afford insurance.

BIBLIOGRAPHY

Jensen, Derrick, and Lierre Keith, eds. *Building a Resistance Movement to Save the Planet*. Crescent City, CA: Flashpoint Press, 2012.

Perkins Marsh, George. *Man and Nature: Or, Physical Geography as Modified by Human Action*. 1864; UK: Andesite Press, 2015.

Naess, Arne, and George Sessions. 'The Deep Ecology Platform', 1984, http://www.deepecology.org/platform.htm.

Wilson, Edward O. *Half-Earth: Our Planet's Fight for Life*. New York: Liveright, 2016.

Chapter Eight

Dirty Your Media

Artists' Experiments in Digital Bio-Sovereignty

Tiffany Funk

On December 14, 2017, the U.S. Federal Communications Commission (FCC), an independent agency of the U.S. government regulating national communications by radio, television, satellite and cable, voted on the 'Restoring Internet Freedom Order', a rule concerning the reclassification of broadband Internet access as a telecommunications service[1]. Despite overwhelming public and bipartisan support for the regulation and many last-minute requests to delay the vote, the FCC voted to repeal Title II protection for net neutrality. Title II, a decades-old regulatory clause that explicitly classified Internet service providers (ISPs) as telecommunications companies, had previously maintained that Internet access was governed by the same regulatory standards as utilities; ISPs *could not* discriminate by user, website, platform, application or content by intentionally slowing, blocking or charging fees for access to online content. The repeal of Title II abdicates the FCC's authority to regulate Internet service providers, significantly curtailing oversight of U.S. broadband access[2]. Though its mandated jurisdiction covers the United States and its territories, the U.S. FCC also provides varied degrees of cooperation, oversight and leadership for similar communication bodies in other countries of North America; furthermore, if the Title II repeal is left unchallenged, it will not only fundamentally alter how people access and use the internet in the United States, it will also deeply influence the progress of Internet regulations in developing countries, promoting isolationism and marginalisation of already disenfranchised populations. Most alarmingly, it will incentivise ignoble political and economic practices by global telecommunications companies.

Amongst these concerns is the accelerated aggregation of user data by telecommunications companies, particularly given recent events revealing global infringements on data privacy. While there is no single agreed-upon event that led to mass awareness of data security, a confluence of incidents in the early 2010s have led to a sharp increase in public anxiety over the security of private data, culminating in the 2013 reveal of global surveillance programmes sponsored by the U.S. National Security Administration (NSA) and the Five Eyes intelligence alliance (FVEY), in cooperation with global telecommunications companies and worldwide government administrations. When former CIA employee and government contractor Edward Snowden leaked these documents to *The Guardian* in June 2013, the exposure set off worldwide insecurities about data, particularly concerning how governments and corporate entities exploit data to dictate how we live and die. Even before the Snowden incident, many artists and activists working in the abstraction, encryption, destruction and obfuscation of data recognised the profound connections between surveillance, privacy and autonomy. The exploitation of personal data is an exceptionally invasive form of necropower that *automates* violence toward already marginalised bodies; through a merging of biopolitics and psychopolitical practices, bodies are subjugated through the design of algorithms that normalise invasive forms of data surveillance and transform all aspects of user identity into data and emotional capital.

Artists and activists recognising these pervasive and malicious methods used in gathering our personal information practice data resistance by *dirtying their media*: subverting, disrupting, camouflaging and destroying data to evade or expose the algorithms involved in datamining. These practices expose the violence perpetuated by proprietary algorithms through methods informed by historical modes of resistance: artists and activists practicing glitch aesthetics disrupt the hegemonic systems that produce and are reproduced by technological convention through practices informed by the indeterminate performances of John Cage; activists practicing data camouflaging obfuscation methods recall the radical *détournement* techniques of the Paris Situationists and culture-jammers by turning media against itself. Even when artist/activist methods perform the violence of data destruction, the act of dirtying media inscribes ethical values in their methods through prioritising the exposure of the denigration perpetrated by automated, data-driven necropolitical practices. The aesthetics of these radical forms of digital bio-sovereignty—many arising from the collaborative spaces of alternative economic networks—trace a path from the low-fi and lossy to the bent and broken, obfuscating, glitching, jamming and annihilating data in a new kind of radical social practice.

BIG DATA IN PSYCHOPOLITICS AND BIOMETRICS

In his 2003 essay 'Necropolitics', Achille Mbembe claims contemporary governance maintains authority not only through regulating life but also through regulating and ensuring death to 'undesirable' populations. By offering a reading of biopolitics from a Global South perspective, he advances an alternative to the discourse of modernity that relies on reason as truth, turning to 'other foundational categories that are less abstract and more tactile, such as life and death'[3]. The transformation of the tactile categories of life and death into aggregable data also reflects the increasingly pervasive neoliberal capitalist acceleration of psychological exploitation. Byung-Chul Han observes that technological domination currently thrives through the practice of psychopolitics; the participatory surveillance demanded by social media platforms necessarily 'means stripping people of interiority' because interiority 'blocks and slows down communication'[4]. The acceleration of communication networks binds consumers to 'voluntary self-organisation', the gamification of work, and an unwitting abandonment of free will, which is then transformed into emotional capital[5].

The transformation of the psyche into vast amounts of raw data has led to the rapid acceleration in creating new means of organising and interpreting information. As observed by technology and social media researchers Kate Crawford and danah boyd in their article 'Critical Questions for Big Data', these methods have fundamentally altered the way we interpret knowledge and objectivity; as big data remains meaningless without the mediation of algorithms to search, share, query, transfer and interpret it, the market has rushed in to exploit its manipulability despite the mythos of objectivity it maintains[6]. As mathematician Cathy O'Neil observes, the 'data economy' is particularly vulnerable to the implementation of algorithms that *encode* prejudices and biases; though designing predictive algorithms is justified as producing rational outcomes, the interpretive methods of data scientists can result in the repetition of past discrimination and produce destructive feedback loops that remain largely invisible to the public they impact[7]. O'Neil's name for these damaging algorithms—'Weapons of Math Destruction', or WMDs—are often the product of outsourcing to private technology companies, employed by overstrapped government agencies without any oversight regarding how they regulate local and global infrastructures that dictate the lives and deaths of populations. For example, as observed by O'Neil and further explored by mathematicians Faisal Kamiran and Toon Calders, proprietary algorithms routinely calculate recidivism risks based on data skewed by discriminatory policing methods and other factors of longstanding racial discrimination in the U.S. justice system; these algorithms directly contribute to the ongoing crisis of mass incarceration of black populations in the United States[8]. WMDs such as these perpetuate inequities and violence worldwide even as they are cloaked in the language of science and reason.

Nowhere is this more evident and pervasively employed than in the realm of biometrics. In her *Governing through Biometrics: The Biopolitics of*

Identity, Btihaj Ajana applies the mediation taking place to the very bodies that populate the system: 'what concerns me primarily is how forms of identity, citizenship and belonging, and how modes of identification, are increasingly being redefined and reconfigured in the name of risk and security, and made amenable to various modes of securitisation and control through technology'[9]. Bodies are not only identified by the processing of biometric data but fundamentally *transformed* as either 'neoliberal citizens' or 'asylum seekers' dependent on how their data is mediated. For example, personal health care information is increasingly available through the use of electronic health records (EHRs). However, the data presently remains largely unstructured and difficult to interpret. Currently, data scientists/machine learning technicians are tasked with developing and implementing algorithms meant to aid health care facilities to improve quality and maximise efficiency[10]. As observed by artist and theorist micha cárdenas, the practice of 'medical surveillance' that provides EHR data is often especially precarious for vulnerable populations; she states, 'physical bodies in the contemporary world are tracked through networks, biometrically analysed and electronically surveilled, and often the result of these forms of observation is violence'[11]. Algorithms applied to health care may not only predict what kinds of care are provided to certain individuals—*who* receives care, *how* that care is administered and *where*—but also dictate their identity as measured by biometric health data, whether it's by gender or specific illness or disorder (HIV-positive, breast cancer survivor, autistic, etc.). For example, cárdenas's hybrid poetry/bioart project *Pregnancy* presents a vision of trans Latina reproductive futures based on her own experiences of cryogenic tissue banking after having been on hormones. The work forms a response to Morgan Robyn Collado's statements at the 2014 Civil Liberties and Public Policy Conference regarding how violence against trans women of colour becomes a reproductive issue as they are prevented from living long enough to have children[12]. Her 2011 performance *virus.circus.laboratory*, a collaboration with Elle Mehrmand, explores speculative futures involving do-it-yourself (DIY) medicine and virus hysteria to reflect on the history of HIV and its impact on the medicalisation of queer culture[13]. cárdenas's plea for the visibility of transgender women and queer HIV-positive identities as more than medicalised gender or diseased bodies reflects on how the violence endemic in medical history is undoubtedly inscribed in our futures; as predictive algorithms used in health care have the ability to fundamentally *restructure* the lives of disenfranchised populations, it is necessary to resist those feedback loops that continue to marginalise and neglect those labelled 'undesirable'.

ALTERNATIVE ECONOMIES

How can we enact the possibility of digital bio-sovereignty, and where can we develop effective networks outside of neoliberal capitalist models to learn techniques in dirtying media? A number of artists and activists have taken the approach of hybrid theory/practice methods, emphasising collaborative approaches to what, without exaggeration, should be called survival. micha cárdenas's project *find each other: local autonomy networks/autonets* is one such project: as her practice concerns preventing violence so often committed on targeted bodies, cárdenas's *Local Autonomy Networks (Autonets)* creates autonomous communication networks to reduce violence against women, LGBTQI people and people of colour. The Autonet unit began as a handmade, networked, wearable prototype, constructed with conductive thread and wireless transmitters. Each autonomous Autonet unit feeds into a mesh network that, when activated, alerts everyone in range who is wearing another Autonet garment that someone needs help and indicates that person's direction and distance[14]. Each *find each other: local autonomy networks/ autonets* event functions as the performative realisation of the local autonomy network; workshops and performances of *find each other* have been enacted around the world, involving trans and gender nonconforming people of colour, sex workers, artists and students in Los Angeles, São Paulo, San Jose, Toronto and Detroit[15].

Find each other: local autonomy networks/autonets provides one example of the methods employed by the growing movement of alternative economies, economic networks based on a collaborative, socially oriented model. These community-based alternative economies necessarily 1) function independently of the dominant, neoliberal capitalist model; 2) reorient the concept of transaction to multiple ways in which exchange can be negotiated, replacing formal market transactions with alternative markets in which considerations other than supply and demand influence the terms of exchange[16]; and 3) provide physical spaces of exchange, education, collaboration and safety[17]. As artists/activists are increasingly enmeshed in social practice methods that include the development of digital bio-sovereignty networks, alternative economic strategies provide fuel and safety for marginalised bodies that benefit most from these collaborative environments. For example, *find each other* combats violence through providing an alternative to corporate infrastructure. As LGBTQI people and people of colour—interconnected communities cárdenas calls 'trans of color' to emphasise the experiences of individuals who are trans and gender nonconforming people of colour—are often the victims of abuses perpetrated by both local and federal law enforcement, the prison-industrial complex or corporations, safety can only be enacted through *independent networks* designed by and for targeted populations. By emphasising the importance of maker-centric alternatives to the neoliberal capitalist model, alternative economies can function as trade-based economies relying on work exchange and skill sharing. *find each other* reframes the concept of the transaction to include collaborative and pedagogical workshops that empower individuals through art and design. Rather than functioning as a commodity, the Autonet is produced through workshops focusing on DIY skills that in turn develop safety networks. These alternative production spaces create empowerment through providing physical spaces of safety and also agency through awareness of the individual's role as cultural labour producer[18]. Rather than remain passive participants in the dominant capitalist market, these spaces have spawned related artist/activist communities that forgo commodity markets for economies fuelled by ethical action.

GLITCH AND DIRTY NEW MEDIA

These kinds of alternative economic spaces have spawned a number of art movements, particularly those based on the DIY methods first popularised by the punk and hacker communities of the 1970s and 1980s. For example, those involved in the glitch and 'Dirty New Media' movement use programming as a platform for radical performance art, relying on alternative economic spaces for collaborative hacking workshops and performances. The international GLI.TC/H conference and festival, held in Chicago in 2010, 2011 and 2012, celebrated all varieties of radical software and hardware intervention. The 2011 event's accompanying text, *GLI.TC/H 20111 READER[R0R]*, features articles and manifestos by artists who interrogate technological systems 'to examine the politics embedded in technological systems, to create digital psychedelic and/or synesthetic experiences, to practice hacktivism, to explore themes of failure, chance, memory, nostalgia, entropy, etc.'[19]. Similar glitch practices and glitch art events, screenings, and festivals continue to take place in numerous cities and online venues throughout the world, including exhibitions such as the Bring Your Own Beamer (BYOB), first organised by Anne de Vries and Rafaël Rozendaal in Berlin in 2010, and the various circuit-bending workshops sponsored by organisations like the V2 Institute for the Unstable Media in Rotterdam, the now defunct Free Art and Technology (F.A.T.) Lab, and the Eyebeam Art and Technology Center in New York. Artists like Rosa Menkman, Legacy Russell, Jon Satrom and jonCates use programming, data and circuit bending toward radical performance art methods, employing their knowledge of programming to interrogate and subvert proprietary software production through diverse methods of computational intervention. Alongside its commitment to media archaeological methods, glitch performances are heavily couched in art historical references and (political) aesthetics. The act of experimentally revising and corrupting technology lends much to early video and conceptual art of the 1970s, particularly the work of artist and activist Phil Morton[20]. However, glitch and Dirty New Media performances also pay homage to the experimental music performances and compositional practices of the mid-twentieth century and the legacy of indeterminacy. For example, Jon Satrom's prepared desktop real-time performances, such as his series *100 Force Quit Noise Cancel Calculators* (2013) and *Plugin Beachball Success* (2012), bear the mark of John Cage's 'prepared piano' pieces wherein Cage inserted screws, nuts and bolts and a variety of other objects between the strings of a piano to replicate nonpiano sounds. Satrom's prepared laptop instead places criticism squarely on the *personal computing paradigm*. He performs solo with his laptop, its display mirrored with the digital projection viewable by the audience. He begins with a fake-out: he struggles to access the desktop from the login window, tries to install a plugin and fails repeatedly, culminating in a choreography of download windows, errors and dissonant sonic feedback echo and blend into one another[21]. Satrom's broken workflow, morphing into stacking, choreographed feedback loops, place clear emphasis on the vulnerabilities of data systems.

The many references to Cage are not merely frivolous, art historical in-jokes but studied aesthetic choices based on his concept of indeterminacy, process-based aesthetics and dematerialisation. He freed performance from the suppositions of rigid musicianship to involve the spectator and the everyday object, revelling in the notion that even silence is always filled with sound. Just as Cage popularised the concept of chance operations, the process of glitching or 'dirtying media' relies on chance. Cage's *4'33"*, first performed by David Tudor in 1953 in Woodstock, New York, couched the performance in the expected tropes of music performance: Tudor sat at a piano, opened its lid to signal the beginning of each movement and closing it to mark its ending. Any sound that occurred within that time frame became part of the performance[22]. Cage's *Variations VII* performance with E.A.T. 9 Evenings: Theatre and Engineering (1966) bears even more relevance to glitch, if only for the frenetic energy and impenetrability of the once familiar technologies transformed through performance; for example, during his *Variations VII* performance, Cage's rapt focus on manipulating the photocells that triggered whines and bleats from the hacked consumer-grade transistor radios distracted him from the fact that his tie had caught fire from an unprotected soldered connection[23].

Similarly, jonCates manipulates electronic equipment that produces effects fluctuating between chaos and order. He constructs multimedia performances that reference current DJ and VJ culture but also pays homage to earlier Cage works such as *Water Walk* (1959) and *Variations VII* (1966)[24]. Cates references Cage's influence not only in the profusion of equipment he manipulates but also in his intention of creating a meditative experience through noise abundance. In his *ERRORRUNNINGWWWATERNOISES* (2012), Cates creates a droning audio feedback loop on a sound mixer and tends to stacks of audio-visual equipment as he is recorded by a black-and-white security camera feed. The quality of the droning sound and his poetic monologue delivery into a feedback-prone microphone also evoke Cage in their meditative quality, his voice fading in and out of the feedback. But the work also constitutes a significant update of Cage for the digital era. Cates wrote of the performance,

> as Douglas Kahn says in his *Noise, Water, Meat*: 'Water flowed in the arts prior to midcentury, of course' + by this he means not our century but the century before ours 'but it was restricted almost entirely to programmatic, depicted, or discursive water: water music, water scenes, water talk'. i want to make this a realtime water talk, flowing in datastreams of mountainfalls
> if almost a memory already
> . . .
> waterfall
> waterflow.[25]

Cates recognises that to reflect digital data flows, contemporary performances have to reflect immediacy, functioning as real-time processes. This focus on immediacy replicates the acceleration of technological adoption so embedded into neoliberal capitalist markets; glitch and Dirty New Media communities are nothing if not cognisant of how aesthetic is so quickly reified and reinscribed into these dominant market systems. As the glitch aesthetic has rapidly appeared on Adidas's shoe designs and Speedo board shorts, glitch artists continue to produce work critiquing these systems[26]. In tandem with the M0N3Y AS AN 3RRROR exhibition curated by Vasily Zaitsev, jonCates sold bodycon one-pieces with glitched prints to explore 'why . . . Glitch Art [became] profitable and for whom' and how this 'expanded concept of glitch' can still functions as radical performance[27]. While so much of glitch is identified through the aesthetics of digital error—broken pixels, lossy and jagged media, dissonant noise—the movement fundamentally disrupts media in an effort to reflect disruption of the more fundamental, hegemonic systems that produce, and are reproduced by, technological convention. Glitch artist and theorist Rosa Menkman explains, 'the art works within this realm can be disturbing, provoking and horrifying. . . . These works stretch boundaries and generate novel modes; they break open previously sealed politics and force a catharsis of conventions, norms and believes [*sic*]'[28]. Of these norms, Menkman is particularly interested in piercing the myth that glitches pertain only to digital media; her media-archaeological practice involves outdated technologies, both analogue and digital. Her live audio-visual performance *The Collapse of PAL* (2011) pays tribute to the end of the analogue video coding system Phase Alternating Line (PAL). The glitches and feedback resulting from the PAL compression are coupled with an astounding variety of both analogue and digital artefacts and methods, including a Nintendo Entertainment System, digital photo cameras, Casio keyboards, European telephone signals and Morse code[29]. *The Collapse of PAL* explores the struggle for agency, relevance and visibility through frequent characterisation of the corroded, outdated PAL signal as a slowly, painfully dying *female* presence, as her own face is often violently distorted in real time during live performance. Menkman emphasises the deep embeddedness of culture within material as a means of expression, and it is difficult to ignore how patriarchal values are so embedded within the histories of our current media technologies.

Artist and curator Legacy Russell emphasises how forcing malfunctions to create glitches exemplifies an agency so often unavailable to media users; employing the error as a radical performance act is 'breaking from the hegemony of a "structured system" infused with the pomp and circumstance of patriarchy'[30]. Her research and artistic practice of Glitch Feminism (#GLITCHFEMINISM) aims to turn the focus of glitch from technological systems to our digitally embedded social systems. Russell's 'Digital Dualism and The Glitch Feminism Manifesto' describes an artistic, activist practice in which she

> embraces the causality of 'error', and turns the gloomy implication of glitch on its ear by acknowledging that an error in a social system that has already been disturbed by economic, racial, social, sexual, and cultural stratification and the imperialist wrecking-ball of globalization—processes that continue to enact violence on all bodies—may not, in fact, be an error at all, but rather a much-needed erratum.[31]

Russell emphasises the ways in which hegemonic structures homogenise communication in the interest of user-friendliness, acceleration and automatisation; despite deep frustration with how these homogeneous platforms restrict communication, perpetuate biases and normalise surveillance, Russell recognises the impossibility of breaking free from these systems in everyday life. In her performative essay '10 Things the NSA Has Seen Me Do', Russell lists ten instances of celebration and vulnerability that would fit within the normal experiences of any young adult, from streaking down 5th Avenue in

Manhattan after the election of Barack Obama to the U.S. presidency, posing for 'effortless' selfies in Apple's PhotoBooth application, enjoying a relaxed dinner gathering and impromptu dance off to hosting a raucous, punk rooftop party. However, Russell recounts how each of these private and public moments could easily be subject to the one-sided data gathering methods of government organisations such as the NSA and FVEY through the accidental and intentional actions of the user:

> Ever tried to cut your own hair using a YouTube video as an instructor? Tried to private message someone on Twitter and instead put yourself on blast to the world beyond? Sent a text about someone else to that person—or texted someone you positively abhor accidentally—simply because you neglected to pay attention to the task at hand? Yeah, NSA, during those moments you could have intervened and thrown me a bone. You could have said something—anything, anything at all.
>
> NSA—thanks for positively nothing.[32]

OBFUSCATION AND CAMOUFLAGE

Whereas glitch demonstrates the circuitous, reflexive flow of one's personal relationship with technology and relationship to accelerationism, contemporary social practice movements emphasise the production and distribution of digital tools for the purpose of promoting and practicing data sovereignty. The 'obfuscation movement', coined by philosopher and activist Helen Nissenbaum, camouflages data by designing and employing programs and plugins. In Nissenbaum and Finn Brunton's text *Obfuscation: A User's Guide for Privacy and Protest*, they describe obfuscation as a kind of data camouflage:

> The production of noise modelled on an existing signal in order to make a collection of data more ambiguous, confusing, harder to exploit, more difficult to act on, and therefore less valuable. . . . Camouflage, whether seeking the complete invisibility of mimicry or the temporary solution of hiding a shape in a mess of other, ambiguous, obfuscating possible shapes, was always a reflection of the capabilities of the technology against which it was developed.[33]

Obfuscation, rather than encryption (blocking or shielding one's data from detection), means enabling privacy by using the method of data aggregation against itself. For example, Nissenbaum, Daniel C. Howe and Vincent Toubiana's browser extension TrackMeNot runs a low-priority background process that sends randomly generated search queries to search engines. TrackMeNot overwhelms search engines with a wealth of data, thus obfuscating user information from corporate policies enacting the collection of personal data. Nissenbaum states, 'we have developed TrackMeNot as an immediate solution, implemented and controlled by users themselves. It fits within the class of strategies, described by Gary T. Marx, whereby individuals resist surveillance by taking advantage of blind spots inherent in large-scale systems. TrackMeNot may not radically alter the privacy landscape but helps to place a particularly sensitive arena of contemporary life back in the hands of individuals, where it belongs in any free society'[34]. Similarly, the browser extension AdNauseum automates ad clicks on each visited webpage, camouflaging meaningful user data from advertisers[35]. Both TrackMeNot and AdNauseum function by blending seamlessly within a sea of already-available free browser extensions. They are meant to be easy to use but also serve as a power balance corrective. Nissenbaum writes,

> AdNauseam joins a broader class of technical systems that attempt to serve ethical, political, and expressive ends. In light of the industry's failure to self-regulate or otherwise address the excesses of network tracking, AdNauseam allows individual users to take matters into their own hands, fighting back against unilateral surveillance. Taken in this light, the software follows an approach similar to that of TrackMeNot, employing obfuscation as a strategy to shift the balance of power between the trackers and the tracked.[36]

Nissenbaum's obfuscation movement borrows from a long history of performative *détournement*, and later, 1980s culture-jamming, meant to subvert mainstream cultural institutions through 'rerouting' or 'hijacking' their means of communication. The Situationist Internationale, active globally from 1957 to 1972, involved a number of artists and intellectuals interested in revolutionary artistic practices, predominantly through experimental methods like psychogeography and hypergraphics[37]. Situationist Guy Debord's *The Society of the Spectacle* drew on a number of antecedents, amongst them earlier twentieth-century art movements such as Dadaism and Surrealism, the philosophies of Georg Hegel and George Lukacs and the anti-authoritarian Marxist theories of social alienation and commodity fetishism. The Situationist method of advancing *détournement* as a necessary critique of advanced capitalism asserts agency through subverting images such as advertisements and political propaganda. The practice of *détournement*—a French term meaning both 'reversal' and 'diversion'—served to tactically deface, reproduce and remix material to create self-reflexive, recontextualised activist media. The practice had many related art historical influences, from agit-prop Weimar collages to early conceptual art practices. The most obvious guide was Marcel Duchamp's readymade sculptures, such as his infamous *Fountain* (1917): a readymade urinal most often recognized as the *Ur*-conceptual art sculpture poked fun at the deification of art and artist while reinscribing the artists' power to alter and manipulate meaning. As the anti-commodity fetishism focus of Situationist *détournement* was its most vital component, examples such as Hannah Höch's iconic photomontage *Cut with the Kitchen Knife Dada through the Last Weimar Beer-Belly Cultural Epoch in Germany* (1919) provided an especially relevant template: it *détourned* advertisements by chaotically collaging images into startling political satire, skewering both the failed attempt at democracy imposed by the Weimar Republic and the restrictive confines of patriarchal society. Debord asserted that *détournement* disrupted corporate, commercial media by negating the ideological conditions of artistic production, as all artworks ultimately become commodities but also produce politically educative material. This could be done through adding details to existing works, thus revealing an obscured ambiguity in its message, or collage many previous works to create new and surprising juxtapositions[38].

There exists a tendency to attribute to Debord predictions of the current Internet-based society (he defined the *spectacle* as 'a social relation among people, mediated by images') and the normalisation of the Global War on Terrorism ('The story of terrorism is written by the state and it is therefore highly instructive . . . compared with terrorism, everything else must be acceptable, or in any case more rational and democratic')[39]. However, his claims of the power of the spectacle and terrorism came from his own timely sources: the acceleration of communication ushered in by the proliferation of newspapers and cinema, the early- and mid-century mobilisation of media for propaganda, as well as how these provided pervasive methods for the governments of Soviet Russia and Maoist China to maintain control of their populations. The spectacle of Debord denoted lived experience and authentic desire fulfilment, giving way to individual expression by proxy through the exchange or consumption of commodities. The current psychopolitical turn ushered in by digital media forms an accelerated, extensive spectacle that permeates not only our consumption of media but also our very free will; the societal terrorism of Debord has transformed into an internal struggle in which we are conditioned to no longer trust our own instincts.

This transformation is reflected in the evolution of tactical media strategies employed by counterculture communities; while the anti-capitalist, activist practices of the Situationists greatly influenced the aesthetic of anarchist, communist, punk, and hacker communities from the 1970s to the present, the techniques they employ have continued to evolve. The related technique of *culture-jamming*, greatly popularised by the anti-advertising methods of the Adbusters Media Foundation and its global network of social activists, further promoted guerrilla tactics attempting to, according to the Adbusters manifesto, 'pull off a radical transformation of the current world order'[40]. While early culture-jamming methods included the satirical refiguring of corporate logos and product images, more recent digital culture-jamming obfuscation lives predominantly as user-uploaded videos on social media platforms: users perpetuate memes meant to transform and abstract popular—or infamous—media, ultimately weaponising social media tools to subvert or disrupt mainstream cultural and corporate institutions.

Just as the meme-ification of corporate and political media shields individual users through spontaneous crowdsourcing, obfuscation also depends largely on shifting agency from outside hegemonic forces to users by giving them the choice between invisibility but also *radical visibility*, in which collaborators shield their identities by creating a highly conspicuous but camouflaged presence. Knowbotic Research, a collective comprising of Yvonne Wilhelm, Christian Huebler and Alexander Tuchacek, devised various performances in which actors dressed in a camouflage costumes—called 'Ghillie Suits'—are situated in urban settings (*macghillie_just a void*, 2010). While the Ghillie Suit originated in the nineteenth century as a mobile, wearable hunting blind, its usage became popularised during World War I. Knowbotic Research *détournes* the suit to interrogate modes of subjectivity and identity:

> Its camouflage effects the anonymisation and the neutralisation of the person who wears it in public. macghillie, a -prefer not to- figur [*sic*], an actor without idenity [*sic*], transforming past and future into here and now, oscillating between the hyperpresence of a mask, and visual redundancy. It traverses the modern urban environment in which conspicuity holds ambivalent currency, wavering between cumbersome affirmation and visual arbitrariness. It is a variation of types like 'Bloom', 'Bartleby', or the 'man without qualities', which have transgressed their original literary existence and have become the tropes of philosophical debates around the postmodern politics of subjectivity.[41]

Art historian and curator Andreas Broeckmann situates this oscillation between 'public visibility and strategic camouflage' as *opaque presence*: just as 'transparency is no longer a sign of democratic openness, but rather one of administrative availability', the mask wearer is conspicuous yet anonymous[42]. Other camouflaging tactics concentrate on disrupting surveillance methods through various forms of appearance modification[43]. Artist Adam Harvey seeks to disrupt the violence perpetuated by biometric surveillance systems by blocking algorithmic detection entirely. Harvey's project CV Dazzle *détournes* the aesthetic of avant-garde fashion and makeup by combining it with World War I geometric 'dazzle' camouflage patterns to escape biometric detection. He analysed the Viola-Jones algorithm used for the popular

OpenCV face detection system in order to design 'anti-face' methods for avoiding being recognised by biometric surveillance monitors[44]. Performers apply bright, geometric makeup swatches, rhinestones and hairpieces to break up the algorithmic detection of facial signifiers like the bridge of the nose, symmetry of the eyes, and ovular facial shape. Though the combination of costuming, hairstyling and makeup application is startlingly conspicuous to humans, Harvey instructs anti-face activists that algorithms such as the Viola-Jones biometric scanning method 'expect[s] symmetry between the left and right sides of the face' and 'analyse[s] gradations in skin tone and texture' to differentiate faces from noise[45]. The biopolitical resistance performed is both conceptual and practical; while the facial data the CV Dazzle method creates is dirtied to the point of digital unrecognisability, the user maintains a radical visibility that signifies protest and resistance.

Opaque presence and urban camouflage reflect the lived realities of victimised populations within digital surveillance networks that function using facial recognition software. For example, despite protests from civil liberties organisations, London's Metropolitan Police deployed real-time biometric tracking at the November 12, 2017, World War I Remembrance Event, thought to be attended by 10,000 former and current service personnel, foreign dignitaries, as well as members of the public[46]. Biometric surveillance systems are frequently used in the workforce to discourage overtime fraud, and credit card companies are currently testing the use of biometric data for identity authorisation. More pervasive still is the regular use of biometric data by U.S. police forces to provide 'virtual line-ups' of perpetrators; the Georgetown Law Center on Privacy and Technology reports that unrestricted facial recognition monitoring by American law enforcement is widespread, despite very real concern regarding the accuracy of such software when analysing diverse racial groups. As explained previously, micha cárdenas's thesis regarding trans of colour poetics focuses on the kinds of visibility offered to victimised populations; while trans people become visible targets for violence, they remain invisible in discussions of protection and sovereignty. Regarding glitch practice and aesthetics, Legacy Russell's curatorial efforts interrogate cultural assumptions about agency and digital media by exploiting the parallels between digital glitches and glitches in hegemonic systems, exploring how they are continuously enacted through cultural, economic, racial, social and sexual means; her recent exhibition 'WANDERING/WILDING: BLACKNESS ON THE INTERNET' interrogates the dichotomies of white/black, *flâneur*/loiterer, safe/endangered to investigate how the transformation of bodies of colour from real to virtual either enacts agency or replicates the errors encoded in social, cultural and political systems[47].

ACTIVIST DESTRUCTION

Perhaps the most fittingly necropolitical activism is that of annihilation; as necropolitics dictate how we live and die, the ultimate *détournement* would be to destroy all personal data as a form of absolute resistance. Though total digital annihilation may be impossible, it is practical to identify how precautions can be taken to effectively limit leaks in private data. Are we truly concerned about the security of our personal data and the implications of its misuse, or is our compliance with these aggregative systems a signal of passive acceptance? If we don't actively refrain from sharing our data or take control through effectively purging or destroying private, sensitive materials, are we culpable in its lack of security? As Nissenbaum posits in her study 'Measuring Privacy: An Empirical Test Using Context to Expose Confounding Variables', respondents express their concern regarding the security of their data but regularly act against their best interests:

> Yet when confronted with actual choices involving the capture or exchange of information few people demonstrate restraint: but when confronted with actual choices involving the capture or exchange of information few people demonstrate restraint: we sign up for frequent flyer and frequent buyer programs, we are carefree in our use of social networks and mobile apps, and we blithely hop from one website to the next, filling out forms, providing feedback, and contributing ratings.[48]

While sceptics claim that this indicates users are not actually concerned about data privacy, Nissenbaum argues that privacy is highly contextual; when faced with a series of vignettes, respondents rated situations that indicated that privacy expectations are extremely fine-grained depending on how and why data is being shared. What's more, she recognises that many people simply don't know enough about technology to understand how things work and also don't feel they have the aptitude or outlet to learn about technology in order to defend themselves from the aggression and theft of private data. Troublingly, public policy regarding data privacy is determined on models that do not take contextualisation into account and vary in their responses to how important it is that data aggregators supply transparency in how data is used. Without this information, and worse yet, *misinformation* as to how data is aggregated and shared, users are at a disadvantage in judging what they consider safe or breeches in their privacy.

Artist and game designer Zach Gage makes custom software and video games that interrogate our relationship to our personal data, often penetrating social media through aggregation algorithms to uncomfortable ends. Gage describes his work, *My Best Day Ever*:

best day ever
is a twitter project by zach gage
Each day at 6:30pm EST
it automatically searches twitter for the phrase
'best day ever'
and then picks a tweet it likes, and re-twitters
the tweet as it's [*sic*] own.
best day ever arose out of my desire to find a twitter feed that always held meaning.
it is a compilation of all our happiness[49]

Veiled in friendly verbiage, *My Best Day Ever* essentially steals Twitter users' tweeted happiness to create what constitutes an abstracted, aggregated database of emotional currency: it is given anthropomorphic agency as it actively 'picks a tweet it likes', fulfilling a desire to create 'meaning' from the happiness of other users who willingly give it away. *My Best Day Ever* comments on social media, privacy and our conceptions of personal digital identity. Miguel Sicart, in his book *Play Matters*, claims that *My Best Day Ever* 'somehow disrupts Twitter as a medium without destroying it, revealing the self-imposed honesty of these media. The activity needs to exist, to be finished, for the playful disruptiveness to be effective. Otherwise it is just destruction, a nihilist attitude different from the creative approach that playfulness affords'[50].

While the message inherent in *My Best Day Ever* at first seems positive, it ultimately questions how users interpret their participation in Twitter: Is it an intentional giving away of oneself? Is it a misguided attempt to assert agency over one's identity? Or is the original sentiment of the tweet simply gone into the ether, out of sight, out of mind? Is it as Nissenbaum asserts, all of these at one time or another, based on context? Is the final product of *My Best Day Ever* a meaningful reconstruction of 'all our happiness' or is the original intention of the tweets simply destroyed in the process? Zach Gage's video game *Lose/Lose* (2009) perpetrates a much more hostile interpretation of data security, committing the ultimate act of disruption. By playing ('at your own risk'), the user enters into an irreversible agreement: every time the player kills an alien starship, the game will randomly and permanently delete a file—*any file*—from the hard drive. Though *Lose/Lose* touches on a variety of heavy topics concerning consumption, culpability and mediation, Gage's final questions perfectly encapsulate the anxiety and apathy surrounding the data debate: 'what real objects do we value less than our data? What implications does trusting something so important to something we understand so poorly have?'[51]. Surprisingly, many have asked these questions with real consequences: the top scorer to date is user name *alvernus*, having 'slaughtered 412 alien(s)'[52]. Ultimately, the top scorers may have already realised what the rest of us have not: that our analogue and digital lives are already involved in a game of *Lose/Lose* until we find effective, collaborative methods to permanently opt out.

DIRTY YOUR MEDIA: *DÉTOURNE,* DECENTRALISE AND DIY

Dirtying media constitutes a crucial recognition of the political challenges at the intersection of life, technology and art by exploiting openings in which the possibility of data sovereignty can be performed. The practices engaged in by these artists and activists transcend disciplinary boundaries to explore how the modes of digital necropolitics can be disrupted and *détourned* with ethical values inscribed in their methods. The current increase in DIY, self-organising movements regarding data privacy reflects the possibilities for successful, ethical activism and political action on a global scale. The nature of current hybrid alternative economic entities and political activism groups ensure the nimbleness of their communication networks so that they can engage in the most pressing online civil rights violations, from the fight for net neutrality to ensuring safety for victims of cyber- and doxing attacks. For example, the CryptoParty, a global, grassroots organisation focused on cryptographic pedagogy through workshops and literature distribution functions as a crowd-sourced, decentralised platform for local activism[53]. Their handbook, available online and actively updated, pays homage to the past political and legislative actions of the nonprofit digital rights group the Electronic Frontier Foundation (EFF) by including a passage from co-founder John Perry Barlow's 1996 manifesto:

> Cyberspace consists of transactions, relationships, and thought itself, arrayed like a standing wave in the web of our communications. Ours is a world that is both everywhere and nowhere, but it is not where bodies live.

We are creating a world that all may enter without privilege or prejudice accorded by race, economic power, military force or station of birth.

> We are creating a world where anyone, anywhere may express his or her beliefs, no matter how singular, without fear of being coerced into silence or conformity.[54]

While the CryptoParty acknowledges that the goals of their predecessors may seem naïve in their optimism, they recognise that providing evolving, practical tools and methods for resistance is crucial to enact free expression both online and off. Ultimately, they—and all those that practice data resistance as a matter of life and death—perform the act of dirtying media through individual and collective optimism, glitching, obscuring and destroying data as means to effect positive change on the online and real world.

NOTES

1. Federal Communications Commission, 'Restoring Internet Freedom Order', *WC Dock*et No. 17-108 (2017).

2. Title II was first applied to ISPs in 2015, after a hard-won fight largely by grassroots methods. The 2017 vote was made during an especially embattled time; during FCC chair Ajit Pai's remarks, the room was evacuated for ten minutes due to an unspecified security threat.

3. Achille Mbembe, 'Necropolitics', trans. Libby Meintjes, *Public Culture* 15, no. 1 (2003): 14.

4. Byung-Chul Han, *PSYCHOPOLITICS: Neoliberalism and New Technologies of Power*, trans. Erik Butler (London and New York: Verso, 2017), 9.

5. Ibid.

6. danah boyd and Kate Crawford, 'CRITICAL QUESTIONS FOR BIG DATA: Provocations for a Cultural, Technological, and Scholarly Phenomenon', *Information, Communication & Society* 15, no. 5 (2012): 664–67.

7. Cathy O'Neil, *Weapons of Math Destruction* (New York: Broadway Books, 2016), 3.

8. Ibid.; Faisal Kamiran and Toon Calders, 'Data Preprocessing Techniques for Classification without Discrimination', *Knowledge and Information Systems* 33, no. 1 (October 2012): 1–33.

9. Btihaj Ajana, *Governing through Biometrics: The Biopolitics of Identity* (New York: Palgrave McMillan, 2013), 2.

10. Travis B. Murdoch and Allan S. Detsky, 'The Inevitable Application of Big Data to Health Care', *JAMA* 309, no. 13 (April 2013): 1351.

11. micha cárdenas, 'Trans of Color Poetics: Stitching Bodies, Concepts, and Algorithms', *The Scholar & Feminist Online* 13.3–14.1 (2016), http://sfonline.barnard.edu/traversing-technologies/micha-cardenas-trans-of-color-poetics-stitching-bodies-concepts-and-algorithms/ (accessed 3 January 2018).

12. micha cárdena, 'Pregnancy: Reproductive Futures in Trans of Color Feminism', *Transgender Studies Quarterly* 3, no. 1–2 (May 2016): 48–57.

13. micha cárdenas and Elle Mehrmand, *virus.circus.laboratory*, in *Speculative*, ed. Zach Blas and Christopher O'Leary (Los Angeles: Los Angeles Contemporary Exhibitions, 2011), 92.

14. micha cárdenas, 'Local Autonomy Networks: Post-Digital Networks, Post-Corporate Communications', *Media-N Journal* CAA Conference Edition (2013).

15. More information about the *Local Autonomy Networks (Autonets)* project and workshops can be found at https://faculty.washington.edu/michamc/autonets/.

16. J. K. Gibson-Graham, *A Postcapitalist Politics* (Minneapolis: Minnesota University Press, 2006), 71.

17. David Harvey, *Spaces of Hope* (Berkeley: University of California Press, 2000); Andrew Leyshon and Roger Lee, 'Introduction: Alternative Economic Geographies', in *Alternative Economic Spaces*, ed. Andrew Leyshon et al. (London: Sage, 2003), 1–26.

18. Tiffany Funk, 'Exploration of Alternative Economies', *Media-N Journal* Conference Edition (Summer 2015).

19. *GLI.TC/H 20111 READER[R0R]*; 'GLI.TC/H–the F.A.Q. Page', http://gli.tc/h/faq/ (accessed 13 January 2016); 'GLI.TC/H', http://gli.tc/h/ (accessed 13 January 2016).

20. The name 'Dirty New Media' has been employed throughout the Chicago glitch community to differentiate the associations of 'new media' with the slickness of corporate culture and the kind of software/hardware interrogation they mean to enact. jonCates, 'Re: Copying-IT-RIGHT-AGAIN', in *Relive: Media Art Histories*, ed. Sean Cubitt and Paul Thomas (Cambridge, MA: MIT Press, 2013), 337–45.

21. Documentation of these performances can be accessed on Jon Satrom's portfolio website: 'Jon Satrom', http://jonsatrom.com/ (accessed 13 January 2016).

22. Richard Kostelanetz, *Conversing with John Cage* (New York: Limelight, 1988), 70.

23. Details such as these are shared throughout the documentary *Experiments in Art and Technology and ARTPIX Present 9 Evenings: Theatre & Engineering: John Cage: Variations VII* (ARTPIX, 2008), DVD, 41 minutes.

24. Cates's many references to Cage's performances *Water Walk* (1959) and *Variations VII* (1966) reflect a deep interest in bridging the mundane and technological: both Cage performances relied on an abundance of technological performance materials, from the commonplace—rubber ducks, bathtubs, and tea kettles—to the electronically advanced, including equipment wired to create both biometric and environmental feedback loops. The technologically ambitious *Variations VII* (1966) was conceived after an invitation from engineers Billy Klüver and Fred Waldhauer, and the artists Robert Rauschenberg and Robert Whitman, the organizers of Experiments in Art and Technology (E.A.T.). In a collaboration with the Bell Telephone Laboratory engineers, Cage 'played' photoelectric cells and electronic equipment, amplifying the sounds of the heart, lungs, brain, as well as Geiger counters, radios, televisions and telephones. 'The John Cage Trust,' database of works, http://www.johncage.org/ (accessed 17 January 2018).

25. Here Cates references sound artist Douglas Kahn's criticism of Cage's aesthetics presented in Kahn's account of the history of sound art in his text *Noise, Water, Meat*. Kahn observes that Cage's concept of silence 'was dependent from the very beginning on silencing', suggesting that he privileged some sounds over others, constituting

a silencing of the social, political, and ecological power of performance. jonCates, '*ERRORRUNNINGWWWATERNOISES* . . . Realtime: Reflections and Render-Times by jonCates (2012) DE:SCRIPT', http://gl1tch.us/files/ERRORRUNNINGWWWATERNOISES.pdf (accessed 13 January 2016); Douglas Kahn, *Noise, Water, Meat: A History of Voice, Sound, and Aurality in the Arts* (Cambridge, MA: MIT Press, 2001).

26. jonCates, '_ṗ◉şƮ-g └!┼ɧ ʂɄ/\/\/\/\/\/\ƌ (2014)—jonCates (SEPT, 2014, CHI IL USA)____', *Medium*, 24 April 2017, https://medium.com/@joncates/%E1%B9%97-%C8%BF%CA%88-g-%C9%A7-%C8%BF%CA%89-%C6%8C-%C2%B2%E2%81%B0%C2%B9%E2%81%B4-joncates-sept-2014-chi-il-usa-1e8d7d59098f (accessed 30 January 2018).

27. jonCates, 'MØN3¥-Δ$-3RRRØR—jonCates (2013-...)', last updated 14 November 2016, https://medium.com/@joncates/m%C3%B8n3-%CE%B4-3%C9%8D%C9%8D%C9%8D%C3%B8%C9%8D-joncates-2013-9da5841b2eb2 (accessed 4 February 2018).

28. Rosa Menkman, 'Glitch Studies Manifesto,' in *Video Vortex Reader II: Moving Images Beyond YouTube*, ed. Geert Lovink and Rachel Somers Miles (Amsterdam: Institute of Network Cultures, 2011), 341.

29. Rosa Menkman, 'The Collapse of PAL', Transmediale performances archives, https://transmediale.de/content/the-collapse-of-pal-by-rosa-menkman (accessed 3 February 2018).

30. Legacy Russell, 'Digital Dualism and the Glitch Feminism Manifesto', *Cyborgology*, 10 December 2012, https://thesocietypages.org/cyborgology/2012/12/10/digital-dualism-and-the-glitch-feminism-manifesto/ (accessed 3 January 2018).

31. Ibid.

32. Legacy Russell, '10 Things the NSA Has Seen Me Do,' http://www.berfrois.com/2013/06/legacy-russell-10-things-the-nsa-has-seen-me-do/ (accessed 4 January 2018).

33. Finn Brunton and Helen Nissenbaum, *Obfuscation: A User's Guide for Privacy and Protest* (Cambridge, MA: MIT Press, 2015), 46–48.

34. Gary T. Marx, 'A Tack in the Shoe: Neutralizing and Resisting the New Surveillance', *Journal of Social Issues* 59, no. 2 (2003): 369–90; TrackMeNot browser extension, NYU Computer Science project, https://cs.nyu.edu/trackmenot/#marx (accessed 3 February 2018); Brunton and Nissenbaum, *Obfuscation*, 13–14.

35. Brunton and Nissenbaum, *Obfuscation*, 26–27.

36. As of 1 January 2017, AdNauseum has been banned from the Chrome web store; Nissenbaum claims Google's explanation was based upon the web store's 'terms of service' that claims extensions should 'have a single purpose that is clear to users', without any further comment. AdNauseum Chrome extension, https://adnauseam.io/ (accessed 3 February 2018).

37. Jean-Paul Curtay, *Letterism and Hypergraphics: The Unknown Avant-Garde 1945–1985* (New York: Franklin Furnace, 1985); Sadie Plant, *The Most Radical Gesture* (New York: Routledge, 1992).

38. Guy Debord, 'Definitions', *Internationale Situationniste* 1 (June 1958); Guy Debord, *Comments on the Society of the Spectacle* (London: Verso, 1988), 24.

39. Debord and Gil J. Wolman, 'A User's Guide to Détournement', *Les Lèvres Nues* 8 (May 1956), http://www.cddc.vt.edu/sionline/presitu/usersguide.html (accessed 4 January 2018).
40. Adbusters Manifesto, http://www.adbusters.org/about/ (accessed 4 January 2018); Marilyn Bordwell, 'Jamming Culture: Adbusters' Hip Media Campaign against Consumerism', in *Confronting Consumption*, ed. Thomas Princen et al. (Cambridge, MA: MIT Press, 2002), 237–53.
41. Knowbotic Research, 'macghillie_just a void', http://knowbotiq.net/macghillie/ (accessed 2 January 2018).
42. Andreas Broeckmann, 'Action *en passant*', *Opaque Presence/Manual of Latent Invisibilities*, ed. Andreas Broeckmann and knowbotic research (Berlin: diaphanes, 2010).
43. Ranran Feng and Balakrishnan Prabhakaran, 'Facilitating Fashion Camouflage Art', Proceedings of the 21st ACM international conference on Multimedia, Barcelona, Spain, 2013.
44. Paul Viola and Michael J. Jones, 'Robust Real-Time Face Detection', *International Journal of Computer Vision* 57, no. 2 (May 2004): 137–54.
45. Adam Harvey, 'Face to Anti-Face', *New York Times*, 14 December 2013.
46. Mark Townsend, 'Police to Use Facial-Recognition Cameras at Cenotaph Service', *The Guardian*, 11 November 2017.
47. Legacy Russell, Image Music Text Gallery, 'Wandering/WILDING: Blackness on the Internet,' exhibition December 2016, http://www.imagemusictext.com/exhibitions/next-wandering-wilding (accessed 4 January 2018).
48. K. Martin and Helen Nissenbaum, 'Measuring Privacy: An Empirical Test Using Context to Expose Confounding Variables', *Columbia Science and Technology Law Review* (2017).
49. Zach Gage, 'Best Day Ever', http://stfj.net/data2010/bestdayever.html (30 January 2018).
50. Miguel Sicart, *Play Matters* (Cambridge, MA: MIT Press, 2014), 27.
51. Zach Gage, 'Lose/Lose', http://www.stfj.net/art/2009/loselose/ (13 December 2017).
52. Ibid.
53. CryptoParty wiki, https://www.cryptoparty.in/index (accessed 18 December 2018).
54. *The CryptoParty Handbook*, Version: 2013-08-21, 13-14, http://key.cryptoparty.is/files/cryptoparty-handbook-2013-08-21/cryptoparty-handbook-2013-08-21.pdf (accessed 18 January 2018).

BIBLIOGRAPHY

Adbusters. 'Adbusters Manifesto.' http://www.adbusters.org/about/.

AdNauseum Chrome extension. https://adnauseam.io/.

Ajana, Btihaj. *Governing through Biometrics: The Biopolitics of Identity*. New York: Palgrave McMillan, 2013.

Bordwell, Marilyn. ‘Jamming Culture: Adbusters’ Hip Media Campaign against Consumerism’. In *Confronting Consumption*, edited by Thomas Princen et al., 237–53. Cambridge, MA: MIT Press, 2002.

boyd, danah, and Kate Crawford. ‘CRITICAL QUESTIONS FOR BIG DATA: Provocations for a Cultural, Technological, and Scholarly Phenomenon’. *Information, Communication & Society* 15, no. 5 (2012): 664–67.

Broeckmann, Andreas. ‘Action *en passant*’. In *Opaque Presence/Manual of Latent Invisibilities*, edited by Andreas Broeckmann and knowbotic research. Berlin: Diaphanes, 2010.

Brunton, Finn, and Helen Nissenbaum. *Obfuscation: A User’s Guide for Privacy and Protest*. Cambridge, MA: MIT Press, 2015.

cárdenas, micha. *Local Autonomy Networks (Autonets)*. https://faculty.washington.edu/michamc/autonets/ (accessed 4 February 2018).

———. ‘Pregnancy: Reproductive Futures in Trans of Color Feminism’. *Transgender Studies Quarterly* 3, no. 1–2 (May 2016): 48–57.

———. ‘Trans of Color Poetics: Stitching Bodies, Concepts, and Algorithms’. *The Scholar & Feminist Online* 13.3–14.1 (2016). http://sfonline.barnard.edu/traversing-technologies/micha-cardenas-trans-of-color-poetics-stitching-bodies-concepts-and-algorithms/ (accessed 3 January 2018).

cárdenas, micha, and Elle Mehrmand. *virus.circus.laboratory*. In *Speculative*, edited by Zach Blas and Christopher O’Leary. Los Angeles: Los Angeles Contemporary Exhibitions, 2011.

Cates, jon. ‘_ṗ●ȿʈ-g└!┼ɧ ȿʉ/\/\/\/\/\/\ƌ (2014)—jonCates (SEPT, 2014, CHI IL USA)____’. *Medium*. Last updated 24 April 2017. https://medium.com/@joncates/%E1%B9%97-%C8%BF%CA%88-g-%C9%A7-%C8%BF%CA%89-%C6%8C-%C2%B2%E2%81%B0%C2%B9%E2%81%B4-joncates-sept-2014-chi-il-usa-1e8d7d59098f (accessed 30 January 2018).

———. ‘Re: Copying-IT-RIGHT-AGAIN’. In *Relive: Media Art Histories*, edited by Sean Cubitt and Paul Thomas, 337–45. Cambridge, MA: MIT Press, 2013.

CryptoParty. *The CryptoParty Handbook*, Version: 2013-08-21, 13-14. http://key.cryptoparty.is/files/cryptoparty-handbook-2013-08-21/cryptoparty-handbook-2013-08-21.pdf.

Curtay, Jean-Paul. *Letterism and Hypergraphics: The Unknown Avant-Garde 1945–1985*. New York: Franklin Furnace, 1985.

Debord, Guy. *Comments on the Society of the Spectacle*. London: Verso, 1988.

———. ‘Definitions’. *Internationale Situationniste* 1 (June 1958).

Debord, Guy, and Gil J. Wolman. ‘A User’s Guide to Détournement’. *Les Lèvres Nues* 8 (May 1956). http://www.cddc.vt.edu/sionline/presitu/usersguide.html.

Feng, Ranran, and Balakrishnan Prabhakaran. ‘Facilitating Fashion Camouflage Art’. Proceedings of the 21st ACM international conference on Multimedia, Barcelona, Spain, 2013.

Funk, Tiffany. ‘Exploration of Alternative Economies’. *Media-N Journal* Conference Edition, Summer 2015. http://median.newmediacaucus.org/caa-conference-edition-2015-new-york/explorations-of-alternative-economies-panel-report/.

Gage, Zach. 'Best Day Ever'. http://stfj.net/data2010/bestdayever.html (30 January 2018).

———. 'Lose/Lose'. http://www.stfj.net/art/2009/loselose/ (13 December 2017).

Gibson-Graham, J. K. *A Postcapitalist Politics*. Minneapolis: Minnesota University Press, 2006.

GLI.TC/H 20111 READER[R0R]. Tokyo: Unsorted Books, 2011.

Han, Byung-Chul. *PSYCHOPOLITICS: Neoliberalism and New Technologies of Power*. Translated by Erik Butler. London and New York: Verso, 2017.

Harvey, Adam. 'Face to Anti-Face'. *New York Times*, 14 December 2013.

Harvey, David. *Spaces of Hope*. Berkeley: University of California Press, 2000.

Kahn, Douglas. *Noise, Water, Meat: A History of Voice, Sound, and Aurality in the Arts*. Cambridge, MA: MIT Press, 2001.

Kamiran, Faisal, and Toon Calders. 'Data Preprocessing Techniques for Classification without Discrimination'. *Knowledge and Information Systems* 33, no. 1 (October 2012): 1–33.

Knowbotic Research. 'macghillie_just a void'. http://knowbotiq.net/macghillie/.

Martin, K., and Helen Nissenbaum. 'Measuring Privacy: An Empirical Test Using Context to Expose Confounding Variables'. *Columbia Science and Technology Law Review* (2017).

Marx, Gary T. 'A Tack in the Shoe: Neutralizing and Resisting the New Surveillance'. *Journal of Social Issues* 59, no. 2 (2003): 369–90.

Mbembé, Achille. 'Necropolitics'. *Public Culture* 15, no. 1 (2003): 11–40.

Menkman, Rosa. 'Glitch Studies Manifesto'. In *Video Vortex Reader II: Moving Images Beyond YouTube*, edited by Geert Lovink and Rachel Somers Miles. Amsterdam: Institute of Network Cultures, 2011.

Murdoch, Travis B., and Allan S. Detsky. 'The Inevitable Application of Big Data to Health Care'. *JAMA* 309, no. 13 (April 2013): 1351.

O'Neil, Cathy. *Weapons of Math Destruction*. New York: Broadway Books, 2016.

Plant, Sadie. *The Most Radical Gesture*. New York: Routledge, 1992.

Russell, Legacy. 'Digital Dualism and the Glitch Feminism Manifesto'. *Cyborgology*, 10 December 2012, https://thesocietypages.org/cyborgology/2012/12/10/digital-dualism-and-the-glitch-feminism-manifesto/ (accessed 3 January 2018).

———. '10 Things the NSA Has Seen Me Do'. http://www.berfrois.com/2013/06/legacy-russell-10-things-the-nsa-has-seen-me-do/ (accessed 4 January 2018).

Russell, Legacy, Image Music Text Gallery. 'Wandering/WILDING: Blackness on the Internet'. Exhibition December 2016, http://www.imagemusictext.com/exhibitions/next-wandering-wilding (accessed 4 January 2018).

Townsend, Mark. 'Police to Use Facial-Recognition Cameras at Cenotaph Service'. *The Guardian*, 11 November 2017.

Viola, Paul, and Michael J. Jones. 'Robust Real-Time Face Detection'. *International Journal of Computer Vision* 57, no. 2 (May 2004): 137–54.

Chapter Nine

Ignorance, Intimacy and Mourning in Iowa Hog Confinement

Malin Palani

> Grief, praise: one grunt, even under the brilliant pupil of this wide blue eye of sky?[1]

I should know how to provide care for—to practice care with—pigs because I grew up on a pig farm and have been charged with their care for short periods of time. The farm initially provided only minor income and food for the family but was part of the broader shift in agriculture to contract farming—a model in which companies own livestock animals and contract employees to provide care. During the shift (that began in the United States in the early 1970s) from small- and medium-sized farms with outdoor facilities to large sites with indoor concentrated systems, hogs were known as a farmer's most profitable 'mortgage-burner'. Large-scale agribusiness corporations that were not exposed to the instability of market fluctuations attracted many farmers with assurances of stable income and the relatively low financial risks associated with contract farming. The confinement system—along with the routine use of antibiotics to prevent disease brought on by confinement conditions—made it possible for livestock animals to gain weight faster, making them market ready sooner and in greater quantities[2].

The U.S. Environmental Protection Agency designates numbers in a concentrated animal feeding operation (CAFO) as 2,500 hogs over or 10,000 hogs under 55 pounds[3]. Even though the hog industry often uses the jargon of 'farm/ing', there are marked differences between farms and confinements. In confinements, the quantity of hogs is calculated per square footage for maximum animal numbers in the minimum amount of space (that is, for efficiency). A confinement building (called a 'barn' though not the red barn of farming imagery that houses a diverse range of animals) is an enclosed indoor climate-controlled space for year-round production with slotted floors for the transference of waste into storage areas. In contrast, farms often have indoor-outdoor space for various animals to inhabit in far fewer numbers. Historically, farms have depended on the unpaid labour of a family that lives on and knows the full operations of the farm, while confinements depend on low-wage hired employees that do not live on site and often are compartmentalised according to specialisations of knowledge. While the mythology of living off the land in tandem with nature associated with the 'family farm' is perhaps nostalgic and plays on a jargon of authenticity for a vision of farming that has limited historical reality, confinement rejects the potential of farms as embedded within rather than closed off from a more-than-human community and habitat. Configuring the farm as a habitat requires a long-term vision of farming that recognises ecosystem processes, supports biodiversity and cultivates an approach that considers the quality of life and death for *all* inhabitants—such as pollinators and plants, rocks and microbes, bodies of water, deer, mosquitoes and pigs—expansively and inclusively construed[4].

While hog confinements are now located within one quarter mile of the farm where I grew up in Iowa, the farm is not a conventional confinement operation. The pigs can go indoors and outdoors—yet remain on concrete floors—and have room to run around. They are overflow animals, sometimes injured or ill, from confinements that have run out of space. Each hog carries with them the conditions of confinement that manifest in aggression, in not knowing how to go outside or inside a building, and in fair skin that burns easily from not having been in the sun. Some of the pigs would have otherwise been euthanised—killed and disposed of—rather than nursed to a modicum of health and marketed—killed and consumed. While I have taken care of hundreds of pigs at a time[5], I would like to mention one pig whom I cared for through my daily duties, which included feeding, shovelling excrement, separating out weakened pigs and hauling out 'deads'. Certainly, the pig whom I remember here was an expendable 'kill and dispose of' pig sent to the farm to see if she could be salvaged. One of her back legs had been severely injured (perhaps getting stuck in a fence or loading on a truck), which made her unable to stand once she laid or sat down. This pig, with no name, was kept alive (by me and others) in a state of injury. While not naming this pig might have served me in avoiding feelings of attachment or in dealing with the inevitability of her death or just as a matter of the inability to name each and every pig under my care, none of these reasons prompted my reluctance to name her. I could have named her, but the act of naming is not what activates care or companionship. She persists in my memory with no name or, perhaps better stated, with a name that I do not know. I could recall the daily work of lifting her body to stand for a short time; the way the bedding, feces and feed would stick and form a crust on her backside; how her leg hung from the hip as she struggled to walk and find balance; or the deep sorrow that I felt (and continue to feel) for this pig. Still, her bones cannot be unearthed from or buried in a place of remembrance.

What follows is an auto-ethnographic approach in thinking through the aesthetic, embodied, power-infused and necropolitical practice of hog confinement. The chapter is composed of four sections—'Touching this Decomposing Body', 'Modes of Partitioning the Perceptible', 'Unknown Knowns', and 'With (Death) Care'—in which I take up the intimacy of touching (and being touched by) death and decomposing bodies, the subjugation of bodies and subjects to processes of instrumental efficiency, the rhetorical strategies of distraction and ignorance in the creation of discourses of truth in agribusiness and mourning as a potential address to the violence of industrial agriculture and its particular death worlds.

TOUCHING THIS DECOMPOSING BODY

When providing care for another sentient being, a bodily sense of sharing temporal and spatial material realities is generated. Healing is cultivated when you attune your body to another body (no matter their species or identities)—to their breathing, movement, warmth and coolness, their guttural voices, their efforts to get and be well. Together this pig and I are embedded in a death world. This is not to say that our lives, experiences, bodies, perceptions or status as subjects or objects are the same but that the situation that bears on our encounter is necropolitical: life here is subjugated to the power of death. Achille Mbembe takes up the necropolitical in the colonial context in order to assess the contemporary 'creation of *death-worlds*, new and unique forms of social existence in which vast populations are subjected to conditions of life conferring upon them the status of *living dead*'[6]. Each and every time I pushed and lifted this pig to stand, I carried out a practice of deathcare, which realises the fusion of the living and the dead body—a body living through its own decomposition and (prolonged) death.

The definitions and parameters of animal abuse and care are socially and culturally constructed; they are often dealt with through animal welfare laws and programmes which foreground the psychology of a person that learns (or does not learn) 'cognitive, empathetic, and behavioural skills'[7]. Despite the socially institutionalised and technologised acceptability of animal care in agricultural production, deathcare and care practices for 'savable' lives are intimately bound together. Healing and hope are as integral to deathcare practice as they are to care practices that have as their goal saving the life of the individual or animal receiving care. Healing is an ongoing process rather than an end result to be achieved. Likewise, hope is a practice, something we do, rather than something we have. Even so, the process of healing and the practice of hope in a small pen with this pig does little to confront and disrupt the business of agriculture as a pervasive system that bears on everyday death/care practices and bodies as well as on public perceptions of grievable and killable lives and species.

Sus domesticus might be considered a particular population well matched for xenotransplantation; their bodies are easily conditioned to become the living dead. Humans do not so much eat meat as consume the bodies of the living dead and digest the necropolitical practices that create death worlds weighted with the bodies of livestock animals. The clean and brightly lit meat case contrasts the dead box at the confinement site (formerly the rendering truck that visits the small farm) with its strong smell, swarms of flies and maggots. Neatly cut, cleaned, stacked and labelled (finished) cuts of meat contrast the haphazard pile of entire, whole yet disordered (unfinished) corpses. The dead box is often enclosed to limit access and visibility of dead bodies while the perfect slant of the meat display enables better viewing. The clear shiny glass creates a window that directs the eyes and activates the senses. One is constructed to induce consumption, the other to hide disgust. However, this decrepit pig whom I was charged to take care of, whom I tried to practice care with, bridges these aesthetic regimes and places them within the same death world operating through a form of commerce in which life is not a force belonging to a particular being but an object of incessant capitalisation.

The capitalist model of production operative in hog confinements is based on efficiency and the maximisation of profits; it requires standardised spatiotemporal control of biogenetics and conditions of existence. This injured pig brings to mind another well-known pig, Number 6707, from a USDA experiment meant to create a more efficient and profitable 'superpig' through bioengineering. The transgenic alteration (using a human growth gene) in pig Number 6707 resulted in a deformed physiology that prevented the pig from standing on his own. Number 6707 lived in a pen at the Agriculture Research Service in Beltsville, Maryland, and was housed with a companion pig that could walk. The intersecting paths of injury, engineering and companionable touch (from humans and pigs) permeate and condition the death world of livestock confinement. In this system, a pig materialises both as life *in potentia* and *in absentia*, a genetic abstraction and hypermobile concrete material whose presence/absence is at best emergent and at worst reified. Insofar as concrete genetic material is configured as abstract plastic physicality devoid of emerging sensual and relational qualities in a quantitative differentiation, life is taken up as *raw material* that signifies pure potential, which generates and decomposes physical bodies. 'Pig' and this Pig Number 6707 become genetically modifiable material that represents the emergence of a new animal with new potential, an animal reified as a commodity for feeding the world[8] in an ideological move that reproduces the right to kill and produces the living dead.

Biotechnology, science, juridical and market forces work together to control the in/visible parameters of violence and to establish the mutual embedment of power and domination. New technologies configured as responding to market demands become the norm by which human and nonhuman animal bodies are or might be engineered for 'optimum aptitude to the fabrication of cellular, organic, genetic, and combinatory individuality'[9]. Through a progressive technologisation[10] that hierarchises the lives and deaths of species and bodies in a naturalising process meant for a 'global good', life becomes increasingly commodified; rationality becomes increasingly irrational, giving rise to a sociality in which domination and (capitalist) production are inextricably intertwined. The commodity form becomes the structuring principle of society as bodies and spaces are reduced to the calculus of their end—profit, capital, debt (repayment) and death. The hierarchical ordering of bodies and species materialises conditions for the living dead, constructs the acceptable parameters for killing and further enacts the calculation of what counts as a livable life and a grievable death. For Judith Butler, 'the differential allocation of grievability that decides what kind of subject is and must be grieved, and which kind of subject must not, operates to produce and maintain certain exclusionary conceptions of who is normatively human: what counts as livable life and grievable death?'[11] Grieving oriented around an ordering of species, lives and bodies determines the parameters of acceptable and recognisable grievability according to normative (anthropocentric) expressions of grief and the proximity of the life lost to the human. The social fabric and deathcare industry recognises and makes place for mourning and sorrow that surrounds the death of a human set within micro-hierarchies that make distinctions along lines such as race, class, age and social status. The deaths of companion animals[12] exist on the margins of grievability, making families of pets often ashamed to openly express grief because their grief falls outside recognisable norms for attachment, love and mourning. Further, there is very little to no place in the normative social order for grieving the lives and bodies of road kill or livestock animals (including the living dead) in confinement systems.

MODES OF PARTITIONING THE PERCEPTIBLE

Confinement embodies a social and architectural formation devoid of a place for mourning in which the spatiotemporal conditions and realities for human and swine bodies are shaped through biotechnological instrumentalisation. The ordering of seeing, hearing, smelling, touching—perceiving in all modalities—partitions the perceptible. It makes seemingly healthy and clean, scientifically coded bodies visible while placing other, damaged bodies beyond the boundaries of perceptibility. The placement of bodies within channels of perceptibility triggers phobia and fascination embedded in necrorealities. Landscapes and bodies of ruin both compel and repel attention. The living dead (decomposing bodies) activate necrophobia and necrofascination. While necrophobia materialises through the operation of fear—the fear of intimacy with the dead and the dying as well as proximity to one's own death—necrofascination occurs through captivation with and attraction to the liveliness of dead things (the coincidence of the living and the dead that activates the imagination and excites a kind of pleasure). Contemporary death worlds such as sites of ecological disasters, oceanic garbage patches or animal confinements are made in part through the work of phobia and fascination, which risks overlooking supra-empirical, imperceptible decay and suffering.

Gases of decay bloat bodies, distend abdomens and expel beyond boundaries with frothy liquids that run from the nose, anus and mouth. Orifices are not enough to release the building pressure and the marbled skin ruptures. The body splits. *Odour*. Odour is difficult to contain and easily ruptures the perceived frames of visibility. Odour passes through bodies across thresholds of imperceptibility and is difficult to reject. Odour activates pleasure—in salivation—and inconveniently confronts and invades the senses—in feces and decomposition. While a body bag might hide the visibility of the decomposing body, it will not hide its smell[13]. Conditions of hog confinement transform bodies through necrophobia and fascination, taking up strategies of invisibilisation that determine what must and must not be seen, heard, smelled, tasted and felt. A person can travel across the state of Iowa easily without seeing a pig or confinement building. Someone unfamiliar with Iowa agriculture might wonder what the long buildings at the roadside or on the horizon might contain or what 'the other crop' growing in the fields might be[14]. Although hog confinements certainly mark the Iowa landscape[15], the buildings are couched amongst fields and farms, rivers and marshes.

It is *easy* not to see hog confinements and slaughter facilities. We hardly notice the semi-trucks (with their characteristic odour and oval openings revealing glimpses of pink skin) that continually transport hogs along the same network of roads that we travel. Hog confinements are much greater in number and have been more uniformly constructed than slaughter facilities as sites with single-level buildings that often do not have gated fencing (thefts of hogs do occur) or obvious signage that indicates a company name. Slaughter facilities (processing plants) tend to be much larger warehouse-looking build-

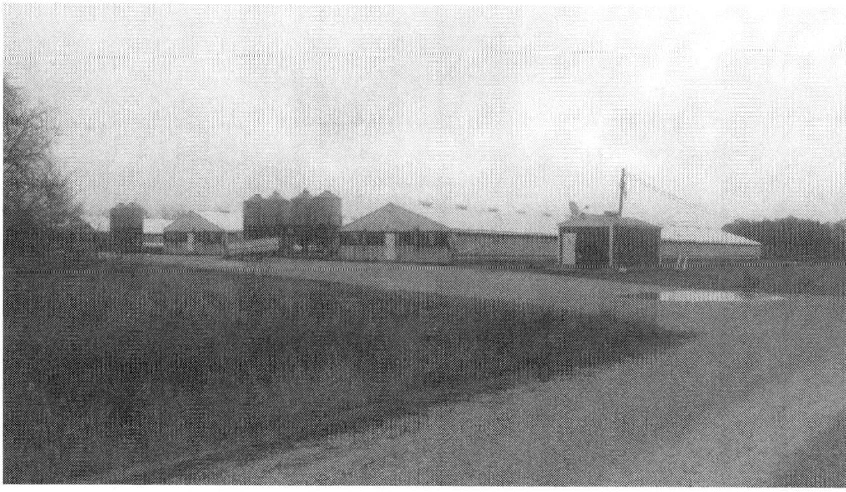

Figure 9.1. The confinement site near the farm in Iowa on 22 January 2018. Photographer anonymous.
Source: Courtesy of the author.

ings with refrigeration, fencing and regulated entries that receive hogs from multiple sites. The plants are usually located in rural areas or on the margins of small cities unlike the Rath Packing Company, which was located in downtown Waterloo, Iowa, until the company's closure in 1985.

It would seem that pork somehow appears at the meat counter through some mysterious work of magic rather than the intersectional work of (formally union) labour, architecture, technology, markets, governments, consumers, producers and politicians. Despite the ease of not seeing hogs in Iowa, there are 22,400,000 hogs in the state as compared to just over three million humans. In the United States, swine farms decreased from over one million in 1967 to just short of 158,000 in 1996. Meanwhile, the average number of pigs per farm (a term that persists in the industry) grew by nearly 500 percent[16]. Yet calling a hog confinement a farm is a misnomer. A more accurate term is 'site'.

Pork industry employees—from caretakers and specialists to technicians—manage several disparately located sites rather than cultivate a single proximately consolidated farm. The implications of the historical transformation of farm to site are manifold, not the least of which includes the professionalisation of the pork producer as site manager and the transformation of swine bodies to weight-gaining units and quantities of production in swine populations. The transition from farm to site marks a cognitive and aesthetic shift from the proximate, intimate and relational to that of the distant, superficial, and inconceivable. Under the architecture of 'site' the nearly 10 billion domesticated livestock animals slaughtered each year in the United States are encountered and felt as beyond our own personal realities. They are made distant and inconceivable; they appear to fall outside the boundaries of political life. Confinements inhabit the social order and the physical landscape as sites without place and belonging—numbers on a grid that temporarily holds a quantity of units (of the living dead) in a system of units[17].

The aesthetics of hog confinement sites shape their political dimensions; they also shape power formations. For Jacques Rancière, politics—as a process in which contingently contested spaces and times form through a 'distribution of the sensible'[18]—is inherently aesthetic. Rancière describes the distribution of the sensible as

> an order of bodies that defines the allocation of ways of doing, ways of being and ways of saying, and sees that those bodies are assigned by name to a particular place and task; it is an order of the visible and the sayable that sees that a particular activity is visible and another is not, that this speech is understood as discourse and the other as noise.[19]

Thus a distribution of the sensible pertains to 'all the activities which create order by distributing places, names, [and] functions'[20] in an active regime that continues to shape the behaviour of humans and nonhuman animals every day. The aesthetic regime that assigns places and tasks in the order of hog confinement extends from unitised geographies of rural land separated by property lines and site parameters to the unitised building architecture that creates a controlled/controlling environment to the unitised body of a pig set along the farrow to finish assembly line of production. A general process of unitisation—which hinges on efficiency, quantification, specialised (technologised) care practices and automation[21]—comes to characterise the aesthetic regime of hog confinement and authorises strategies of invisibilisation. A variety of climate-controlled buildings are constructed specifically for particular stages in the lifespan of pig and swine populations. The buildings enable year-long breeding and continuous pig production. After breeding, which is commonly done through artificial insemination, pregnant sows are kept in individual two-foot by seven-foot crates for approximately three and a half months until a few days before they are due to farrow. Sows are then moved to individual farrowing crates where they give birth and remain for two weeks with their litters until the piglets are weaned. The newborn pigs are moved to a nursery building for one month, then to a growing building, and finally to a finishing building where they stay until they are five to six months old, at which time they are marked as market ready, sorted and loaded onto semi-trucks for transport to slaughter.

The architectural-temporal partitioning of breeding, farrowing, nursing, growing, finishing, transporting and slaughter allocates particular places for particular functions—divisions of pig growth set alongside divisions in labour and employment that enable the abstraction of knowledge and care practices within the processes of production. The aesthetics of measured, partitioned, productive, efficient spaces are evidenced in the assembly line formation as well as in small enclosures constructed for containing forty 250-pound pigs. For Mbembe, necropolitics operates through an exercise of sovereignty in partitioning spatial relations[22]. Mbembe writes, 'Space was . . . the raw material of sovereignty and the violence it carried with it. Sovereignty meant occupation, and occupation meant relegating the colonized into a third zone between subjecthood and objecthood'[23]. The raw material of sovereignty indicative of colonial occupation is not fully implied in hog confinement insofar as a/the pig's geography is not occupied but rather produced. In contrast to colonial occupation, the space, time and bodies of or present in hog confinement operate as raw materials of capital markets *as* sovereign power. Violence does not operate in the form of capitalisation in a distribution of the sensible that digitises, technologises, in/visibilises and globalises the time and space of this injured pig subject to and object of (my incapable and inculpable) practices of care. Therefore, violence does not just take that which is subjectively situated or possessed, such as land or freedom, but instead produces conditions of death that make a claim on generation after generation of pigs engineered in conditions of injury and exploitation. This well-organised system in turn determines the naturalised and normative parameters and visibility of, in Rancière's words, 'doing, being, and saying' and the interactions that can be thought and performed concerning swine and human bodies integrated in the confinement system.

While developments in confinement architecture, waste management, biotech and pharmaceutical industries enabled the growth and homogenised the aesthetics of confinement facilities, a discourse of species distinctions further informs the operations of biosecurity that appear to be essential for the continuance of industrial agriculture. Under a mandate for biosecurity, bodily proximity and physical contact shape the aesthetic order of confinement and its strategies of invisibilisation. The corporeal intimacy and viral affective immediacy of swine and human bodies feeds concerns about the spread of disease in confinement systems. In a study of avian flu, Celia Lowe demonstrates that agricultural biosecurity generates anthropocentric, impossible ideals of meticulously ordered 'biosocial worlds'[24]. Despite disconcerting realities of hypermobile, invisible and uncontainable reciprocity evident in avian flu, swine flu or mad cow disease, biosecurity is founded on a fantasy of separation, of 'enclos[ing] humans and animals in specific, sterile, and segregated spaces'[25]. The performativity of biosecurity in hog confinements—as seen in the extensive labour and assiduous practices of power washing[26] buildings between swine populations and showering before entering disparate sites—exposes the bond between controlled separation, which supposedly ensures efficient and globally secure production of food, and the intimate proximity of species and bodies that produce unexpected and sometimes threatening (necrofascinating) effects. The performative effect of measures taken in the name of biosecurity—such as wearing Tyvek suits to enter a trailer of weaned pigs or routine showering on entering and exiting barns—inaugurates a seemingly transparent and secure reality that absolves consumers and the public from responsibility of enquiry into the insecurity and violence of animal consumption and care practices. The topography and geography of the distribution of confinement bodies and species functions temporally in a mode that can immediately shift from perceived separation to sudden and viral intimacy.

Writing on disciplinary and biopolitical regimes of power, Michel Foucault theorises *sécurité* as a regime of power less concerned with spatial partitioning and more with pathways of circulation in between spaces[27.] Power operates through the technology of security that controls, inhibits and allows circulation specifically for the shaping of a population within the space of the city[28]. In hog confinement, the technology of biosecurity shapes a swine population, which becomes normalised as a species that must be controlled (biosecured) individually and collectively for interspecies and global health. The in/visible and viral threats of circulations that biosecurity is meant to quell activate necrophobia and necrofascination as evident in the imagery of burning livestock bodies that contract viruses such as H1N1 and of handling infected and infectable bodies through the mediation of biohazmat suits. Health and safety laws for handling these risks function as ideological frames that foreground the role and capacity of juridical power to confine and control viral threats brought on by industrial agriculture. In the midst of changes meant for more responsible animal practices, animal welfare regulations and research universities invested in agribusiness work together to provide knowledge validating the ability of technology to provide solutions to biothreats while avoiding or distracting from the economic centre that gives rise to insecure conditions that demand measures for security.

Iowa Select Farms, a leading hog producer in Iowa, details the key responsibilities of the Production Well-Being Specialist as training 'farm personnel to develop techniques that will positively affect animal care and overall production'[29]. These techniques are described as: the proper ways to handle animals and perform injections, assessing and performing timely euthanasia, the identification of sick or compromised pigs, daily observations and biosecurity[30]. The discourse, techniques and knowledge (as truth) of biosecurity is deeply embedded in the architecture and the practices of observation and assessment. Biosecurity operates as a grid of intelligibility that advertises the company's commitment to responsible, innovative and ethically motivated farming practices. In a branding modality, it ideologically forms an imaginary relationship to the real conditions of existence within the confinement system and its particular death world. Enabled by spatiotemporal partitioning, the techniques of observation and collecting records on swine populations and each individual pig are meant to quell the threat of sudden dis-order, decomposition and deviation from the norm of 'health' set within the regulatory policies and visibilities of the confinement system. The techniques that Iowa Select Farms indicate as working for the well-being of 'the animal' and 'overall production' work to reinforce the corporation's power formation and the normative distribution of the sensible in livestock confinement. The recursive performative work of normalising the aesthetic and technological norm also creates circuits of necrophobia and necrofascination that call into question the security of the normative distribution.

UNKNOWN KNOWNS

Hog confinement is not just a 'peculiar spatial institution scientifically planned for the purposes of control'[31] but also an institution of biotechnologically enabled capitalisation that enables market sovereignty 'to define who matters and who does not, who is *disposable* and who is not'[32]. The realities of disposability and waste are significant in Iowa. In 2008, Iowa's 5,000 (at that time) hog confinements generated over 50 million tons of raw waste, or 16.7 tons of animal manure for every resident[33]. Run-off from manure spread on fields and nitrate fertilizers—used for producing corn and soybeans, mostly for livestock feed—are not considered point source pollution under the Clean Water Act but easily feed into waterways through tiling systems, contributing to hypoxia in the Gulf of Mexico and the contamination of 634 Iowa waters[34]. A single 10,000-head finishing operation that averages a 2 percent mortality rate results in approximately 14 tons of animal carcasses per year. While these statistics might appear transparent in their categorization of materials and their flows, the concrete (ruining) realities remain opaque even in the well documented and publicised place of hypoxia in the Gulf of Mexico. Concerning explicit and implicit death worlds, Mbembe argues that 'new technologies of destruction are less concerned with inscribing bodies within disciplinary apparatuses as inscribing them, when the time comes, within the order of the maximal economy', represented by the massacre with a 'patchwork of interests' and actors that render destruction, injury and suffering opaque[35]. The opacity (that, paradoxically, also seems transparent) of damage, injury and suffering further permeates the issues of perceptibility in modern agriculture and informs what Timothy Morton understands as the ecological crises of global warming. In *Dark Ecology*, Morton examines the logistics of agricultural sociality in a critique of the foundations of ecological crises and thinking. Agrilogistics evokes a metaphysics of presence in which existence is 'constantly present' and 'separated from nonhuman systems' and asserts that 'human existing is always better than any quality of existing'[36]. It is a loop that in its attempts to map the world within a grid of intelligibility generates the unintelligible and the unknown. Agricultural ecological damage occurs on scales above and below human perception that might be incomprehensibly shown in the build-up of nitrates (and plastics) across thousands of miles and years of application or in deforestation that decreases absorption of carbon while impacting salmon populations. Impacts not only spread across geological times and places but also weave through multiple ecologies that cannot be wholly determined or made transparent or fully comprehensible.

Within this context, the Iowa Select Farms Web site shapes a discourse of knowledge based on four 'pillars of care'—People, Animal, Community and Environment. The knowledge formation and its discourse of truth realised through the online website extends the power, violence and domination of confinement partitioning insofar as it does not make visible or sayable the ecological impact of corporate agriculture and the realities of care*less* dying and injury. Underlying profit and market forces are rendered as noise—except in terms of providing good jobs—in the company's model of care that formulates a network of power and knowledge linked to on-site practices, legislative regulations and processes and public performances. The partitioning of confinement in terms of units and the website reinforce necropolitical tendencies in an imperative for a discourse of care as truth, factuality and performativity of taking care (rather than *practicing with care*), thus creating a sense of the system operating with no human or corporate actors, which strategically absolves everyone of culpability. While the website labours to make transparent and innocuous the confinement model (and innocent the public and the consumer), the economic interests and business operations involved in making decisions remain opaque. The seeming online transparency of hog care practices performs objectivity; it is a strategy that garners legitimacy[37].

The study of ignorance—agnotology—aims to expose 'the power at work in practices of knowing'[38] and the operations of culturally and institutionally induced ignorance for the strategic and political manipulation of public values. Forms of ignorance arise contextually and are employed through management strategies that uphold social and power formations invested in particular interests for controlling what might or might not be known. For Sarah Lucia Hoagland, the denial of relationality contributes to problematic forms of ignorance that render relationality invisible[39]. A strategy to address criticisms of industrial agriculture is to craft a positivist (provable and local) demonstration of knowledge (as truth) of hog production. Knowledge formations work in conjunction with aesthetics to create zones of knowability and obscurity (and distraction). Moreover, technologised globalised existence and social order submits the operation of truth to forces of technodetermination and acceleration, which constrain the provable and the local to the un/timely functions of available technology. Facts that might be proven, in a positivist manner, with the aid of available technology and online branding stand in stark contrast to knowledge encountered in pragmatic enquiry of critical and (embodied) relational thinking.

The formation of human subjectivity as responsible consumer, industry competitor, corporate entrepreneur and care(less) provider disperses responsibility across platforms of subjectivity that generate social and public participation through flexibility without critical and expanded relational thinking for decisions that are made for and by public interest. In a mode of public plasticity, the 'public' becomes an amorphous and indeterminate entity that implicates no one and is addressed via a rhetorical strategy that drains the political import of what is being said (and decided) and how it is being said (and de cided) in the public sphere. In *The Ignorant Schoolmaster*, Rancière suggests that rhetoric, operating according to a principle of war, distracts and casts 'a veil of prejudice over the truth' that prevents another intelligence from seeing[40]. For Rancière, rhetoric motivates perceptions and feelings of contingent superiority and has as its goal the silencing and marking of inferiors. Of import here is the function of distraction rather than ignorance in the shaping of public discourse and knowledge concerning the treatment and conditions of confinement animals. Slavoj Žižek suggests 'disavowed beliefs, suppositions and obscene practices we pretend not to know about, even though they form the background of our public values' or 'unknown knowns' are primary dangers because they sustain American values and way of life[41]. Reading Žižek and Rancière together, unknown knowns—including the suffering and deaths of livestock animals and the expanse of ecological damage tied to industrial agriculture—are not knowledge of which the public is ignorant but knowledge and practices that we *deny* equality within, *pretend* not to know about and through which we *affirm* public values bound to violence and the living dead. Ignorance is a knowledge formation saturated with the (necro)political that necessarily must operate through what Rancière might call 'verification' of equality through sensory contact and enquiry. While Rancière focuses on the recognition of equality between men[42], the *practice* or verification of equality, which Rancière suggests cannot be given or claimed, must include nonhuman bodies, lives and life—a verification continually enacted with this injured pig whom I touch and who touches me.

WITH (DEATH) CARE

For Rancière, politics are performed through acts of subjectivation and the speech of those who through a vocalisation of dissent negate the negation of their existence[43]. Power formations that negate or do not recognise the existence of those who have no place within the normative social order are disrupted through the voices of dissent set against (rather than consent to) the normative order. If we follow Rancière's argument that politics can only occur 'out of place and in a place which was not supposed to be political'[44], hogs *act politically* not because all life is *zoë* in differentiation from *bios* but because equality must be verified through a practice, which activates attunement and attention to others. Dawn Coppin raises the question of whether Foucault's thinking—with its distinction between relationships of violence and power—is applicable to relationships between humans and other animals. Coppin concludes that because Foucault situates resistance at the level of the body, resistance can be theorised and understood as an animal's biophysical response to the situation[45]. In terms of confinement, hogs might resist through bodily actions such as tail biting, belly ruptures and blow outs. These bodily acts do not as much violate this or that law but nonetheless lay bare the violence of the sovereign agricultural corporation that attempts to silence and disallow the confrontation of the damage that it performs. This injured pig whom I hold to standing protests the social order and death world in which she touches me and within which we are both embedded. While human bodily acts such as self-harm, self-immolation and suicide perform protest and are sometimes spectacularly public (and therefore demand visibility and journalistic circulation), the responsive injuries affecting this pig enact a quiet protest to forgetfulness. They demand personal and public attention in the midst of a system and cadre of individuals (including me) who look with a blind eye and an ethic of 'business (interests) as usual'.

I have taken up the phrases 'take care' and 'with care' as indicators of my encounter with this pig on the farm. By way of a distinction, I would like to suggest that the phrase 'take care' is an absolution. By this I mean, if I were to say 'take care' I absolve myself of you, of others, of this pig. I send you on your way, so to speak. I say that you must take care where you can find it, that care is not a matter or condition of our encounter. In choosing to write and practice 'with care,' I say that I hold you in my mind and my body as I (carefully) choose my words and that your presence/absence persists in me beyond the writing and publishing of this text. I reveal that my words might touch you as my hand or eyes might if we were to be physically close. 'With (death) care' is a binding condition of our strange friendship and a practice of attunement and attention that sheds the tears of melancholy—awakening a death that dies little by little, a death that stays in us and in the bodies of the living dead—always carrying the seeds of remorse.

A New York–based movement artist, Eiko Otake, whose work engages with place, empathy and stillness, describes sustained mourning as an antidote for human aggression and a quiet protest to forgetfulness in which one gives attention to what has been lost[46]. Eiko writes, 'Though I realize there is a logical difference in mourning for someone I have loved and mourning for victims I have not met . . . what I call *mourning* is both quieter and more sustainable than the way Freud describes either mourning or melancholia'[47]. For Sigmund Freud, the grieving process associated with mourning is a test of reality that proves that the loved one no longer exists and thereby requires the libido to withdraw its attachment[48]. The withdrawal of the libido from the loved object and its transference to a new loved one occurs with the completion of mourning[49]. In mourning, one completes the grieving process once the loved object is proved *in reality* to no longer exist and

> passes its verdict upon each single one of the memories and hopes through which the libido was attached to the lost object, and the ego, confronted as it were with the decision whether it will share this fate, is persuaded by the sum of its narcissistic satisfactions in being alive *to sever its attachment to the non-existent object*.[50]

The work of grief is to impel the ego to give up the object—to declare the object dead so that the ego can go on living after undergoing the required process of detachment and reality testing of the loved object's nonexistence. However, mourning is not just concerned with those who we recognise as human, 'lovable' or as really 'living'. Mourning is not just a practice that can be sustained beyond the parameters of the living and the dead, the human and the nonhuman. It is a practice that *is sustaining*—not a cure but an ongoing process of healing and care with others. Mourning is not a process that *ought* to be completed in order for one to detach the ego from the dead in reality. Rather, the (living) dead are loved, attended, attuned with and listened to beyond death with no transference of attachment (and desire) onto other objects. The loved, the dead and the living dead do not leave reality and become nonexistent. In a practice of deathcare, one maintains relation with the (living) dead and does not detach the existent reality of the living from the 'nonexistent' realities of the dead and the living dead.

Mourning might sustain bodies in a death world and encourage care—a place where one continues (rather than transfers desire or distracts from violence) to feel loss, to remember, to love and to acknowledge another's dying not pathologically but as giving time and adjusting attention to this one that continues to be a part of one's own living and dying, learning and enquiry. Mourning that might sustain life/death is not about transference of love and desire in order to end grief or to delimit the parameters of grievable lives. Mourning in deathcare, in death worlds, encourages finding care with the living dead. In this modality, ignorance must not function to distract from or make strategically invisible and unknowable the realities and histories of our agricultural system and its service to structures of power and violence that uphold a market vision of relationality, which subsumes bodies to the commodity form and the mandates of business operations. Instead, ignorance embedded in our practices of knowing (this pig, this dispensable low-wage employee, this immigrant labourer, this place of confinement) might affirm relational intimacy with others and disrupt the strategic ignorance of agribusiness that obtains policy favour and legitimation through the distributive values of profit, technology and capitalisation on bodies embedded within and systematically produced and consumed in death worlds.

NOTES

1. Mona Van Duyn, 'Last Words of Pig No. 6707', *Grand Street* 7, no. 3 (Spring 1988), 140–42.
2. In 2012, the state of Iowa marketed more than 49 million hogs (nearly seventeen for every Iowa resident) that consumed an average of 39 million bushels of feed made primarily from corn and soybeans.
3. The EPA also marks concentrated quantities for other animal feeding operations as 1,000 head of cattle, 55,000 turkeys, 125,000 chickens and 82,000 laying hens.
4. Dana Jackson, 'The Farm as Natural Habitat', in *The Farm as Natural Habitat Reconnecting Food Systems with Ecosystems*, ed. Dana L. Jackson and Laura L. Jackson (Washington, DC: Island Press, 2002), 19.
5. Fifteen hundred at most spread across three buildings with seven separate indoor-outdoor pens, a small number in terms of confinement practices in which a single employee in worst-case scenarios takes care of thousands of pigs across several sites with multiple confinement buildings at each site.
6. Achille Mbembe, 'Necropolitics', *Public Culture*, trans. Libby Meintjes, 15, no. 1 (2003): 35.
7. Emphasising the link between human and animal violence, Ascione and Shapiro describe animal abuse as 'nonaccidental socially unacceptable behavior' and indicate with critical reflection pathways for combating violence through education, prevention and programs for learning skills and empathy through animal assisted activities

and therapies. Frank R. Ascione and Kenneth J. Shapiro, 'People and Animals, Kindness and Cruelty: Research Directions and Policy Implications', *Journal of Social Issues* 65, no. 3 (2009): 569–87.

8. Advocates for the agribusiness model of agriculture often base advocacy in a greater capacity to provide food for growing human populations who struggle to meet food needs.

9. Michel Foucault, 'The Means of Correct Training', in *The Foucault Reader*, ed. Paul Rabinow (New York: Pantheon Books, 1984), 204.

10. Martin Heidegger describes the essence of technology as a way of revealing that the modern age is tied to an ordering of knowledge defined as Enframing [*Ge-stell*]—a self-revealing—that challenges-forth the world as a picture. Heidegger states, 'In such producing, man contends for the position in which he can be that particular being who gives the measure and draws up the guidelines for everything that is'. In Martin Heidegger, *The Question Concerning Technology and Other Essays*, trans. William Lovitt (New York: Harper and Row, 1977), 134. Heidegger argues that, through modern technology, man's challenging [*Herausfordern*] 'puts to nature the unreasonable demand that it supply energy which can be extracted and stored as such' for maximum yield at minimum expense. In Martin Heidegger, 'The Question Concerning Technology,' *Basic Writings from Being and Time (1927) to The Task of Thinking (1964)*, ed. David Farrell Krell (New York: Harper and Row, 1977), 296.

11. Judith Butler, *Precarious life: The Powers of Mourning and Violence* (London: Verso, 2004), xiv–xv. See also Judith Butler, *Frames of War: When Is Life Grievable?* (London: Verso, 2009).

12. Donna Haraway argues for the broader more heterogeneous phrase 'companion species', which concerns the relational composition of subjects and objects through 'co-constitution, finitude, impurity, historicity, and complexity'. In Donna Haraway, *The Companion Species Manifesto: Dogs, People, and Significant Otherness* (Chicago: Prickly Paradigm Press, 2003), 16. While Haraway emphasises that beings do not 'preexist their relatings', relationality has been taken up in many philosophical and scholarly texts. Influenced by the writings of William James and Gilles Deleuze, Brian Massumi conceptualises relation as preceding distinct interrelating correspondences in an open-ended sociality. Massumi draws on James's argument that relation is perceived as such in embodied activity, which occurs always in the midst of already ongoing participation. Relation therefore precedes recognisable correspondences, disrupts subject-object positioning and appears as an 'unspecified . . . *intensity* of total experience'. Relation is described as 'a measureless gap in and between bodies and things, an incorporeal interval of change.' In *Parables for the Virtual Movement, Affect, Sensation* (Durham, NC: Duke University Press, 2002), 58, 168, 231–32. Massumi draws on Gilles Deleuze's formulation of relation as external to terms in *Empiricism and Subjectivity: An Essay on Hume's Theory of Human Nature*, trans. Constantin Boundas (New York: Columbia University Press, 1991), 66, 101, and William James argues that 'Relations are feelings of an entirely different order from the terms they relate,' in *The Principle of Psychology*, vol. 1 (New York: Dover, 1890/1950), 149. Understanding relationality as a shared realm from which distinct terms and interactions emerge refuses the assumption that the

identities relating precede their interrelating as already-constituted entities. Insofar as bodies are embedded in relation as 'real potential to be actualized', perhaps it might be best to approach *all* life and materials as companionable *and* power infused—bound up in processes of heterogeneous relational emergence—especially because 'species' as conveniently as 'animal' or 'kinship' inclusions and exclusions can and have historically operated to sanction violence and inaugurate exploitation and domination instead of and in the midst of companionable encounter.

13. When picking up animals for cremation at the Garden of Memories pet cemetery where I formerly worked, a veterinarian (a person and profession for animal care) once asked with a hint of disgust, 'Does it smell like dead animal in here?' Often bags of pet bodies were haphazardly stacked about—an indicator marking the parameters of grievability.

14. Visitors often ask about 'the other crop' (soybeans as opposed to corn, both of which are primarily used for feed).

15. I cannot recall a single confinement in the area in the 1970s and 1980s, but there are many now.

16. Dawn Coppin, 'Foucauldian Hog Futures: The Birth of Mega-Hog Farms', *The Sociological Quarterly* 44, no. 4 (2003): 597–616. Coppin cites a paper done for the 1997 U.S. Meat Export Federation Pork Conference: Ronald Plain, 'Trends in U.S. Swine Industry'.

17. The Iowa Select Farms website (http://www.iowaselect.com/) states: 'Geographical Information System (GIS) software allows our team the ability to view all 700 production sites and the neighboring fields receiving the nutrients. Every parcel of ground is mapped into the system including creeks, building sites, terraces or tile outlets. Aerial imagery is used as the base maps and layers are then added for contours, county tile lines, flood area, water sources and cemeteries. GIS technology ensures manure is applied responsibly and in compliance with all state regulations'.

18. Rancière argues that politics is 'a delimitation of spaces and times, of the visible and the invisible, of speech and noise, that simultaneously determines the place and the stakes of politics as a form of experience. Politics revolves around what can be seen and what can be said about it, around who has the ability to see and the talent to speak, around the properties of spaces and the possibilities of time'. Jacques Rancière, *The Politics of Aesthetics, the Distribution of the Sensible*, ed. and trans. Gabriel Rockhill (London: Bloomsbury, 2013), 7–14.

19. Jacques Rancière, *Disagreement: Politics and Philosophy*, trans. Julie Rose (Minneapolis, MN: University of Minnesota Press, 1999), 29.

20. Jacques Rancière, *The Names of History: On the Poetics of Knowledge*, trans. H. Melehy (Minneapolis, MN: University of Minnesota Press, 1994), 173.

21. The phrase 'factory farm' indicates the form of automation that characterises confinement. In the industrial context of the mid-1800s, the word 'factory' was designated as 'the combined operation of many orders of work-people . . . in tending with assiduous skill a system of productive machines continuously impelled by a central power. . . . [T]his title, in its strictest sense, involves the idea of a vast automaton, composed of various mechanical and intellectual organs, acting in uninterrupted concert for the production of a common object, all of them being subordinated to

a self-regulated moving force'. In Andrew Ure, *The Philosophy of Manufactures: Or an Exposition of the Scientific, Moral, and Commercial Economy of the Factory System of Great Britain* (1861; Whitefish, MT: Kessinger Publishing, 2010), 13–14.

22. Mbembe, 'Necropolitics', 25–26. Mbembe affirms that '*colonial occupation* itself was a matter of seizing, delimiting, and asserting control over a physical geographical area—of writing on the ground a new set of social and spatial relations. The writing of new spatial relations (territorialisation) was, ultimately, tantamount to the production of boundaries and hierarchies, zones and enclaves; the subversion of existing property arrangements; the classification of people according to different categories; resource extraction; and, finally, the manufacturing of a large reservoir of cultural imaginaries. These imaginaries gave meaning to the enactment of differential rights to differing categories of people for different purposes within the same space; in brief, the exercise of sovereignty'. For Mbembe, colonial occupation redefines the relationship between sovereignty and space and is regulated through surveillance and control.

23. Ibid., 26.

24. Celia Lowe, 'Viral Clouds: Becoming H5N1 in Indonesia', *Cultural Anthropology* 25, no. 4 (2010): 625–49.

25. Javier Lezaun and Natalie Porter, 'Containment and Competition: Transgenic Animals in the One Health Agenda', *Social Science & Medicine* 129 (2015): 100.

26. Power washing uses high-pressure water spray to clean hog buildings in order to help ensure the nontransmission of illness or disease between populations.

27. The technology of security shapes circulations of capital and people and bears on what Foucault calls a milieu. The (human) population takes shape within a milieu, which becomes at the end of the eighteenth century the object of police and state power. Therefore the population is the object of biopolitics rather than society or the individual. In Michel Foucault, *Sécurité, territoire, population: Cours au Collège de France, 1977–1978* (Paris: Seuil/Gallimard, 2004), and Michel Foucault, *Il faut défendre la société: Cours au Collège de France, 1976* (Paris: Seuil/Gallimard, 1997), 218.

28. For Foucault, society—the modern formation indicative of the space of the city—forms as a normalised population through the regularization of the milieu of individuals as members of a biological species. Michel Foucault, 'Governmentality', in *Essential Works of Foucault, 1954–1984*, vol. III, *Power* (Harmondsworth: Penguin, 1994), 123, 201–22, 416.

29. The Iowa Select Farms website.

30. Ibid.

31. Mbembe, 'Necropolitics', 25.

32. Ibid., 27.

33. Daniel Imhoff, 'Introduction', in *The CAFO Reader: The Tragedy of Industrial Animal Factories*, ed. Daniel Imhoff (Berkeley, CA: University of California Press, 2010), xvi.

34. A call for a moratorium on new confinements in Iowa in order to reduce the number of impaired waters to one hundred has recently gained public support. Also see the Des Moines Water Works lawsuit No. 5:15-cv-04020 against thirteen Iowa counties for nitrate runoff in the Raccoon River.

35. Mbembe, 'Necropolitics', 31–34.

36. Agrilogistics also functions by 'excluding (undomesticated) lifeforms'. Timothy Morton, *Dark Ecology for a Logic of Future Coexistence* (New York: Columbia University Press, 2016), 46–59.

37. Similarly, Michael Karlsson argues that in the online age in which traditional journalism is challenged, a 'rival sometimes overlapping strategy for truth telling and the garnering of legitimacy has been proposed, namely transparency'. In Michael Karlsson, 'Rituals of Transparency', *Journalism Studies* 11, no. 4 (2010): 535.

38. Susan Dieleman, 'Review Essay of "Agnotology: The Making and Unmaking of Ignorance". Robert Proctor and Londa Schiebinger (editors) and "Race and Epistemologies of Ignorance". Shannon Sullivan and Nancy Tuana (editors)', *The Social Epistemology Review and Reply Collective* (2012), 1.

39. Sarah Lucia Hoagland, 'Denying Relationality: Epistemology and Ethics and Ignorance', *Race and Epistemologies of Ignorance*, ed. Shannon Sullivan and Nancy Tuana (Albany: State University of New York Press, 2007), 99.

40. Jacques Rancière, *The Ignorant Schoolmaster Five Lessons in Emancipation*, trans. Kristin Ross (Stanford, CA: Stanford University Press, 1991), 82.

41. Slavoj Žižek, 'What Donald Rumsfeld Doesn't Know that He Knows About Abu Ghraib', *In These Times*, 21 May 2004.

42. Rancière, *The Ignorant*, 137.

43. Jacques Rancière, *Dissensus: On Politics and Aesthetics*, ed. and trans. Steven Corcoran (London: Bloomsbury, 2010). Subjectification is the process through which the normative order is ruptured by 'the part of those who have no part' who perform the wrong of negating the negation of their existence. Rancière, *Disagreement*, 36.

44. Jacques Rancière, 'The Thinking of Dissensus, Politics and Aesthetics,' in *Reading Rancière: Critical Dissensus*, ed. Paul Bowman and Richard Stamp (London: Continuum, 2011), 4.

45. Coppin, 'Foucauldian', 612. Coppin addresses the question of whether confinement animals can be thought to resist industrial technologies by arguing that if 'we can see resistance at a biological level, then this opens the concept to a notion of nonhuman resistance'. Coppin bases her argument in Foucault's theorisation that resistance materialises in the body and marks a gap in power rather than is enacted by subjects or agents.

46. Eiko Otake, 'Sustained Mourning', unpublished manuscript, 2007, http://eikoandkoma.org/sites/ek/images/ek_3506_pdf. Eiko makes solo and duo performance as part of Eiko and Koma.

47. Ibid., 2.

48. Freud draws an uncertain and ultimately unsuccessful clinical distinction between mourning and the pathological disposition of melancholia. He outlines mourning as a reaction to the loss of a loved one or the loss of an abstraction that has taken the place of a loved one or object. In contrast, Freud attributes melancholia to a loss that—although might have been activated by a conscious loss—created a wound in the unconscious. Sigmund Freud, 'Mourning and Melancholia', *Collected Papers IV* (London: The Hogarth Press, 1925/1953).

49. The melancholic transfers the libido to the ego instead. Significantly, Freud emphasises detachment and transference of the libido from a nonexistent loved object for mourning and for melancholia.
50. Ibid., 166; emphasis added.

BIBLIOGRAPHY

Ascione, Frank R., and Kenneth J. Shapiro. 'People and Animals, Kindness and Cruelty: Research Directions and Policy Implications'. *Journal of Social Issues* 65, no. 3 (2009): 569–87.

Butler, Judith. *Frames of War: When Is Life Grievable?* London: Verso, 2009.

———. *Precarious life: The Powers of Mourning and Violence*. London: Verso, 2004.

Coppin, Dawn. 'Foucauldian Hog Futures: The Birth of Mega-Hog Farms'. *The Sociological Quarterly* 44, no. 4 (2003): 597–616.

Deleuze, Gilles. *Empiricism and Subjectivity: An Essay on Hume's Theory of Human Nature*. Translated by Constantin Boundas. New York: Columbia University Press, 1991.

Dieleman, Susan. 'Review Essay of "Agnotology: The Making and Unmaking of Ignorance". Robert Proctor and Londa Schiebinger (editors) and "Race and Epistemologies of Ignorance". Shannon Sullivan and Nancy Tuana (editors)'. *The Social Epistemology Review and Reply Collective* (2012).

Foucault, Michel. 'Governmentality'. *Essential Works of Foucault, 1954–1984,* Vol. III, *Power*. Harmondsworth: Penguin, 1994.

———. *Il faut défendre la société: Cours au Collège de France, 1976*. Paris: Seuil/Gallimard, 1997.

———. 'The Means of Correct Training'. In *The Foucault Reader*, edited by Paul Rabinow. New York: Pantheon Books, 1984.

———. *Sécurité, territoire, population: Cours au Collège de France, 1977–1978*. Paris: Seuil/Gallimard, 2004.

Freud, Sigmund. 'Mourning and Melancholia'. *Collected Papers IV*. Translated by J. Riviere. London: The Hogarth Press, 1953.

Haraway, Donna. *The Companion Species Manifesto: Dogs, People, and Significant Otherness*. Chicago: Prickly Paradigm Press, 2003.

Heidegger, Martin. *The Question Concerning Technology and Other Essays*. Translated by William Lovitt. New York: Harper and Row, 1977.

———. 'The Question Concerning Technology'. In *Basic Writings from Being and Time (1927) to The Task of Thinking (1964)*, edited by David Farrell Krell. New York: Harper and Row, 1977.

Hoagland, Sarah Lucia. 'Denying Relationality: Epistemology and Ethics and Ignorance'. *Race and Epistemologies of Ignorance*, edited by Shannon Sullivan and Nancy Tuana. Albany: State University of New York Press, 2007.

Imhoff, Daniel. 'Introduction'. In *The CAFO Reader: The Tragedy of Industrial Animal Factories*, edited by Daniel Imhoff. Berkeley, CA: University of California Press, 2010.

Iowa Select Farms. http://www.iowaselect.com/.

Jackson, Dana. 'The Farm as Natural Habitat'. *The Farm as Natural Habitat Reconnecting Food Systems with Ecosystems*, edited by Dana L. Jackson and Laura L. Jackson. Washington, DC: Island Press, 2002.

James, William. *The Principle of Psychology*, vol. 1. New York: Dover, 1890/1950.

Lezaun, Javier, and Natalie Porter. 'Containment and Competition: Transgenic Animals in the One Health Agenda'. *Social Science & Medicine* 129 (2015).

Lowe, Celia. 'Viral Clouds: Becoming H5N1 in Indonesia'. *Cultural Anthropology* 25, no. 4 (2010): 625–49.

Massumi, Brian. *Parables for the Virtual Movement Affect Sensation*. Durham, NC: Duke University Press, 2002.

Mbembe, Achille. 'Necropolitics'. *Public Culture*, trans. Libby Meintjes, 15, no. 1 (2003): 11–40.

Morton, Timothy. *Dark Ecology for a Logic of Future Coexistence*. New York: Columbia University Press, 2016.

Otake, Eiko. 'Sustained Mourning'. Unpublished manuscript, 2007. http://eikoandkoma.org/sites/ek/images/ek_3506_pdf (accessed 12 April 2017).

Rancière, Jacques. *Disagreement: Politics and Philosophy*. Translated by Julie Rose. Minneapolis, MN: University of Minnesota Press, 1999.

———. *Dissensus: On Politics and Aesthetics*. Edited and translated by Steven Corcoran. London: Bloomsbury, 2010.

———. *The Names of History: On the Poetics of Knowledge*. Translated by H. Melehy. Minneapolis, MN: University of Minnesota Press, 1994.

———. *The Politics of Aesthetics, the Distribution of the Sensible*. Edited and translated by Gabriel Rockhill. London: Bloomsbury, 2013.

Sullivan, Shannon, and Nancy Tuana, eds. *Race and Epistemologies of Ignorance*. Albany: State University of New York Press, 2007.

Ure, Andrew. *The Philosophy of Manufactures: Or an Exposition of the Scientific, Moral, and Commercial Economy of the Factory System of Great Britain*. 1861; Whitefish, MT: Kessinger Publishing, 2010.

Van Duyn, Mona. 'Last Words of Pig No. 6707'. *Grand Street* 7, no. 3 (Spring 1988): 140–42.

Žižek, Slavoj. 'What Donald Rumsfeld Doesn't Know that He Knows About Abu Ghraib'. *In These Times*, 21 May 2004.

Epilogue

Archipelagoes of the Unseen

May Joseph

Writing about Medieval Europe's production of spatial organisation, Michel Foucault identifies the leper and the plague as two logics that created the modern sensibility of the systematised ordering of society[1]. What was normal was spatialised in relation to what was out of the norm. In New York, the archipelagic nature of the eighteenth-century imagination perpetuated structures of isolation and quarantine, modes of hiding populations within plain sight amidst its numerous islands. New York's agglomeration of wetlands, sandbars, barrier islands, mudflats and rocky protuberances activated an unplanned fluid urbanism[2]. Shaped by the dense interface of water and land, New York's coastal development was a disconnected series of archipelagic planning strategies over four hundred years, organised around making unwanted populations disappear in the densest city in the world by the mid-twentieth century. These modes of containment were social engineering experiments situated across the city's numerous smaller islands lacing Manhattan's shores. Prisons, asylums, cemeteries, homes for the destitute, orphanages and hospitals for contagious diseases like smallpox and yellow fever were all located away from the density of the thriving metropolis. Over time, New York emerged as a peripatetic necropolis, a place where one walks through former histories of biopolitical management.

Nowhere is this sensation more viscerally felt than when walking along Gansevoort Street in what today is the West Village district of New York. One is immediately accosted by the ghosts of historic Sapokanikan, the Lenape village that was situated around a cove that Gansevoort Street emerged from. Walking south along Greenwich Street downtown, one walks at the edge of the sixteenth-century Lenape island of Manahatta. Strolling along the 1609 water's edge that captured Henry Hudson's awe is a peripatetic engagement with a lost history of the Munsee at one of their larger settlements along the verdant island. Winona LaDuke's words echo along the cobblestoned streets, 'but we never forgot our place'[3]. Writing about the Ojibwe's sentiments of their forced removal from Madeline Island in Canada, LaDuke records, 'We left that island with the understanding that we would never hold lodge there again'[4]. These words resonate with the violent history that is Manhattan island's memory, as descendants of the early Manhattan now reside far away from their rightful home, on reservations in Oklahoma, Wisconsin and Ontario[5]. The memory of a peripatetic knowledge of island habitation has continued to shape the unconscious becoming of life across the New York archipelago. To walk the necropolis is to actively immerse oneself in a decolonial methodology of reenvisioning what lies below the surface of ecological meaning. One has to look for the buried traces of former ecologies. Seek the buried rivers, the paved rivulets.

In their exhaustive research documenting the rich archaeological traces of millennia of Native American life around New York City, Anne-Marie Cantwell and Diana diZerega Wall painstakingly unearth traces of the decimated indigenous past over which layers of modernity now coexist[6]. At downtown Manhattan's Stadt Huys Block, on Governors Island, along Staten Island's Port Mobil, at Wards Point, New Jersey, around the Collect Pond of Manhattan's Chinatown, artefacts and chemical residues of Lenape, Canarsie and Munsee habitations fill the archipelago with what Tina Campt calls 'quiet soundings'[7]. Campt's technique of ontological excavation through listening to the erased spaces of possibility is useful to cultivate as a practice of peripatetic knowledge making. Listening to the quiet soundings of the archipelago's historic past is an invaluable tool for a decolonial understanding of New York's necropolitan imaginary.

ISLANDS OF THE FORGOTTEN

Over forty islands shape the New York archipelago. To walk across New York's island ecology is to constantly engage with the materiality of settler colonialism. The ghosts of genocide haunt as one takes the boat from one island to another, demanding that we shift how we see by reckoning with the thick opacity of what lies below the water's surface, approaching the task of thinking through New York's transforming archipelagic consciousness, I am spurred by Macarena Gómez-Barris's methodological challenge to find submerged viewpoints, 'ways to see what lies within the ecologies around us, and how to perceive those things that are not usually available to the naked eye'[8]. Circumnavigating Manhattan's ring of small islands threading its shoreline, an entire epistemology of forgotten islands rise to the surface. Roosevelt Island, North Brother Island, Ward Island, Randall's Island, Rikers Island, Hart Island, Governors Island, the Far Rockaways. These formerly ghostly islands were presences at once visible but discursively hidden from the consciousness of the anchoring big island of Manhattan. Strung along Manhattan's peripheries across the harbour and up the East River, these smaller islands surrounding the jewel in the New York estuary functioned as strategic biopolitical enclaves of contaminants. Ward Island has two psychiatric hospitals, numerous homeless shelters, cemeteries and a wastewater treatment centre. Rikers Island is a system of prisons with no access to the public. Hart Island is a cemetery for indigents and the urban poor. Governors Island was a military facility for over three hundred years and was closed to the public until 2003. The Rockaways were originally used to house the urban poor in large public housing projects built by Robert Moses with no amenities and poor connectivity to the mainland islands of Brooklyn and Manhattan.

The island-ness of each small landmass emerged in relation to its proximity to Manhattan, as well as to each other, beginning with Dutch colonisation. Originally purchased in 1637 from the Munsee Indians by Wouter Van Twiller, Governor General of New Netherlands, for his personal property, many of the smaller islands accrued marginal status as destinations for the unwanted of Manhattan. Outside the public eye, these smaller islands mutated from floating mud flats to military islands, to private farms and informal potters fields after independence from the British. Propelled by their necropolitical importance to Manhattan, the uneasy emergence of interrelationality between these small islands generated distinctive structuring linkages. For one, these small islands shared a coastal topography closer to a marine wilderness, borne out of a culture of neglect from the 'mainland' of the island of Manhattan: affectively, infrastructurally as well as hydrologically. The particular estuarine environment of salt water and fresh water created distinctive currents that made the waters around some of the islands treacherous to navigate for swimmers or small boats, adding to their isolation. Roosevelt Island is such a case in point, with strong currents swiveling around it. It consequently became an ideal prison location. Other small islands neighbouring Roosevelt became accompanying locations for internment, segregation, incarceration, quarantine, social engineering and punishment in all their brutish informality of the eighteenth century. Rikers Island remains the most notorious. Today, these small islands buoy deeply enmeshed within the archipelagic consciousness of the city as hovering presences along the East River and the New York harbour. Their psychologically remote yet proximate landmasses are gradually transforming into prime real estate with dramatically shifting futures. For the moment, however, most of them loom silently as unmarked sentinels of a watery world protecting the larger landmass on either side of their shorelines from the grimmer realities of life in the city, which they encompass.

Of the small islands around New York, Castle Clinton was one of the first geological islands to be designated a place of isolation. Originally a rocky promontory equipped for a military battery, it was quickly transformed to become the first immigration depot and place for quarantining immigrants who were deemed infectious on arrival from the old world. Geologically separated from the mainland of Manhattan by water, Castle Clinton's function as the island of immigration and quarantine marked its biopolitical function as container of migrants, pollutants and the sick. Following the pattern in which Castle Clinton's relationship to Manhattan developed, other islands around Manhattan emerged as a graded archipelago of disappearance. The farther away from downtown Manhattan's visual span the island was, the more hopeless the social cause defining the island. In this unconscious structuring of the necropolitan imaginary across the Hudson River, the once pristine but soon forbidding long sliver of island called Roosevelt Island is the most notorious case of such an island of ghosts transforming into one of the more desirable places to relocate to today. Formerly known as Blackwells Island and Welfare Island, Roosevelt Island is etched in the minds of older New Yorkers as the island of the forgotten. It contained a notorious prison, an infamous mental asylum, The Octagon and James Renwick's Small Pox Hospital. Prominent as a landmass adrift between Manhattan and Brooklyn on the East River, Roosevelt Island developed a distinctive visual ecology of invisibility despite its proximity to the two densest islands of the early twentieth century, Brooklyn and Manhattan. North of the island, the melancholic windswept landscape of the former psychiatric hospital held a large number of women. The aura of its sinister reputation for conducting some of the earliest shock therapy treatments and lobotomies, particularly on resistant women, permeates the moody terrain of windswept red brick and grey river. The island's dark eighteenth-century history of inhumane treatment of the mentally ill, along with its history of housing a penitentiary and the city's quarantine for smallpox patients, kept its presence along the East River a mystery for much of the last hundred and fifty years[9].

WALKING THE ARCHIPELAGIC NECROPOLIS

Islands like Ward Island, Hart Island, Rikers Island and Randolph's Island, all islands with histories of quarantined communities and graveyards of the dispossessed, bore the burden of their necropolitan histories through their ecological topographies. Waterlogged and low lying, many of these islands are provisional mudflats whose liveability has been under threat as sea levels rise. The barrier islands of the Far Rockaways are another case in point in which the history of the dead converges with the dreams and worries of the living. The Rockaways were one of the last holdouts of Munsee Indians against the Dutch colonisers during the seventeenth century. At the time geographically far away from Dutch New Amsterdam, the Munsee clung to their disappearing land longest along its outer edges. Along the Rockaways, an ecology of *thanatos* courses its way through the landscape, licking the decrepit sea-worn walls on one street, washing the shoreline's edges along the beach elsewhere. At Breezy Point, an entire community was destroyed by the storm fires of Hurricane Sandy. Large swaths of the Jamaica Bay and the Rockaway islands lie waterlogged and filled with mold. The Rockaways are a living example of precarity and risk along barrier islands. Along the Rockaway coastline, devastated coastal communities are still struggling to restore normality to their radically altered lives after the fury and storm surge damage of Hurricane Sandy. Provisionally protected by imported dunes that have been replaced twice at great cost by the Army Corps of Engineers, the Rockaways will be the test case for New York's grappling with climate refugees. Do they stay or do they move?

Not far from the Rockaway barrier islands are the lesser-known floating cemeteries of Hart Island and Ward Island, Governors Island and Roosevelt Island, Rikers Island and Lower Manhattan. At Hart Island the unknown remain buried while at Ward Island the disinterred remains of indigents from Manhattan's burial sites are laid to rest. Governors Island is a forgotten Lenape terrain whose indigenous artefacts trace a thousand-year history of occupation, while at Roosevelt Island the disturbed and forgotten souls of disease and madness were laid to rest. Together, these sites comprise an aesthetics of *thanatos*, where the voraciously alive ghost the entrails of the dead. Burial grounds across the New York archipelago articulate a hidden emotive life that underlies the banality of everyday life in the city. To live in New York is to walk among the dead, at Washington Square Park, at Bryant Park, at Liberty Park, at Ground Zero. New York's archipelago is a perpetually transforming necropolis whose palimpsest ecology has never been more endangered. Each of its islands presents an ecological lesson in how death, nature and urban artifice converge to shape environmental futures.

NOTES

1. Michel Foucault, 'Of Other Spaces: Utopias and Heterotopias', *Rethinking Architecture: A Reader in Cultural Theory*, ed. Neil Leach (London: Routledge, 1997), 330–36.

2. May Joseph, *Fluid New York: Cosmopolitan Urbanism and the Green Imagination* (Durham, NC: Duke University Press, 2013).

3. Winona LaDuke, *Chronicles: Stories from the Front Lines in the Battle for Environmental Justice* (Ponsford: Spotted Horse Press, 2016), 9.

4. Ibid., 10.

5. Robert S. Grumet, *First Manhattans: A History of the Indians of Greater New York* (Norman: University of Oklahoma Press, 2011), 3.

6. Anne-Marie Cantewell and Diana diZerega Wall, *Unearthing Gotham: The Archaeology of New York City* (New Haven, CT: Yale University Press, 2001).

7. Tina Campt, *Listening to Images* (Durham, NC: Duke University Press, 2017).

8. Macarena Gomez-Barris, *The Extractive Zone: Social Ecologies and Decolonial Perspectives* (Durham, NC: Duke University Press, 2017).

9. Nellie Bly, *Ten Days in a Mad-House*. (New York: Ian L. Munro, 1887).

BIBLIOGRAPHY

Bly, Nellie. *Ten Days in a Mad-House*. New York: Ian L. Munro, 1887.

Campt, Tina. *Listening to Images.* Durham: Duke University Press, 2017.

Cantewell, Anne-Marie, and Diana diZerega Wall, *Unearthing Gotham: The Archaeology of New York City*. New Haven, CT: Yale University Press, 2001.

Foucault, Michel. 'Of Other Spaces: Utopias and Heterotopias'. In *Rethinking Architecture: A Reader in Cultural Theory*, edited by Neil Leach, 330–36. London: Routledge, 1997.

Gomez-Barris, Macarena. *The Extractive Zone: Social Ecologies and Decolonial Perspectives.* Durham: Duke University Press, 2017.

Grumet, Robert S. *First Manhattans: A History of the Indians of Greater New York.* Norman: University of Oklahoma Press, 2011.

Joseph, May. *Fluid New York: Cosmopolitan Urbanism and the Green Imagination.* Durham: Duke University Press, 2013.

LaDuke, Winona. *Chronicles: Stories from the Front Lines in the Battle for Environmental Justice.* Ponsford: Spotted Horse Press, 2016.

Index

abstraction, 8, 10, 31, 77, 79, 81, 83–85, 87, 89, 91, 93, 95, 100, 102, 110, 115, 125, 130, 158, 184, 189, 200
acceleration, 80, 82, 147, 159, 164–165, 168, 193
Ackroyd, Heather, 115
AdNauseum, 167, 176–177
aesthetics, 1, 5–6, 12–14, 17–21, 23, 25, 27–31, 33, 35, 58–59, 65–66, 69–75, 83, 92, 111, 113, 115, 117, 148, 158, 163–164, 170, 175, 188–189, 193, 198, 200, 202, 207
Agamben, Giorgio 13
agency, 5, 9, 21, 30, 43–44, 46–48, 53, 88, 99, 105, 111, 143, 157, 159, 162, 165, 167, 169–170, 172, 181
agents, 20, 132, 200
aggression, 40–41, 81, 88–90, 171, 182, 195
Ajana, Btihaj, 177
algorithm, 4, 84, 158–160, 169–170, 172, 174, 178
amnesia, 7, 31–32
Anders, Günther, 87, 94–95
Anthropocene, 105–106, 114, 116–117
aphasia, 7, 31, 35–36
apparatus, 28, 41, 62, 89, 101, 103–104, 191
archipelago, 10, 204, 206–207
attention, 2–3, 51, 80–82, 97, 145, 152, 166, 186–187, 194–196
authenticity, 64, 67, 120–121, 182
automaton, 79–81, 93, 198
autonomy, 6–8, 55–63, 65–75, 81, 129, 158, 161, 175, 178

Balibar, Étienne 7, 18, 22–26, 33–35
bare life, 11, 13, 47–48
Baucom, Ian, 53
Berardi, Franco, 13, 95
Beuys, Joseph, 7, 12, 126–127, 131, 135, 137
biodigital (inorganic) becoming, 121, 130, 132–133
biometrics, 158–159, 174, 177
biopolitics, 7, 17–19, 26–27, 29–30, 34, 36, 100, 110, 120, 124, 133, 149, 155, 158–159, 174, 177, 199
biopower, 2, 18–20, 26, 28
biosecurity, 10, 189–191
biosphere, 79, 84, 97, 113
biotechnology, 100, 109, 120, 127, 130, 135, 137, 185
Bishop, Claire, 74
Black Liberation Army 153
Black Lives Matter, 7, 37–38, 41, 45, 50

blackness, 17, 32, 170, 177, 179
bondsman, 43–45, 48
Bourriaud, Nicolas, 13
Broadwater Farm riot, 29
Broeckmann, Andreas, 178
Brown, Vincent, 53
Buck-Morss, Susan, 53
Butler, Judith, 53, 201
Butler, Octavia, 95

caesura, 19, 29
CAFO, 181, 199, 201
Cage, John, 115
camouflage, 107, 166, 169–170, 177–178
capital, 4, 8, 25, 27–28, 37, 49, 53, 57, 64, 66–68, 70, 81–82, 84, 94–95, 128, 130–131, 158, 185, 189, 199
captivity, 22–23
cárdenas, micha, 160–161, 170, 174–175, 178
Cates, jon, 162, 164, 175–176, 178
Césaire, Aimé, 32
Chamayou, Grégoire, 18, 28, 33, 35
citizen, 7, 19–20, 24–25, 29, 38, 84, 100, 150, 154, 160
climate change, 32, 100, 110–111, 118, 150
cloning, 121–122, 129, 132
Clooney, George, 91
coding, 20, 127, 165
cognition, 81, 112, 142
collectivity, 24, 56, 66–71, 73, 83
colonialism, 8, 25, 204
Communism, 87
community, 6, 21–22, 24–25, 29–30, 43, 46, 48, 55, 58, 65–69, 72, 74, 91, 106, 114, 117, 152, 161–162, 164, 168, 175, 182, 192, 206–207
consciousness, 5, 42–43, 45–47, 51–52, 54, 79, 105–106, 142, 146, 148, 204–205
consensus, 3
consumption, 1, 11, 110, 131–132, 151, 168, 172, 177–178, 184, 190
contemporaneity, 6, 8, 58, 69–70
corpse, 8, 29–30, 52, 79–81, 83, 85, 87, 89, 91, 93, 95, 184
Cowan, T. L., 35
culture-jamming, 167–169
cyberspace, 80, 173
cyborg, 9, 142–146, 154

data, 1, 9, 103, 106, 108, 130–131, 142–143, 145, 157–160, 162–164, 166–167, 170–174, 178–179
death, 1–2, 7–10, 17–19, 26–27, 29–33, 36–40, 42–54, 68–69, 71, 74, 80, 82, 93, 110, 114, 117, 119, 126–129, 131–133, 143, 146–147, 149, 151–154, 159, 174, 182–187, 189, 191, 193–196, 207
Debord, Guy, 178
Debray, Régis, 104, 113, 115
decay, 186–187
decolonial understanding, 204
Décosterd, Jean-Gilles, 107, 114, 118
dehumanization, 20, 41
delegated performance, 64, 66–67
Deleuze, Gilles, 13, 53, 136, 201
demonetization, 85–86, 93
denigration, 2, 5, 90, 158
deregulation, 83
desire, 8–9, 50, 58, 60, 65, 97, 119–121, 123, 125, 127–135, 137, 141, 144, 148, 168, 172, 195–196
determination, 56, 63
deterritorialisation, 5, 89, 124–126, 133
detournement, 158, 167–168, 171, 177–178
devaluation, 27, 37–38, 42, 45
digital unconscious, 9
Dirty New Media, 9, 158, 162–164, 175
discrimination, 20, 40–41, 159, 174, 179
disease, 19, 30, 92, 121, 129, 131, 181, 189, 199, 203, 207
diversity, 106, 147–148, 151
DNA, 8, 119–135, 137
Doherty, Gareth, 115
domination, 25, 131, 143, 154, 159, 185, 192, 198

Dubois, W. E. B., 46, 48, 52–54
Duchamp, Marcel, 62, 72, 107, 114, 117, 167
Duggan, Mark, 29
Dunn, Joshua, 35

ecology, 97, 105, 107, 110–111, 113, 115, 117, 136, 147, 156, 192, 200, 202, 204, 206–208
econihilism, 149
economy, 6, 11, 14, 26, 52, 65–66, 84–87, 93, 102, 112, 115, 118, 120, 131, 135–136, 148, 151, 159, 161–162, 175, 178, 191, 199, 202
EFF, 173
Eliasson, Olafur, 74
empathy, 3, 8, 92–93, 195–196
Engels, Friedrich, 57, 71, 74
ENP, 30
entrainment, 4
environment, 81, 83, 86, 90, 97, 103, 113, 118, 142, 146–150, 152, 161, 169, 188, 192, 205
epistemic deconstruction, 100
ethnicity, 21–25
EUROSUR, 30
euthanasia, 190
existential refrain, 4
exploitation, 2, 20, 25, 27, 29, 40, 67–68, 81–83, 85, 110, 145, 158–159, 189, 198
expropriation. 27, 66
extermination. 9, 85–86, 88–89, 91, 93, 147
extinction. 82, 93, 147, 150

Fascism, 86–89
Faulkner, William, 25
FCC, 157, 174
fetish, 8, 97, 102
financialisation, 5, 8, 28–29, 31
Foucault, Michel, 13, 36, 74, 201, 208
Frankenstein, 80, 144
Franzen, Jonathan, 95
Fraser, Andrea, 74
FRONTEX, 30
Futurism, 79
FVEY, 158, 166

Gage, Zach, 179
gender, 7, 12, 15, 20, 22–23, 25, 129, 160–161
genealogical scheme, 23–24, 26, 34–35
genealogy, 24–25
genetics, 125–126, 129, 132
genocide, 2, 90–91, 151, 204
genotypes, 124–125, 133
ghetto, 30
Gilroy, Paul, 54
Glissant, Édouard, 39
glitching, 158, 163, 174
global South, 29, 159
globalization, 58, 69, 84–85
Goethe, J. W., 101, 112, 118
Goodman, Nelson, 116
governance, 3, 60, 93, 158
grammatisation, 4–5, 104
green, 8–9, 20, 55–57, 67, 70, 74, 97, 99, 115, 117–118, 147, 149, 208
grievable life/death, 184–185, 196–197, 201
Guatarri, Félix, 4, 11–13, 124, 127–128, 131, 134–137
Guerra, Ciro, 103, 112, 116

habeas corpus, 22, 30
habeas viscus, 22, 30, 34, 36
Haitian Revolution, 39, 44, 50, 53–54
Han, Byung-Chul, 13, 179
Haraway, Donna, 116, 201
Harvey, Adam, 179
Harvey, Dan, 107, 114
Hegel, G. W. F., 43–48, 50–51, 53–54, 167
HeHe, 107–108, 111, 114, 116
HIV, 160
Hjelmslev, Louis, 136
hog confinement, 181, 183, 185–191, 193, 195, 197, 199, 201
holocaust, 86

human, 1–6, 8–9, 12–13, 18–19, 21–22, 26, 28, 30, 32–34, 36–38, 40, 44, 49, 52, 56, 68, 79–83, 86 88, 90, 93, 97, 99, 101, 103–109, 111, 113, 115–117, 121–122, 124, 126–133, 141–152, 154–156, 170, 182, 184–185, 187–189, 192–197, 199, 201
Human Genome Project, 122, 126
hyperconnected body, 79
hypernature, 130, 133

ignorance, 9, 181, 183, 185, 187, 189, 191–193, 195–197, 199–202
immobility, 23
immortality, 8, 79, 82–83, 146, 155
imperceptibility, 4, 7, 9, 186–187
instituent practice, 60–62, 69, 71
institution, 26, 28, 38–39, 56, 60–64, 68, 72, 74, 167, 169, 191
instrumentalisation, 58, 110, 186–187
interdependence, 142–143
intimacy, 9, 22, 181, 183, 185–187, 189–191, 193, 195–197, 199, 201

Kac, Eduardo, 116
Keith, Lierre, 9, 149, 152, 156
Kester, Grant, 13
Kittler, Friedrich, 117
Knowbotic Research, 169, 177–179
knowledge, 1, 3, 7, 11, 17, 29, 31–33, 43, 57, 60–61, 64, 71, 81, 100, 104, 106, 114, 116, 135–137, 142, 159, 162, 174, 179, 182, 189–193, 197–198, 202, 204
Kojève, Alexandre, 7, 43–44, 51, 53–54

labour, 7–9, 21, 26–27, 29, 39, 52, 57–58, 62–68, 70, 72–75, 81–82, 84–85, 89, 130, 133, 152, 155, 162, 182, 187, 189–190, 192
LaDuke, Winona, 208
law, 21, 26, 28, 32, 35–36, 38, 45, 51, 54–56, 84, 124, 128, 144, 151, 161, 170, 177, 179, 183, 190, 194
Lefort, Claude, 3, 11
Lowe, Celia, 202
Lütticken, Sven, 59–60, 62, 65, 71–72, 74

machine, 1, 4, 11–13, 27, 46, 79–82, 88, 122, 127–128, 130, 132–133, 142–145, 154, 160, 198
Malzacher, Florian, 62, 72
Marder, Michael, 117
marginalization, 85, 89, 157
Marx, Karl, 57, 66, 71, 74, 82, 94–95
Massumi, Brian, 136, 202
master-slave dialectic, 7, 44, 46, 48
materiality, 10, 102, 104, 108, 113, 124, 204
Mbembe, Achille, 13, 36, 54, 74, 117, 137, 202
McCarthy, Paul, 6, 10, 12
McKittrick, Katherine, 36
media, 8–9, 11–13, 29–30, 64–65, 83, 91, 103–104, 107–109, 111–113, 116, 122, 125–126, 130, 157–159, 161–165, 167–175, 177–179
mediality, 106
mediation, 90, 104, 106, 109, 159–160, 172, 190
MEND, 5–6, 152–153
migrant, 19–20, 24–26, 28–29, 55–58, 60–61, 64, 66–67, 70–71, 90, 206
miscegenation, 26
Modi, Narendra, 8, 85, 94
money, 73, 75, 84–85, 91
Moravec, Hans, 145
mortality, 11, 14, 43, 142, 191
Morton, Timothy, 117, 202
mourning, 9–10, 49, 53, 139, 181, 183, 185, 187, 189, 191, 193, 195–197, 199–202
Moynihan Report, 21
Mukherjee, Siddhartha, 129, 135, 137
multispectivism, 132

Naess, Arne, 156
nationalism, 23, 85, 88
Nazism, 86–89
NCC, 30

necro-art, 7–8, 55, 66, 68
necro-zones, 33, 35
necroaesthetics, 7, 18, 27–28, 30
necrocapitalism, 21, 28–29, 31–32, 49
necrofascination, 186–187, 190–191
necrophobea, 186–187, 190–191
necropolis, 203–204, 206–207
necropolitics, 2, 7–13, 17–19, 21, 23, 25–39, 45, 47, 49–52, 54, 56–57, 68, 70, 74, 97, 100, 110, 117, 119, 126, 131, 133–135, 137, 141, 143, 145–147, 149, 151–155, 158, 171, 173–174, 179, 189, 196, 199–200, 202
necropower, 18, 26–28, 33, 38–39, 47–48, 158
necroreality, 186–187
necrosis, 79–80, 83, 87
negro, 21, 46, 52
neoliberalism, 10, 13, 152, 174, 179
neuro-aesthetic, 101
neurostimulation, 81
Nissenbaum, Helen, 9, 166–167, 171–172, 176–179
normativity, 99
NSA, 158, 165–166, 176, 179

O'Neil, Cathy, 159
obfuscation, 9, 158, 166–167, 169, 176, 178
object-oriented ontology (OOO), 105
odour, 97, 101, 186–187
Ögüt, Ahmet, 57, 61–65, 71–72, 74
oppression, 6, 41, 43, 45–47, 52
Otake, Eiko, 202
otherness, 8, 22, 99, 197, 201
overbidding, 1, 9–10, 139
overcodification, 119–120, 125, 127–128, 133

Parisi, Luciana, 137
Peele, Jordan, 7, 38–39, 50
perception, 3–5, 8, 11, 14, 71, 83, 87, 99, 101, 103, 105, 107, 110–111, 116, 118, 183–184, 192–193
pig number 6707, 184–185
politics, 1, 3, 6, 8–9, 11, 14, 19, 57–60, 63, 65, 67, 69–75, 94, 104, 106, 114, 117, 119, 121, 135, 137, 153, 162, 165, 169, 175, 179, 188, 194, 198, 200, 202
pollution, 6, 83, 108, 151, 191
population, 2, 18–19, 21, 24, 26–28, 30, 37, 55, 82, 84–87, 89–90, 92–93, 97, 142, 147–148, 150, 152–153, 155, 157, 159–160, 162, 168, 170, 183–184, 187–188, 190–192, 197, 199, 201, 203
postcolonial, 19, 25, 37, 67
posthuman, 9, 119, 134, 136, 141, 143, 145, 147, 149–151, 153–155
power, 2, 9–13, 19–20, 22, 25–26, 28, 42–43, 49, 51–53, 60, 68, 73, 75, 79, 81, 86, 88, 91–92, 97, 112, 117, 123–124, 126, 128, 130, 141–143, 150, 153, 167–168, 173–174, 176, 179, 183, 185, 188–192, 194, 196–201
precariousness/precarity, 5, 38, 82, 89, 207
privatization, 32
Protevi, John, 14
public sphere, 20, 155, 193

quiet soundings, 10, 204

race, 7, 15, 17–20, 23, 25, 31, 33–36, 40, 43, 88, 90, 93–94, 120, 129, 173, 185, 200–202
racialization, 18, 20, 22, 25
racism, 17–19, 23–24, 26, 34–35, 40–41, 49–50, 61, 86, 88, 90
Rahm, Philippe, 107, 114, 118
Rancière, Jacques, 3, 11, 14, 58, 73, 188–189, 193–194, 198, 200, 202
recombinant, 1, 144–146
Red Army Faction, 153
refugee, 2, 7, 20, 25, 28–30, 55–56, 61, 65, 67–68, 70–71, 75, 207
reproductive maintenance work, 68
resistance, 7, 9, 18, 37, 39, 43–45, 47–48, 51–53, 56, 152, 156, 158, 170–171, 174, 194, 200

revolution, 39, 44, 50–51, 53–54, 71, 74
riot, 24, 29–30, 35
Rose, Ebony, 36
Russell, Legacy, 179

scientificity, 125
semiocapitalism, 1, 82
servitude, 39
Sessions, George, 147, 149, 156
sex, 9, 23, 25, 119–123, 125, 127–129, 132–137, 144, 161
Silent University, 7, 57, 60–62, 64, 67, 71–72, 74
Situationists International, 158, 167–168
slavery, 7, 26, 37–40, 42, 44–45, 47–54
social creativity, 65
social imagination, 83
social practice, 57–59, 66–69, 73, 158, 161, 166
solidarity, 45, 48, 56–57, 65, 67–68, 72
solutionism, 146–147, 151
sovereignty, 2, 9, 18, 26, 45, 51, 83, 157–158, 161, 166, 170, 173, 189, 191, 199
species, 6, 69, 82–83, 113, 127, 145, 147, 149–150, 183–185, 189–190, 197–199, 201
Spiess, Klaus, 119, 126, 135, 137
Spillers, Hortense, J., 7, 18, 20, 33, 36
Stiegler, Bernard, 14
Stjernfelt, Frederik, 118
Stoler, Ann Laura, 36
Strecker, Lucie, 9, 119, 126, 135, 137
struggle, 39, 43–48, 53, 56, 65, 112, 118, 149–150, 163, 165, 168, 197
suffering, 5, 17, 22, 30–31, 81, 87, 92–93, 155, 186–187, 192–193
surveillance, 5, 9, 30, 144–145, 153, 158–160, 165, 167, 169–170, 176, 179, 199
Symbionese Liberation Army, 153

technocrats, 141, 143, 146, 149
technofatalism, 9
technology, 6, 8–10, 12–13, 26–28, 79, 81, 84–85, 88, 91, 104–107, 109–112, 115–116, 119–121, 123, 125, 127, 129–135, 137, 142–143, 145–146, 151, 159–160, 162–163, 165–166, 170–171, 173–175, 177–179, 185, 187, 190–191, 193, 196–201
technoromanticism, 9
technosphere, 142
terrorism, 10, 27, 47, 168
thanatos, 207
Tottenham riot, 29
TrackMeNot, 9, 166–167, 176
transhumanism, 146, 154
Trump, Donald, 10, 85, 88, 91–93
Trumpism, 8, 89–90
Turner, Nat, 44, 51, 53–54

undesirable, 159–160
undocumented, 55, 58, 70
USDA, 184

Vanouse, Paul, 137
violence, 2, 5–6, 12, 29–31, 38, 44–45, 47–49, 53, 56, 81, 86–87, 89–92, 158–161, 165, 169–170, 183, 185, 189–190, 192–194, 196–198, 201

warfare, 27, 97
Weheliye, Alexander G., 22, 30, 34, 36
Wilson, E. O., 9, 149–151, 153, 156
Wright, Stephen, 66, 73, 75
Wynter, Sylvia, 18, 32–33, 35–36

Žižek, Slavoj, 12, 131, 193, 200, 202
zombie, 7, 39, 46–47, 49–50, 53–54, 80, 142
Zong Massacre, 38, 49

About the Contributors

EDITOR

Natasha Lushetich is an artist and theorist. She is the recipient of numerous fellowships such as Fulbright, Steim and ArtsLink. Currently, she is senior lecturer in interdisciplinary practices and visual studies at LaSalle, Singapore, having previously lectured at the University of Exeter. Her research focuses on intermedia, biopolitics and performativity, the status of sensory experience in cultural knowledge, hegemony, disorder and complexity. She is the author of numerous articles and book chapters and two books: *Fluxus: The Practice of Non-Duality* (Rodopi, 2014) and *Interdisciplinary Performance* (Palgrave, 2016). Natasha is also co-editor of *On Game Structures* (Taylor and Francis, 2016) and editor of *Beyond Mind*, a special issue of *Symbolism, the Interdisciplinary Journal of Critical Aesthetics* (De Gruyter, 2019).

CONTRIBUTORS

Franco 'Bifo' Berardi is a theorist, cultural worker and activist. He is a frequent public speaker at cultural institutions and universities worldwide. He is also the author of dozens of influential books and articles, translated into all major languages. Among his works are *Futurability: The Age of Impotence and the Horizon of Possibility* (2017), *Heroes: Mass Murder and Suicide* (Verso, 2015), *After the Future* (2011), *The Soul at Work: From Alienation to Autonomy* (2009) and *Precarious Rhapsody: Semio-Capitalism and the Pathologies of the Post-Alpha Generation* (2009).

Critical Art Ensemble are tactical media theorists and practitioners. They have exhibited and performed internationally, at the Whitney Museum and the New Museum in NYC; the Corcoran Museum in Washington, DC; the ICA, London; the MCA, Chicago; Schirn Kunsthalle, Frankfurt; Musée d'Art Moderne de la Ville de Paris; and the London Museum of Natural History. CAE have also written seven books, including *Electronic Civil Disobedience & Other Unpopular Ideas* (1996), *Flesh Machine: Cyborgs, Designer Babies, & New Eugenic Consciousness* (1998), *Digital Resistance: Explorations in Tactical Media* (2001), *Molecular Invasion* (2002), *Marching Plague* (2006) and *Disturbances* (2012).

Tiffany Funk is an artist and art historian specialising in the history of computer art, creative coding, interactive performance and video games. She is co-founder of the Interdisciplinary Education in the Arts (IDEAS) program at the University of Illinois, Chicago, where she teaches courses on digital media art history and practice. She is also the editor-in-chief of the *Video Game Art Reader* and associate editor of the *Media-N, Journal of the New Media Caucus*.

Marina Gržinić, author of *Re-Politicizing Art, Theory, Representation and New Media Technology* (Schlebrugge, 2010) and co-author of *Necropolitics, Racialization and Global Capitalism* (Lexington Books, 2014), is a university professor, philosopher and artist. She is a research advisor at the Institute of Philosophy, Ljubljana, and a full professor at the Academy of Fine Arts, Vienna. Her international lecturing and teaching commitments include the Center for Global Studies and the Humanities, Duke University; UCLA, California; IMI, Osaka; Merz Academy, Stuttgart; Haute école d'art et de design, Geneva; and ASAB, Bogota, Colombia.

Jens Hauser is an art curator, critic and associate researcher in the Department of Art and Cultural Studies, University of Copenhagen. He is the author of *Paul Venouse: Fingerprints* (Argobooks, 2011) and has published widely on bio-art and biomediality in such journals as *BioSpektrum*, *Leonardo*, *Plastik* and *Semaine*. Jens's groundbreaking transmedial research has also been published in numerous edited collections, such as Sean Cubitt et al.'s *Relieve: Media Art Histories* (MIT Press, 2013) and Petra Lange-Berndt's *Materiality* (MIT Press, 2015).

May Joseph is a professor of global studies in the Department of Social Science and Cultural Studies at Pratt Institute, New York. Her research combines critical cultural theory and environmental practice. She has written widely on globalisation, urbanism and visual culture. Her books, which explore the junctures between cities, water ecologies and coastal futures, include *Fluid New York: Cosmopolitan Urbanism and the Green Imagination* (Duke University Press, 2013) and *Nomadic Identities: The Performance of Citizenship* (Minnesota, 1999). May is also co-editor of *Performing Hybridity* (Minnesota, 1999) and *The Journal of Space and Culture* (City Corps, 1999).

Sarah Juliet Lauro is an assistant professor of hemispheric literature at the University of Tampa. She is the author of many works that address the figure of the living dead zombie, including *The Transatlantic Zombie: Slavery, Rebellion, and Living Death* (Rutgers University Press, 2015), and she is the editor of *Zombie Theory: A Reader* (University of Minnesota Press, 2017). Her next book project turns from zombies as a figuration of slavery and slave revolt, which is her central interest in the monster, to literal commemorations of slave rebellion in literature, art, film and digital culture.

Malin Palani is a performance practitioner and scholar who teaches courses in performance ecology, theory, history and practice. Her research examines contemporary performance from the perspective of relationality in the encounter with objects, animals, technology/machines and landscapes. She received her PhD from the University of Minnesota and has formerly taught courses at Macalester College in Saint Paul, Minnesota. Malin most recently completed an artist residency for the Hartman Nature Reserve in Waterloo, Iowa, and performed a shadow puppet show based on the movement and stories of animal bodies (including humans) within the reserve. Malin is certified in reiki healing as well as crematory operation and has training in Butoh and *vipassana* meditation practice.

Verónica Tello is a lecturer in contemporary art theory in the Department of Art and Design at the University of New South Wales, Sydney. Her research, which focuses on biopolitics and critical border studies, has been published in *Third Text*, *Afterall* and *Contemporaneity*. Her book *Counter-Memorial Aesthetics: Refugee Histories and The Politics of Contemporary Art* was published by Bloomsbury in October 2016.

Mi You is a writer, curator and associate researcher at the Academy of Media Arts, Cologne. Her research interests include philosophy of immanence in both Western and Chinese neo-Confucian traditions and the philosophy of science and technology. Mi curates media art. Most recently she has curated exhibitions at the Asian Culture Center Theater in South Korea and at the inaugural Media Art Festival in Ulaanbaatar, Mongolia. Her recent writings have appeared in *Performance Research*, *Kaleidoscope* and in the publications of the Sharjah Art Foundation, among others.

Printed in Great Britain
by Amazon

17162012R00132